"IT SEEMED LIKE WE STOOD AND WATCHED A LIFETIME. . . .

They got the Klaxon sounded, and General Quarters went. We were already topside looking and trying to figure out what in the devil was happening.

Well, we saw these durned planes. We thought at first that it was some kind of dummy maneuver, you know. That was the first thing that entered your mind—like the time in the early days of frogmen, when they'd come aboard your ship, and you were supposed to be watching for them. They were very new then. In fact, I don't think they even called them frogmen. They would slip aboard and pretend to blow up your ship, and you were supposed to catch them. We thought it was some kind of maneuver like that, but, when all the flames started busting out on Battleship Row, why, you knew durned well that it wasn't a maneuver."

REMEMBERING PEARL HARBOR

Eyewitness Accounts by U.S. Military Men and Women

Edited by
Robert S. La Forte
Ronald E. Marcello

BALLANTINE BOOKS • NEW YORK

Copyright © 1991 by Scholarly Resources Inc.

All rights reserved under International and Pan-American Copyright Conventions. Published in the United States by The Ballantine Publishing Group, a division of Random House, Inc., New York, and simultaneously in Canada by Random House of Canada Limited, Toronto.

Ballantine is a registered trademark and the Ballantine colophon is a trademark of Random House, Inc.

www.randomhouse.com/BB/

Library of Congress Catalog Card Number: 90-40179

ISBN 0-345-37380-4

This edition published by arrangement with Scholarly Resources Inc.

Manufactured in the United States of America

First Ballantine Edition: March 1992

10 9 8 7 6 5 4 3

Contents

Introduction

For the United States, World War II lasted 1,351 days, but the nation's greatest defeat took only 110 minutes. In about two hours on Sunday, December 7, 1941, Japanese planes from the strike force *Kido Butai* hit hard at the Pacific fleet in Pearl Harbor and at other military installations scattered across the Hawaiian island of Oahu.

That "date which will live in infamy" began for the U.S. military at 7:55 A.M., when Rear Admiral William R. Furlong, commander of the Minecraft Force, Pacific Fleet, noticed an airplane flying low over Ford Island drop a bomb on installations there. At first he thought that an American pilot had erred, but, as the aircraft turned and flew near where he stood on the deck of his flagship, the minelayer *Oglala,* he saw on the plane's side the unmistakable round red emblem of imperial Japan. Within minutes, other officers had sent the fateful message: "Air raid, Pearl Harbor. This is not a drill!" What followed was a well-planned, expertly executed attack on most of the major vessels of the U.S. Navy's Pacific Fleet. Japanese airmen, having prepared several months for the assault, methodically rained death and destruction from the clear, blue Hawaiian skies.

The task force had left Hitokappu Bay in the Kurile Islands on November 26. After arriving at a point two hundred miles north of Hawaii, the armada's six aircraft carriers launched 360 planes between 6:00 and 7:15 A.M. The planes rendezvoused

INTRODUCTION

MAJOR MILITARY INSTALLATIONS
ON OAHU

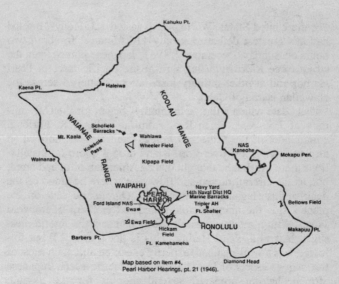

Map based on item #4,
Pearl Harbor Hearings, pt. 21 (1946).

SKETCH OF MOVEMENTS OF
AIR UNITS AFTER THEY CAME IN SIGHT OF OAHU

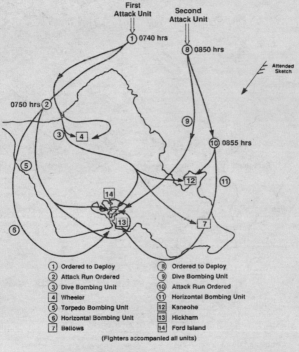

First
Attack Unit

Second
Attack Unit

① 0740 hrs

⑧ 0850 hrs

Attended
Sketch

0750 hrs ②

③

4

⑨

⑩ 0855 hrs

⑤

12

11

14

⑥

13

7

① Ordered to Deploy   ⑧ Ordered to Deploy
② Attack Run Ordered   ⑨ Dive Bombing Unit
③ Dive Bombing Unit   ⑩ Attack Run Ordered
4 Wheeler   11 Horizontal Bombing Unit
⑤ Torpedo Bombing Unit   12 Kaneohe
⑥ Horizontal Bombing Unit 13 Hickham
7 Bellows   14 Ford Island

(Fighters accompanied all units)

Map based on Item #17   Pearl Harbor Hearings, pt. 21 (1946).

PEARL HARBOR ANCHORAGE
7 Dec 1941

① Ramsay Gamble Montgomery
② Trever Breese Zane Perry Wasmuth
③ Monaghan Farragut Dale Aylwin
④ Henley Patterson Ralph Talbot
⑤ Selfridge Case Tucker Reid Conyngham Whitney
⑥ Phelps MacDonough Worden Dewey Hull Dobbin*
⑦ Narwhal Dolphin Tautog Thornton Hulbert
⑧ Jarvis Mugford
⑨ Argonne Sacramento
⑩ Cummings Preble Tracy* Pruitt Sicard Schley
   Grebe Ontario Rigel
⑪ Ramapo New Orleans* San Francisco St. Louis
   Honolulu Bagley
⑫ Bobolink Vireo Turkey Rail

Map based on Item #12.
Pearl Harbor Hearings. pt. 21 (1946)

N

East Loch

Pearl City

Middle Loch

Blue

Phoenix

Detroit
Raleigh
Medusa   Utah
Curtiss   Tangier

Solace   Chew
Allen

Arizona   Nevada
Tennessee   Vestal
West Virginia

Ford Island

Maryland
Oklahoma

Neosho
California

Tank Farm
Pelias

Avocet
Oglala Tern
Helena
Cachalot
Pennsylvania

CINCPACFT

Waipio
Peninsula

Shaw
Naval
Hospital
Downes Cassin

South
East Loch

Sumner
Castor

Merry Point
Landing

West
Loch

U. S. Naval Station

Tank
Farm

Iroquois Point

Hickam Field

Anti-Torpedo and
Anti-Boat Net

south of the task force and then, in two coordinated attacks, made their sorties. Aircraft engaged in the first assault deployed north of Oahu at 7:40 A.M., skirted the northwest coastline, and then divided into several groups to strike different installations. The fighters ("Zekes" in American slang) overflew Haleiwa Field and struck Army pursuit planes parked neatly in rows at Wheeler Field. They were accompanied by a few dive-bombers ("Vals"), some of which attacked Wheeler while others went on to the naval air station at Kaneohe, which lay on the southeast shore of the island.

The bulk of the first force—"Kates," which were used as both horizontal bombers and torpedo bombers, and a small number of dive-bombers that had split off from the group headed for Wheeler—hit the fleet at Pearl Harbor, Ford Island Naval Station, and Hickam Field from 7:55 to 8:25 A.M. They concentrated on the ships, especially those moored on Battleship Row, alongside Ford Island.

Following a so-called lull from 8:25 to 8:40 A.M., horizontal bombers continued the attack. They were succeeded by dive-bombers and more horizontal bombers in a second wave that began its strike about 9:15 A.M. Planes of this group had met some fifteen miles east of the first deployment point and had started on their maneuvers at 8:45 A.M. The horizontal bombers hit Hickam, while the Vals worked over the fleet.

Admiral Samuel Eliot Morison, in his monumental *History of United States Naval Operations in World War II* (1948), separates the air raid into four phases, using torpedo-bomber assaults as his divisor since they were expected to cause most of the damage to shipping. The Japanese employed dive-bombers and horizontal bombers as well because they feared that the U.S. Navy might have placed netting around its battleships in such as way that torpedoes would be ineffective. Their concerns proved invalid, and the horizontal bombers and Vals merely contributed to the day's destruction. At 9:45 A.M., with a few scattered exceptions, the battle ended.

Precision typified the attack. Before the Japanese had finished, they destroyed two battleships and an auxiliary vessel, sank two more battlewagons and three auxiliaries, and severely damaged thirteen other craft. The raid had centered on the heavy ships in Pearl Harbor and on the protection they should have had from nearby airfields. The Army and Navy together saw 183 planes wrecked and another 159 damaged. The majority had been arranged in tidy rows at the two Army Air Forces bases.

Most important, 2,403 Americans were killed, lost, or mortally injured during the attack; 1,178 received nonfatal wounds. Japanese pilots not only bombed vessels and aircraft but also strafed the areas around installations, including Schofield Barracks, the Army's largest post in 1941. Surprised in battle as never before, the U.S. Navy suffered three times its losses in the Spanish-American War and World War I combined.

Aboard the ships, astonishment was the first reaction, with some seamen finding it impossible to believe that they were under a true attack. They assumed that the noise was caused by another mock assault by the Army Air Forces on the Navy, just as those stationed on land explained the racket as a naval exercise against the Army. American forces had been carrying out such maneuvers without warning for several months, and although many of the listeners thought that Sunday morning practice was unusual, they did not imagine that they were hearing enemy bombs. In most instances, but not all, initial confusion gave way to military professionalism. Sailors drew upon their rigorous training and hurriedly took battle stations, even when that may not have been the best action. At the air bases and at Schofield Barracks the reaction was not so quick, for at these sites the men lacked the plans and weapons needed to defend themselves and their sites. Some of these individuals ultimately found ways to fight; only a few, however, fully grasped the significance of the situation. Apparently the eventuality of air raids had not been given much serious consideration by the top brass.

Shocked by the thoroughness of the sudden attack, only a small group instinctively understood what was happening and what had to be done. This handful of soldiers and sailors, officers and enlisted personnel demonstrated a valuable capacity to respond and adjust to the unexpected rapidly, effectively, and skillfully. Such ability may be particularly surprising because many of the men were "depression soldiers" who had enlisted not to pursue military careers but to find security. As one sailor remarked, the Navy for him meant "three hots and a cot!" Others were conscripted under the Selective Service Act, which a worried Congress and President Franklin D. Roosevelt had passed in September 1940 and put into effect the next month.

This book is the story of enlisted personnel and junior officers who tell their own version of the attack. It is not a tale of sweeping maneuvers and magnificent strategy, the usual military history. Rather, what follows tries to grasp the heart of battle—the way people react to war. The reader should not expect a grammatically correct, gripping narrative. For the most part, these individuals had little formal schooling. What they say is nevertheless compelling to us, the editors, and we trust that it will be to the reader. Likewise, the men and women are relating events that happened to them swiftly and without warning thirty to fifty years earlier, and their memory is therefore not perfect; errors occur. But most of what they say is accurate, constituting a reliable chronicle of their participation.

Evidently, no one has previously attempted on such a scale to let the rank and file of the American military tell its story of Pearl Harbor. Others have used interviews, diaries, personal reminiscences, and autobiographies, but in most cases high-ranking officers guide the narrative by relating their own experiences and impressions. Given our purpose it is fitting to ask what manner of men the soldiers in the barracks or sailors below decks were on that fateful day. The descriptions that follow are based on over 350 interviews conducted during the past twenty years by the University of North Texas Oral History Program with Pearl Harbor survivors, a program still in operation.

Each survivor was interviewed individually in private surroundings. A core of questions was asked of everyone; the more precised queries would be made about the action on the particular ship or specific base where the witness saw the attack. No prearranged plan was used to select the interviewees. Those who were easily accessible from the University of North Texas, in Denton, were contacted more frequently than others. Also, witnesses who attended reunions held by the Pearl Harbor Survivors Association were questioned more often, since the interviewer, Ronald E. Marcello, attended many of these gatherings. When opinions are presented as being those of most of the survivors, the reader should remember that the only correct generalization about the interviewees is that no generalization, excepting this one, is absolutely true. The various persons who speak here seem to be representative of the enlisted soldiers and sailors and the junior officers who lived through the attack, and they certainly are a fair cross section of the men and women in the Oral History Program.

At the time of the attack, they were young, like most servicemen, but not so young as the ranks would become as the war progressed and more and more recruits were necessary. They also had been trained for longer periods than would be the norm later on. Sailors spent about four months in boot camp, and many were then sent to special schools; as the war neared, drill became more intense and maneuvers more frequent. Morale was high in this almost entirely volunteer service. The personnel took great pride in what they were doing and, as a result, felt a great shame over what happened on December 7, 1941. Many reacted by wondering not whether their parents or other relatives would be concerned about them but whether the folks back home would understand why the military had let down America. Almost every interviewee blamed higher-ups for the debacle. Some agreed with the governmental committees that were convened later to assign blame: They believed that the problem was at Pearl Harbor, with its military leaders. Others faulted the Washington brass, including the commander in chief himself. Still, only a few thought that, as some writers have implied, President Roosevelt set them up so that he could rally the public for war.

The regulars thought that the military suffered as war neared because so many draftees were being added to their ranks. The naval conscripts were not nearly so well trained as their older shipmates. Some of the reserves, called up in 1941, felt the resentment and answered in kind by denigrating the "lifers." Draftee status did not seem to cause as much trouble or be as important in the Army; during the 1930s the Army had much lower requirements than the Navy for enlistment. At the same time, morale was raised by the perception most held of the field officers who commanded them. Invariably, soldiers and sailors bragged of their company commanders and ship captains. They were particularly impressed by graduates of the service academies at Annapolis and West Point. Less noble sources of esprit de corps were the food and lodging. Sailors especially praised the rations. In fact, some cited the tradition of good meals as their reason for choosing the Navy. Others mentioned cleaner living conditions and better quarters as incentives for going to sea. Despite inhabiting cramped areas below decks and sleeping in hammocks, they maintained that they were better off than lying on the hard ground, choking on dust or freezing in cold rains, hunkered down in hastily dug foxholes.

In all the military branches, athletics were an important part of life. Most of our contacts were involved in sports within their units or among units, and an inordinate number took part in interservice athletic contents. Unlike characters in James Jones's *From Here to Eternity* (1951), none of the survivors felt pressured to be involved, but they all pointed out that such advantages as promotion and better food often came to those who participated. With few exceptions, the interviewees were also avid tourists and at first enjoyed being posted in Hawaii, although the shortage of hotel accommodations made overnight liberty difficult, if not impossible, to get. As the war approached and lines grew longer at attractions and space became harder to secure along beaches, many grew bored and complained.

At times, saloons seemed to be the only refuges they sought in Honolulu. Most admitted that drunkenness existed but was not so frequent or extensive as popularly perceived. That seamen were hung over on December 7 is a notion the survivors universally rejected. Machinist's Mate First Class Rudolph P. Zalman put is best when he said that "young fellows could stay up all night and drink beer, and the minute something happened, they were as alert as if they hadn't drunk a drop. I remember reading a few articles in the paper afterwards about most of the sailors being ashore and having a great time, but this is absolutely not true. There was no such thing." This opinion was echoed by Army and Navy officers. Although about eleven thousand soldiers and sailors were in Honolulu on the night of December 6—approximately 10 percent of the military stationed on Oahu—only a few were arrested for being drunk and disorderly. Police records show that more civilians than military personnel were taken into custody for drunkenness that night. Indeed, sailors below the rank of petty officer first class had to be aboard ship by midnight. For further comments see Admiral Homer N. Wallin, *Pearl Harbor: Why, How, Fleet Salvage, and Final Appraisal* (Washington, DC: Government Printing Office, 1968).

Like most young men, America's soldiery was a cocksure lot. As representatives of the "greatest nation on earth," they felt little need for concern as war clouds developed over Europe and Asia. They expected to go to war one day against Adolf Hitler and Benito Mussolini, but they did not anticipate an attack on Pearl Harbor. In fact, a surprisingly large number did not believe that any trouble would come from Asia. Seaman First Class Nick L. Kouretas expressed this attitude best: "I had no idea that Japan would ever enter the war. Joining the Pacific Fleet, I felt, 'Well, until Hitler gets things going over there, we're not going to have to go over and start fighting.' I had no idea whatsoever."

At first their opinions of the Japanese were unflattering, but that changed. As Seaman First Class William W. Fomby put it: "All Japs wore dresses and flew kites . . . . That was the image that . . . was predominant at the time. As they later proved, they didn't fly kites, and they were pretty good at what they did." Some of those interviewed mistrusted the Japanese and Japanese-Americans in Hawaii. They told of verifiable instances of disloyalty by a few such residents. But on the whole the survivors believed that America had little to fear from its Japanese population and that, despite their ancestral ties, most were U.S. patriots.

These, then, were some of the men who fought at Pearl Harbor and lost, although their defeat was not so devastating as many suspect. The Japanese, satisfied with the damage they had caused in the first two attacks, canceled a third assault and thereby failed to destroy the Navy Yard and fuel supply tanks. Thus, the Navy could repair, refit, and put to sea within a short period of time. It could still engage in battle, as was shown with resounding success a few months later at the Midway Islands.

As noted earlier, Ronald E. Marcello conducted all of the original Pearl Harbor interviews in the University of North Texas Oral History Program over the past twenty years. He is also largely responsible for choosing the forty documents presented in this volume. While questioning the survivors, he asked for much more information than just what related directly to the attack. Anyone wishing to write about the U.S. military of the 1930s and 1940s should consult the oral history collection, which provides a great deal more about the aftermath of the attack than could be given here. And, of course, for those who wish to know about duty at Pearl Harbor, at Schofield Barracks, and elsewhere on Oahu, the program's files form a cornucopia of data.

In the preparation of the transcripts for publication, most were reduced by 50 to 75 percent. Robert S. La Forte performed this task, including all of the writing and most of the research. All documentation came from the personal interviews, survivors' hometown newspapers, the works cited in the bibliographical essay at the end of this volume, or that corpus of knowledge a historian possesses but has forgotten whence it came. In the editing of the documents for this volume, only the pertinent sections were used, but every effort was made to ensure that the final presentation would be representative of each individual's overall reaction during the morning hours of December 7. In addition, information is given about the person before he or she enlisted, the circumstances of joining, and what happened to each after the attack. We fortunately have been able to trace the postwar activities of the forty who were chosen, even though more than one-third died before this work was written.

The interviews have been arranged in seven chapters based on where the speaker was located on December 7. Each chapter is introduced by a brief description of the military installation or installations that define it and by a probable chronological sequence for the events in the area. The brevity of the raid and the confusion it produced make reconstructions difficult; therefore, the times used may not always be precisely accurate, although they do seem closest to being correct. We have tried to keep all the introductory material brief in the belief that most readers want to hear the words of those who survived the attack, not of two historians who years later wish to pass on their views about it. Anyone who wishes to read a scholar's view of World War II should peruse Paul Fussell's

Wartime: Understanding and Behavior in the Second World War (Oxford: Oxford University Press, 1989), which confirms much of what is said in this book.

Unlike Fussell, who fought in World War II, Robert La Forte and Ronald Marcello are veterans of the peacetime military. They hope that they have not let such experience interfere with clear thinking and sound judgment in their response to Pearl Harbor. Operating on the assumption that Alexander Pope was correct when he wrote that "a little learning is a dangerous thing," we realize the burden that service in the Anti-Aircraft Artillery or U.S. Coast Guard may have created.

One person who helped us prepare this volume with his critical commentary and wise opinions on how the entries might be improved is our friend and collegue Professor Edward J. Coomes, Jr., who rarely let us forget that in postwar America and during the Korean conflict he was Yeoman Second Class E. J. Coomes of the USS *Koka* (ATA-185). His knowledge of the sea helped us avoid mistakes, but he should in no way be held responsible for any that may remain.

We also would like to thank Ms. Shannon Peck, student assistant, and Ms. Betty Burch, administrative assistant, Department of History, for their help in copyreading and secretarial matters. Ms. Mary Nash, a media specialist, helped prepare the maps, making them much more useful than two historians could have. And, as is apparent, John Paschetto, project editor at Scholarly resources, did a splendid job of editing the manuscript. Of course, errors of judgment and fact are our own.

Robert S. LaForte
Ronald E. Marcello

Chapter I

Attack at Sea

Although most books about the Pearl Harbor raid begin with the dive-bomber attack on Ford Island at 7:55 A.M., fighting between the United States and Japan erupted slightly more than one hour earlier, in waters near the entrance to the harbor channel. Even before Privates Joseph L. Lockard and George E. Elliott unknowingly observed incoming Japanese planes from their Opana mobile radar station at Kahuku Point, on the northern tip of Oahu, around 6:45 A.M., men on the USS *Condor*, a converted minesweeper, sighted an enemy submarine. At 3:42 A.M. the officer of the deck, Ensign R. C. McCloy, became convinced that he saw a periscope approximately one and three-quarter miles southwest of the harbor entrance buoys, in an area where American submarines were prohibited from operating submerged. By blinker he passed word to the destroyer *Ward*, which was then on patrol at the channel entrance.

Lieutenant William W. Outerbridge, the *Ward*'s captain, searched the area for about one hour. He resumed action around 6:30 A.M., when a message from the USS *Antares*, on its way to Oahu, confirmed the presence of a submarine. Meanwhile, before Outerbridge reacted, Ensign William Tanner, flying a Navy Catalina, sighted the craft and dropped smoke pots to mark the location for the *Ward*. Outerbridge concluded that the submarine was attempting to follow the *Antares* into Pearl Harbor. At 6:45 he fired his number one gun and missed. Number three gun fired next and hit the craft; then, as the *Ward* passed over the target, she dropped depth charges. At 6:53 the lieutenant radioed Fourteenth Naval District Headquarters: "We have attacked, fired upon, and dropped depth charges upon submarine operating in defensive sea area."

Other than dispatching the ready duty destroyer *Monaghan*, closing the net gate at the harbor, and attempting further verification of the sinking, no action was taken. Information about the *Ward*'s attack passed slowly up the chain of command, and Admiral Husband E. Kimmel, commander of the Pacific Fleet, learned of the affair shortly before bombs began to fall on Pearl Harbor.

In the following interview, Fireman William Ellis describes the battle as seen from the deck of the *Antares*.

1
Fireman Third Class William Ellis
USS *Antares*

When Bill Ellis and his shipmates on the USS *Antares* (AG10) left Pearl Harbor on November 3, little did they realize that on their return five weeks later they would witness the opening shots on the day of "infamy," December 7, 1941. The *Antares*, a naval supply ship, had sailed to Canton Island, roughly north of Samoa and near the equator, to deliver foodstuff and military stores to the Navy and Marine commands there. The only excitement in the first half of the passage occurred on the day the crew arrived at Canton, November 20, when they watched a warehouse fire explode cases of beer and whiskey before the sailors were called from the ship to help fight the fire.

The voyage back to Hawaii was considerably livelier. Just outside Canton waters they discovered that a submarine of unknown nationality was following them. The *Antares*'s captain, a lieutenant commander, tried to contact the vessel by radio but got no response. He then informed Pearl Harbor that his ship was being tracked by an unidentified submarine. "In a very short time," according to Ellis, "a destroyer appeared, an older vessel, a four-stacker," and accompanied the *Antares*. "We were in rough seas all the way back, but the submarine stayed with us; it appeared every night. The destroyer also stayed and screened for us, because that darn sub tailed us all the way." What was already an interesting trip became even more exciting for Ellis and his shipmates when they prepared to enter Pearl Harbor.

Ellis had joined the Navy on February 6, 1941, when he was almost eighteen. Although born on February 18, 1923, in Denison, Texas, on the Red River sixty miles northeast of Dallas, he grew up in Saint Louis, Missouri. After his induction, he was sent to the Great Lakes Naval Training Station near Chicago. Following boot camp, he was stationed at Terminal Island, California, and then at Hawaii. It was summer when the Navy assigned him as a fireman apprentice to the *Antares*.

The interview begins with the much-discussed sinking of a Japanese submarine by the USS *Ward* at the mouth of the main channel into Pearl Harbor about one hour before the aerial assault at 7:55 A.M. Ellis was impressed by the presence of a Navy commodore—a "four-striper"—who had joined the *Antares* at Canton Island and apparently played an important role in the destruction of the enemy vessel.

"We were in sight of Pearl Harbor at about a quarter till 4:00 on the morning of December 7. The reason I know that is because I went on a 4:00–8:00 watch that morning in the fireroom. Fifteen minutes before the hour is when I reported for duty, and you could look off the gunwales of my ship and see the lights. The horizon had to be within ten miles, so we were four to six miles from the islands.

"We were looking forward to being in port and having liberty. Of course, there wasn't much left of the weekend since it was Sunday, but we were looking forward to getting ashore. We would probably eat, drink, and sightsee around. I didn't do much bumming around the cathouses, but some of the guys did. I won't say I didn't, but I rarely did. I did get tattoos, quite a few. I was just eighteen years old, and my shipmates, every one of my friends, was tattooed. So I was as stupid as those guys.

"Well, anyway, the lights I saw had to be Honolulu and lights coming off Pearl Harbor. Things weren't any different than when we left; they were well lit that night. We also had our running lights on. It was business as usual. Okay, at some time between 6:00 and 6:30, we got all the way up to the entrance to the channel. We were towing a barge that we had picked up at Palmyra Island, and the Navy had to send a towboat out to pick up the barge before we entered the channel. So we were steaming in circles, waiting for something to come out and get this barge so we could go in.

"We had lost airflow to the fireroom. Since I was on watch and I was a fireman, I was told to go up and trim the vents to the fireroom as we had been doing the entire trip when we lost the wind. We had reach rods from the fireroom that would go up to the vents, and we could trim them by hand down below. But the reach rods didn't work very well. In fact, one was broken, so we had to have somebody go up there occasionally to trim our vents into the wind. We didn't have forced draft in our fireroom; we had natural draft that came out of these big vents up on the boat deck.

"So at 6:00 or 6:30 that morning, I went to the boat deck to trim these vents to the fireroom. During the time I was up there trimming, boy-oh-boy, the scrambling on the bridge just went goofy! The officer of the day, the signalman, and the radioman were all there. The signalman was out on the wing of the bridge throwing signals. We had a PBY bomber* circling above us and dropping flares in the ocean because there was a submarine out there. I thought it was the same submarine that had been tailing us all the time, but there's no proof it was. I don't believe it was a miniature sub, but that's what everyone you read says it was. I thought it was a pretty good sized submarine.

"The conning tower was all I could see. It came up out of the water just about the time that the PBY bomber was dropping flares. A destroyer, the *Ward*, spotted her. I thought the destroyer was the one that had been with us all the while, but it wasn't. I found out since that the *Ward* hadn't been away from Pearl Harbor. I don't know where the destroyer that accompanied us went.

*The PBY, or Catalina, and the PBM, or Mariner, were reconnaissance planes equipped with pontoons and .30- and .50-caliber machine guns; they also could carry bombs and depth charges. They were built for the Navy and first flown in 1935 and 1939, respectively.

"I was on the boat deck, and our guys on the bridge were really active. The signalmen on each of the wings of the bridge were flashing signals to the destroyer and to the plane up above. Since we had a commodore aboard, a four-striper, I got to believe he was in charge.

"Well, with all this happening the submarine comes out of the water with its bow aimed right at us. Here we were, ready to enter the channel, and this is happening. Now it's 6:30. We thought the submarine was trying to get us and sink us just as we entered the mouth of the channel. This would probably have blocked the channel more than the submarine would have. Of course, she might have been trying to get in the harbor, but she had her bow aimed right at us. Our commodore believed the sub was trying to sink us. That's what the guys on the bridge that were communicating with the PBY and destroyer told us.

"I talked to the radioman later. He was a friend of mine. I wish I could remember his name. We went through the Great Lakes training center together. He told me that the communications passed from the officer of the day and the commodore—the signals—to the other vessels were: 'Sink that submarine!' That's what the radioman told me.

"We were communicating and the PBY dropped flares. The next thing I knew was that the destroyer was blasting the conning tower off the sub with a 5-inch gun. I call it a 5-inch gun. I believe it was a 5-inch gun. She fired two shots. Then the destroyer took a different course and came across the top of this submarine and dropped depth charges. At least two depth charges went off. Then the ocean heaved up. I'd never seen a submarine blown up in the water. I believe this was a big submarine, not a small one.

"This all occurred just as the sub's bow was facing us. It looked very much like she was coming out of the water and was going to let us have it right there. That was the word being passed between the officers on the bridge—that's what they surmised. The word that came down to me from the radioman was that the commodore issued the order to sink that thing.

"We weren't two hundred yards from the submarine. If the destroyer hadn't been watching what she was doing, she could have rammed us; that's how close we were. But she didn't. She spun around and did some pretty damned good maneuvering to spin around and come across the top of the submarine and drop the depth charges just exactly in the right spot. But the sub was already going down. They had already blown the conning tower off. The ocean just heaved up with the submarine. You could see the debris and bodies.* The ocean was full of stuff from the sub.

"All this activity didn't take very long. After the sub was sunk, all I could think about was to get below and tell my ship-mates down in the fireroom. When I went down the steel ladders, I never did hit a rung on them. I went from one deck to the other on the handrails. Below decks nobody could believe a word of this without going topside and finding out for himself. All the men below decks, operating the ship in the engine room and fireroom, had to go up one at a time and find out for themselves. This was between 6:30 and 7:00.

"The radioman I talked to told me it was a Japanese submarine. Until then I didn't really have any idea what was going on. It all happened so quickly. It was very few minutes. I stood there watching them drop flares, the submarine came out of the water, and then came the fire from the destroyer, the *Ward*.

"I have read about what happened that day. It is a rare thing to find any information about what exactly happened before the war started. But what I have found to read didn't mention the *Antares*, didn't mention the PBY, didn't mention anything except the *Ward* taking it upon herself to come out there and sink this submarine. Personally, I don't believe that to be the case. There were other things involved, other facts."*

* * *

*No one on the *Ward* made an official report of finding debris and bodies.
*In *Report of the Joint Committee on the Investigation of the Pearl Harbor Attack*, 79th Cong., 2d sess., 1946, S. Doc. 244, Serial 11033, 66, the writer says: "The Navy destroyer *Ward* was informed [by the minesweeper *Condor*] and, after instituting a search, sighted the periscope of an unidentified submarine apparently trailing a target repair ship en route to Honolulu harbor. This submarine was sunk shortly after 6:45 A.M." The *Antares* docked at Honolulu on December 7. It is undoubtedly wrongly identified as a target repair ship in the investigation's report.

The interview concludes with Ellis's comments on the air attack and with the *Antares*'s docking at Honolulu Harbor, which was approximately seven air miles from the center of Pearl Harbor.

"After the sub sank, we didn't enter Pearl Harbor. We stayed at the mouth of the channel for close to an hour. I don't know whether we were anchored, whether we dropped the hook. I think we were steaming around on our own. I went back down below decks, and I don't know why we stayed there.

"The next thing I knew was that we were coming off of watch. We were being relieved by the 8:00–12:00 watch. I went down to my quarters at fifteen minutes till 8:00. I conferred with the guys that had gotten up or were coming off watch about what had happened. Then I was going to take a shower and go and eat breakfast. I was right at the edge of the shower with my shipmate at five minutes to 8:00 or whatever.

"We were just ready to enter the shower, and, boy, here comes the fire from a machine gun through the wooden hatches on the ship. I hadn't heard any planes yet. The first noise I heard was the slugs coming through the wood deck out here. Our engineering quarters were covered by steel decks on both sides of the ship. In the middle of the ship were the wood hatches, and these hatches were taken apart piece by piece when the ship was being loaded or unloaded. There was a ladder that came down to our quarters, which surrounded a hatch, and then the hatch went down to just above the bilge. These wood hatches were both above us and in our quarters. And, boy, the slugs were coming through these hatches, hitting the hatches, and hitting the sides of the ship. Then we started hearing the planes.

"Here I was, standing over at the scuttlebutt with a shipmate of mine. We were talking about what had happened before, and we hear the slugs start hitting the ship. Then the guys start running topside to find out what's going on. As soon as the last guy got up the ladder, about ten of them came flying back down, because, boy, the planes were hot and heavy coming in. They were going right over us, right up to the Fleet Landing and then to the ships in the harbor. We could see the whole harbor from out there.

"We couldn't tell if they dropped any bombs at us or not . . .

there were geysers of water that you could see. I got topside very shortly after this. I snuck up. My shipmate, Bob Marty, and I got into our nest egg up there [*nest egg* is Ellis's term for a hiding place]. There was no General Quarters sounded. We didn't even have training with the term General Quarters until after this day. We never traveled in any convoys. We were a ship all by ourselves, just traveling more like a merchantman. We had drills for safety, for escape if anything happened on ship, but I can't remember that we ever had the term General Quarters. We never had a real gun on board. We had a saluting battery, a 3-inch gun, but no ammunition.

"Marty and I stayed close to the nest egg, but we peered out to try to watch what was going on. We could see the planes coming in over the harbor, dive-bombing. We'd see formations of planes, and then we'd see them, one at a time, coming down through the smoke and dropping their bombs and then going back up. We saw the smoke; that was the first thing we saw. At the time we thought it was just oil drums blowing up or fuel tanks in the harbor. As far as it being ships, we didn't think that they had been hit.

"While the bombing was going on, the skipper decided we were going to go up to the Honolulu docks. I don't know if they were expecting us. It was something like five miles away. We got under way. Our speed was ten knots; that's as fast as we could go. We steamed along the shoreline and around into the docks. We got there sometime between 9:30 and 10:00. As far as we could tell, the attack ended at 10:30 or so. When we got to Honolulu we were ordered back to the fireroom. We secured the fires, the boilers, the main engines, and so on. We thought we'd probably have to go ashore as a rescue party, but we didn't. We stayed aboard ship.

"Nobody was allowed to leave the ship. Everybody ganged up in their own quarters—the engineers stayed in the fireroom or the engine room—whether they were on watch or not. That night there was a lot of surmise going on: 'Suppose they try to invade. What are we going to be able to do?' But nothing was really done that night. There was gunfire all night. Oh, man, there were reports of this guy shot off the top of a warehouse or this guy walking around and being shot by a marine on duty. All night long there was gunfire.

"The next day we took a few supplies, such as food and fuel oil, and went back to Pearl Harbor. Our berth was up beyond the dry docks and the submarine base over to the right of Ford Island where the battleships were. So we steamed back, and we came up the channel in broad daylight. Oh, man, the place had deep oil on top of the water, and motor launches were pulling guys to the Fleet Landing. I guess they had been killed when the planes were machine-gunning. Bodies were being towed out. We had reports that guys trying to get back to their ships were waiting for boats at the Fleet Landing and were killed. They were still taking bodies out from underneath the Fleet Landing and pulling them from the debris around there for days.

"I remember, after we landed, I had the opportunity to walk down to see the *Cassin* and *Downes*, which were in dry dock in front of the *Pennsylvania*. The *Pennsylvania* had taken a bomb. The *Cassin* and *Downes* were totally destroyed in the dry dock; they were just remnants of roasted hulks, burned hulks. Their crews were gone; the dry docks were empty."

Ellis left Pearl Harbor in March 1942 with the *Antares*. Before it sailed, it was overhauled and fitted with armaments: 5-inch, 3-inch, and 20-millimeter guns, as well as .50-caliber machine guns. The crew also learned General Quarters drill. Ellis never returned to Oahu. He and his ship followed the American advance across the Pacific during the war, and his last port of call there was Okinawa. He returned to the United States in May 1945 and, after several months of shore duty, was mustered out of the Navy on February 23, 1946. He reenlisted several times in the Naval Reserve, finishing this phase of military service in the 1960s.

As a civilian, he serviced all types of automotive and electrical systems and then spent twenty years as a product analyst in fuel systems for the manufacturing division of the Borg Warner Corporation. He retired in March 1987 and lives in Robertsville, Missouri.

Battleship Row 11

ing of when each battleship was hit. What is known

Chapter II

Battleship Row

Japanese bombers came to Pearl Harbor on December 7 to destroy the strength of the Pacific Fleet—its battleships and aircraft carriers. Fortunately for the United States, the carriers were at sea that morning. The battlewagons, however, were moored alongside Ford Island in their usual berthings on what was called Battleship Row. Most were tied two abreast in a line extending down from the northeast end of the island.

Southernmost was the USS *California*; it was separated from the rest of the battleships by the oiler *Neosho*, which on December 7 was discharging fuel into Ford Island's tank farm. From that point northward were the following pairs: *Oklahoma* and *Maryland, West Virginia* and *Tennessee, Vestal* (a repair ship) and *Arizona*. Last in line was the *Nevada*. The *Oklahoma, West Virginia*, and *Vestal* were seaward, or farther from the island, and theoretically more vulnerable to torpedo-plane attack.

Since the main thrust of the attack was against Battleship Row, several of these ships were sunk, most before they could get up enough steam to leave their berthings. No one knows exactly how many bombs and torpedoes were loosed on them that day by waves of Japanese aircraft, but the hostile airmen performed with a success that not even their commanders had believed possible.

The confusion created by the raid has prevented any pinpointing of when each battleship was hit. What is known is that the assault opened around 7:56 A.M., soon after the first bomb was dropped on the nearby Ford Island Naval Air Station. Between 7:56 and 8:25, so-called phase one of the air raid, torpedo planes made four distinct runs, two of which were directed at Battleship Row. The first was by far the deadliest. Twelve planes were involved, launching their explosives at low altitudes—50 to 100 feet—and at very short distances. All of the battleships on the outside were effectively hit by one or more torpedoes. During the second run, three struck the *Oklahoma*, which heeled rapidly to port; sporadic strafing also occurred at this time. Meanwhile, an estimated thirty dive-bombers made eight distinct attacks in phase one. In the second of these assaults the forward powder magazine of the *Arizona* was hit, and the resulting oil fire threatened the *Tennessee* and obscured the defenders' vision. The *West Virginia* was struck during the third run by two heavy bombs. In phase two, from 8:25 to 8:40 A.M., fifteen dive-bombers participated in five attacks that included sorties against the *Maryland, Oklahoma,* and *Nevada.* Fighter planes flew in all of these formations and engaged in strafing runs. Dive-bombers, after dropping their loads, also set upon these vessels with their machine guns.

Although horizontal bombers were included in phases one and two, their participation came mainly in phase three, from 8:40 until 9:15, when eight groups dropped missiles (armor-piercing shells fitted with fins) on various targets. The third of these groups followed very closely the line of battleships, and one of its planes probably hit the *California* with the bomb that penetrated to the second deck and exploded.

By 8:30 the *Arizona* was a burning wreck, the *Oklahoma* had capsized, the *West Virginia* had sunk, and the *California* was listing badly. The other battleships also had been hit. The *Tennessee* had taken two bombs and was severely damaged by fires caused by debris from the *Arizona.* The *Maryland* had been hit by a fragmentation bomb on its forecastle and by a missile farther below. Only the *Nevada* got under way. Before casting off around 9:00, she had been struck by one torpedo and by two or three shells dropped by dive-bombers. She headed south for the channel while under attack by a variety of aircraft, suffering several more hits before beaching herself at Hospital Point around 9:40 A.M.

Of the more seriously damaged vessels the *West Virginia*, the newest battleship in the fleet, took six or seven torpedoes on the port side and two bomb hits. She was the first battleship to be attacked, at 7:56. The *Arizona*, however, took the worst beating and suffered the greatest loss of life: 1,103 men, or over one half of the total casualties suffered by the fleet at Pearl Harbor. Eight bombs struck her. A heavy bomb hit beside the number two turret, penetrated the forecastle, exploded the forward magazine, and broke the ship apart. She heaved mightily in the water as flames shot five hundred feet in the air.

The *California* was slow to respond to the attack. At 8:05 she took two torpedoes below the armor belt and by 8:10 had lost power. At 8:25 a bomb penetrated a magazine, and a second bomb ruptured the bow. By 9:10 the ship was engulfed in flames; at 10:02 she was abandoned. The *Oklahoma* was struck by three torpedoes in rapid succession early in the battle. When she began to roll the order to abandon ship was given. As the bombing and strafing continued, she capsized by 8:15 or 8:20.

During the fight the *Neosho* got under way and avoided being hit, a fortunate circumstance considering her high-octane cargo. The *Vestal*, despite her location, also fared better than the rest. She took two bombs and suffered serious flooding but got under way at 8:45, ultimately to be beached on the Aiea Shoal.

Smaller ships near Battleship Row were mostly ignored by the Japanese. The USS *Avocet* (AVP-4), a seaplane tender moored at the naval air station dock near the southern end of Ford Island, escaped unscathed and later went to the aid of the *Nevada*. Water Tender Second Class Emil T. Beran, who was on board the nearby USS *Allen*, noted that the attackers were after "bigger game." As a result, by the time the victors flew back to the ships that awaited them a few hundred miles to the north, the pride of the Pacific Fleet lay mostly in ruins.

2
Private First Class James Cory
USS *Arizona*

James Cory enlisted in the U.S. Marine Corps in his hometown of Dallas, Texas, on Friday, June 13, 1940, the day he heard that France had surrendered to Hitler's Germany. He joined because he had been unable to find a job and because he could see war "looming ahead" and wanted "to get what training I could" before America entered the battle.

Cory was born at Saint Paul's Sanitarium in Dallas on October 27, 1920. After graduating from high school in 1937, he worked sporadically, when he could find employment. In 1940 he first tried to enlist in the Navy but discovered that it had reached its quota for the year. After becoming a marine and completing boot camp in San Diego, he was sent to sea school, where he learned the role of a marine afloat, a duty he described as "providing internal security and spearheading landing forces on hostile shores." He then requested service aboard the USS *Arizona* (BB39) and joined the ship's complement in October 1940 at Pearl Harbor.

For several weeks before December 7, 1941, Cory was busy as a pointer for the two 5-inch guns manned by marines on the ship's secondary aft near the mainmast. At that time, the *Arizona* was on maneuvers with other members of the fleet, and target practice was a major part of the undertaking. As a pointer, Cory was responsible for elevating and depressing the guns. Back in port on the afternoon of the 6th, he pulled watch from midnight to 2:00 on Sunday morning.

Regarding statements he had read that the fleet's sailors were physically spent on Sunday from a night of carousing in Honolulu, Cory, who saw most of the seamen return to the *Arizona* by midnight, stated that no disturbances occurred and nothing unusual happened. Only a few had been drinking. "You see more rowdiness at a high school football game today," he added, "than you'd see in a whole fleet liberty in Honolulu—maximum liberty ashore for the fleet for two days of a weekend."

Because he stood watch from 12:00 to 2:00 A.M., Cory was off duty on Sunday morning, December 7. He arose at 6:30 A.M., shaved, showered, dressed, and ate breakfast. About 7:55, when he heard "Prep for Morning Colors" being blown, he decided to go to Honolulu. Unable to find the seaman from whom he planned to borrow money, he left the main deck and went below to the second armored deck (third deck) where the laundry was located. Since it was closed, he had started to return to his quarters when the battle began. As he notes, he was still on the second armored deck when the word was passed that the Japanese were attacking.

"As I was coming back past turret number two, barbette number two on the third deck, some very husky sailor came down this ladder from the compartment on the first armor deck and shouted: 'Japs! We're being attacked by Japs!' There were people squatted around their coffee pots in their skivvy shirts waiting for the coffee to brew. They had just gotten up. They looked up at him, and somebody started to say something in a kidding voice, but right behind him came another man saying: 'Jap planes! Jap planes! We're being bombed!' Well, these guys were really moving. I don't think anybody in the compartment took more than a second or two to be convinced that this was an attack. Then right on the tail of this came the air-raid siren. Also, over the loudspeaker came the air defense call blown by the field music of the day.

"This said: 'We're in business, boys! No BS!' When you're in port on a Sunday morning and this sounds, you're certain that you're in business. There was no question in my mind because of the previous alerting by the sailors. I had to see this. I wasn't going to miss it. This was a ringside seat on the opening round of the biggest fight we'd ever see in our lives, and I said: 'This is something that you've got to witness, buddy! You can't sit down here!'

"I rushed through the M Division's compartment to the next compartment. I went up a ladder on the aft, starboard side, then aft again on the second deck until I got to the compartment leading up to the Marines' compartment. Immediately above the Marines' compartment was another ladder, and I went up to casemate nine, which was above the Marines' compartment on the starboard side. I knew the *Vestal* was on the other side, and I figured it would screen my view, so I didn't go there. In this casemate was a bay window, in essence, in the shape of a configuration of the hull, really the superstructure. This gave you a bay window–type view out over Ford Island and of the *Tennessee*.

"Some sailor said: 'Look, there's a Jap plane,' and we saw one. I was kind of hesitant to get right out toward the front of the port where the gun was because I didn't know what to expect, but I wanted to see. So I went to this gun port and looked out and saw a Jap plane very plainly. It looked much like a Spitfire, except that the wheels were fixed types sticking down with pants over them. It just cleared the afterdeck of the *Tennessee*. It didn't dawn on me at the time that this might have been a torpedo plane which had come down over Merry's Point, past the sub pens, and launched its torpedo in Merry's Loch. I suspect that the first weapon that was launched at the *Arizona* was probably this plane launching its torpedo.

"We saw a plane over Ford Island start smoking, and then we felt the impact of bullets on the casemate overhead, and you could feel them hitting the quarterdeck and coming up the after superstructure and then pounding into your overhead in the teak deck above the metal overhead on this casemate. The sailors came running back from that hatch. They were white; they were scared!

"I noticed that there was a slow chatter of some of our .50-caliber machine guns from some of the destroyers moored off the landward side of Ford Island. That's a very slow chatter, a .50-caliber. The ship, it seemed to me, lurched to starboard, and you felt her decks being penetrated with an explosion that was a muffled-type explosion. I would say this was the first torpedo, the first blow with which the *Arizona* was hit that would have done any damage other than superficial.

"There was plenty of activity, and I began to get frightened about now. The explosion from the torpedo moved the *Arizona*, lifted the ship, and moved it against the quays. It heaved up the port side, and you could feel the decks—the compartments— being penetrated just like you could hold a taut piece of cloth or two or three pieces separated by your fingers and feel a needle go through them. That's the way it felt. You began to get afraid.

I don't know about other people, but I thought: 'Gee, I might get killed!'

"As I remember, a plane dived over Ford Island heading toward us. It was a dive-bomber. It released something from beneath it. I recognized that this was a bomb, but I was fascinated by the sight of it because this was the first bomb I'd seen in war headed in my general direction. It looked like it was oblong when it left the airplane, but then it began to get like a basketball, then briefly it turned oblong again and flashed into the sea between the stern of the *Tennessee* and the dredge pipeline. This was no more than 100 to 150 yards from where I was. The blast and the Whump and the splashing water and everything *really* excited me, and I turned around and said: 'Hey, look, a bomb hit over there!'

"I had no duties whatsoever at this time. The standard rule in the Navy is, If you're not engaged, stand clear. Now a naval officer came through the compartment from the quarterdeck below. This one was fully clothed. He was waving his hands and saying: 'Everybody below the armor deck! Get below!' Regardless of what you wanted to do, in the naval service at that time, you didn't disobey an officer. I went down the hatch, but just as I put my foot on the ladder to go below, General Quarters sounded. Now that gave me something specific to do, and I'm glad it did because at this point I'd already thought about the exploding battleships in the Battle of Jutland!'"*

As the order "All hands, man your battle stations" sounded over the speaker system, Private First Class Cory ran toward his post in the fire control area of the 5-inch guns, located in the secondary aft. As he made his way through the *Arizona*, he noticed Rear Admiral Isaac C. Kidd, the ship's captain, donning his blouse and skipping a button as the admiral and his aide hurried toward the bridge. The first bomb to strike the ill-fated vessel hit at this time, as Cory began to climb a ladder on a leg supporting the tripod mast.

* * *

*Fought on May 31, 1916, the Battle of Jutland was the single significant engagement between the British and German navies in World War I.

"I started up this inclined leg on the starboard side. When I got about two thirds up, there was a 'slap' aft—a very heavy 'slap'—and then you felt the deck of the *Arizona* being penetrated, and then you heard a bomb explosion. I knew what happened because I observed this on other vessels. A bomb hit aft on the slanting part of turret number four. I saw this when I looked down later. There was a bomb splash, as we called it, because the bomb had hit the slanting side of the turret and glanced off of it and exploded in officers' country and literally wiped out most of the officers aboard the *Arizona*.

"I ran on up the ladder just as fast as I could and came to rest against Lamar Crawford's back because he was blocking my way. I started to step around him and I saw the reason for his delay. There was Lieutenant Carlton E. Simonsen, USMC, one of the most popular officers on the *Arizona*, lying in a pool of blood. I said: 'Oh, my God!' Crawford helped me roll him over. His whole abdomen and lower chest were just torn to bits—probably by splinters. He was losing blood in such volume that he couldn't last much longer. He said: 'Leave me. Go on!'

"By this time I was literally scared out of my wits. There were bullets ringing into the secondary aft, and you could feel the impact of them on the metal as you went up these various ladders and into the secondary aft, which had a trap hatch—you had to push it back to get in. I did that as accurately as I could, and I was on station."

Once at his battle station, Cory performed his duties regarding the guns, which were surface defense weapons and of no use in the battle that was raging. No sooner had he opened several windows to get a better view for setting his guns' elevations than, he believed, several more bombs hit the *Arizona*, near to where he was located.

"The bombs struck forward—forward of us. We were in the mainmast, two thirds of the way back in the ship from the stem. They struck forward of us, and immediately you could feel them penetrating the decks, and then there was this big Whoosh! Now it wasn't a Bang. It wasn't a Boom. It was a Whoosh! You could hear the bombs whistling down and feel them hit and penetrate, and then this Whoosh. It was all very rapid, almost simultaneous.

"The bridge shielded us from flames coming aft. There was at least eight hundred feet of very massive structure that shielded us from this.* But still around the edges in these open windows came the heat and the sensation of the blast. We cringed there. You have an instant, automatic response. I think that at this moment I wanted to flee, but this was impossible. You're on station, you're in combat; you can't leave until you're given permission, and nobody's going to ask permission to leave.

"In desperation for something to do, I went aft. It was all in a matter of seconds, but I can't tell you what the time factor was. I saw the bow of the *Nevada* explode forward of turret number one. I thought: 'My God, there goes another battleship!' She sank under the impact of explosions and came up out of the water. It amazed me because these are big pieces of equipment. A battleship is not just something you toss around.

"About that time Major Allan Shapley gave the order: 'Abandon ship! Let's get below!' I waited until six men got through that hatch. I was right beside it, and I wanted to be the first out; but I forced myself to wait until some other men had gone first. I was confused along with being scared, but not so confused that I wanted to run. Fear had now taken hold, but not to the point to destroy discipline. I went down the proper ladders until I got to the searchlight platform, and then I said: 'To hell with traffic rules! I'm going down this ladder!' I remembered not to touch the hot ladder rails as I raced down that ladder, facing aft, onto the quarterdeck.

"There were bodies of men. I'd seen this from above, but it didn't register clearly until I got down on the quarterdeck. These people were zombies, in essence. They were burned completely white. Their skin was just as white as if you'd taken a bucket of whitewash and painted it white. Their hair was burned off; their eyebrows were burned off; the pitiful remnants of their uniforms in their crotch was a charred remnant; and the insoles of their shoes was about the only thing that was left on these bodies. They were moving like robots. Their arms were out, held away

---

*The *Arizona* was 608 feet long.

from their bodies, and they were stumping along the decks. These were burned men!

"The *Arizona* was settling by now. The problem now that the ship is settling is that the mooring lines are beginning to get very taut. The gangplank has broken and turned over on its side. It's merely a 12-by-2 board, going across to the quay, which is a cement rectangle filled with sand and has some bollards, great big steel posts, on top of it. I didn't want to make the trip across there, from ship to quay, but I had to do something quickly, so I just made up my mind and trotted across that piece of 12-by-2 before it fell off. As I was going across, one of these six-inch cables—a manila rope six inches in diameter*—spatted past my head. It missed by a very small margin. I don't know what would have happened, but at least it would have knocked me off of that gangplank probably back into the ship if it had not killed me, which I think it would.

"I made the quay and scrambled across and down to the fender on the other side, and here were motor launches and people trying to start them. The first thing I thought was: 'That's a nonmotorman. He's not part of that boat's crew, and I'm not going to get into that mess.' So I dived out into the harbor water. When I hit that cold water, I wished I had taken off my shoes because I simply could not swim with those heavy brogans on in the condition I was in. Here I remembered my father saying: 'If you ever get in trouble in water, turn over on your back and throw your head back as far as you can and inhale and try to duck your head and keep your mouth above water until you can think your way out of it.' Well, this is a form of floating, and I eventually floated and swam over to this dredge pipeline pier.

"During this swim some Filipino mess boy came by me at one hundred miles an hour, swimming like a duck. I asked him for help, and he ignored me. I'm glad he did because I'd probably drowned both of us. There were bomb splashes nearby; there was strafing in the water. You could feel the impact of the bullets. There was a tremendous amount of confusion and noise and all this sort of thing. Our own oil was bubbling up and

*Cory probably means six inches in circumference, a much more likely size.

congealing. People who have never seen this at sea cannot imagine what oil is like once it is exposed to cool seawater. It becomes a globlike carpet about six inches thick, gelatinous. It was catching fire slowly and was incinerating toward us.''

After reaching the pipeline, where he was sheltered somewhat from Japanese airmen who were strafing the water, Cory was joined by other sailors and marines. Together, he and Private First Class Don C. Young swam onward to Ford Island.

"I climbed ashore and went looking for Young. I saw him wretching beneath a palm tree, and I said: 'We'd better get under cover.' We went into a garage. He said: 'I've got to get something,' and he started throwing up again. We went outside underneath this tree probably in momentary confusion. He said: 'Help me get my trousers off,' because they were oil soaked and burning his legs. I didn't realize it at the time.

"But we started to get these trousers off, and a bomb exploded quite near. How near I can't say. But we were lifted up into the air and flung down to the ground again. Young got up crying in a sense of anger more than anything else. His trousers were up around his abdomen again, and he says: 'Goddamn, Cory, I'm having trouble today! I can't even get my pants off!' I said: 'Well, leave them on until we get into a house.' After that we just ignored the bomb. We were alive and still functioning, and it hadn't hurt either one of us.''

Cory was ultimately joined by other mates. He was united a bit later with Marine Corps officers and ordered to duty on the USS *Tennessee*. Put on watch on the bow of the ship and armed with a .30-caliber machine gun, he witnessed American planes returning from patrol that night being fired on "by the whole damned harbor. Everybody was trigger-happy. We shot down four of our own planes.'' Below he comments on the many rumors that were circulating among the military after the attack.

"The wildest rumors were going around that night. The Japs had landed on the other side of the island and were pushing across the island, and we'd soon be captured; and they'd sunk all the carriers; and they hadn't got the *Enterprise*, and it'd blown the hell out of the Jap fleet; and so on. They sent some interisland seaplanes out with men with Browning automatic rifles to the Jap fleet. We heard the most fantastic tales about the accomplishments of these unarmed aircraft shooting down numerous Japanese planes. By and large, it was a bunch of stuff you didn't believe, but you wanted to hear everything. This is a normal condition after something like this and after every other battle or near combat that I've been in. You learn to weigh this, and most reasonable men come to discount 99 percent of what they hear."

Cory was promoted to corporal soon after Pearl Harbor. He served in the Pacific theater during the remainder of the war and took part in the occupation of Japan at the conflict's end. He mustered out of the service in 1945 and attended Southern Methodist University under the GI bill. Not finishing college, he married and raised a family. His first postwar job was selling insurance, but he spent most of his days as building director at the world-famous Neiman-Marcus Department Store. James Cory died on July 9, 1978, at age 56.

3
Seaman First Class Clay H. Musick
USS *Arizona*

Clay Musick was born in New Mexico in 1917. His family soon moved to the Texas panhandle and, when he was eight, moved again to Weslaco in the Rio Grande Valley, where he attended school, graduating in 1934. When Congress passed the Selective Service Act in October 1940, Musick joined the Navy rather than wait to be drafted. On November 6 he volunteered for six years. By enlisting he kept his older brother, who had a better job at the time, from having to go. He chose the Navy over the Army because "I couldn't see carrying that seventy-pound pack around on my back."

After boot camp, Musick was assigned to the USS *Arizona*, the only ship on which he would serve. He eventually became port bow hook on the number two motorboat, which carried passengers around Pearl Harbor and ran errands for the ship's complement. His battle station was ammunition hoistman at the port antiaircraft magazine located on the deck just below the *Arizona*'s main deck.

The day before the sneak attack, Musick and three friends went on liberty in nearby Pearl City. After a few drinks he ate "a pork chop with whatever it was that went with it." He returned to the *Arizona* at sundown, about 8:00, and went to bed one hour later at lights-out. The next morning he arose, ate breakfast, and noticed that December 7 dawned a "pretty day" with a "good breeze blowing." He then went to his post on the number two motorboat, which was scheduled to begin carrying men at 8:05 to various church services on other ships. He was topside when the attack began. Upon hearing General Quarters sound, he went below to the antiaircraft magazine to begin sending ammunition up to the guns. His description of the first phase of the battle follows.

"We heard a loud blast of noise. I looked up, and right over there, why, that's the first Jap plane I saw. The first bomb hit Ford Island. He, the Japanese aviator, had his canopy pushed back and had his hand alongside the plane. He was so close that you could have knocked him down with a hand grenade. He had his goggles up, but I really didn't even look at his face. I saw that rising-sun emblem on his plane. The first thing I thought of was: 'How did those damned Japs get over here?'

"There were two other motor launches out there, and the officer of the deck of the USS *Arizona* was telling those guys to come in there so that they wouldn't get machine-gunned. So we got off of the motorboat onto the quays and from the quays to the pilings and from the pilings to the blister* top of the USS *Arizona*, and then we ran down the blister top to a ladder.

"I went directly to the third deck and met two or three others on the way down, and we rigged the hoist and the conveyor before we went down to the magazine. I'd say there were at least six of us in the magazine. The first round of ammunition was

*In naval terminology, a blister is a bulge built into a warship to protect the vessel against torpedoes and mines.

handed to me, and I pushed it onto the conveyor to take it up to the third deck. At about the same time, we took our first hit. I went forward first, then I went backwards, and then forward again, and then I fell and got up. The lights went out except for the battle lights, so that stopped the motor from taking the ammunition up. I reached up to get the crank to start cranking the ammunition up, but I no more than got that crank in my hand, and that's when the second one hit. The second blast was a little bit greater. It seemed like it didn't shove me forward, but it shoved me backwards and then back again and then to the floor.

"They claim that the *Arizona* was hit by torpedoes, but I really don't know. I'd rather think that it was bombs. I got up, and I was trying to find the crank. There was just one battle light still on. I got the crank, and I started to put it in the socket, and that's when a bomb went down the chimney."

Those who participated in the attack on the *Arizona* disagree about a bomb's entering one of the ship's smokestacks, which Musick calls "the chimney." Historians likewise are split concerning the matter, some arguing that an armor-piercing bomb penetrated the decks and exploded in the forward powder magazine. The stack was covered by a wire screen.

Soon after the third explosion the men in the antiaircraft magazine went topside again. Although Musick did not realize it, he had been wounded. At the end of the next passage, he describes how he got to Pearl Harbor hospital.

"Then we went up. We started climbing this ladder up the wall. It was so hot you could hardly touch the rungs. I got to the third deck, but I couldn't find this opening. It was hot down there. Anyhow, I got up there, and the gunner's mate got me out, and he says: 'Musick, can you go the rest of the way?' I said: 'Yes.' The minute he turned me loose I passed out. I went up two ten-foot ladders unconscious. The only thing I can remember was that that man asked me if I could go the rest of the way myself. He had hold of my arm, and he turned me loose. I remember starting up that ladder, but I don't remember another thing until I started to step out on topside.

"There were fires all on the forecastle. Anyhow, I started to step out on topside, and there were people underneath the turret. Some were from the magazines, and some from other parts of the ship. They said: 'Musick, go back down, go back down! They're machine-gunning the deck!' Well, you know, being half-stunned, I just walked on out. I said: 'Well, I'd better go up on the boat deck and see what I can do up there!' So I started wandering all around up there, and everything was silent. I couldn't see any movement. All I could see was flames and fire.

"So I walked to the port side of the quarterdeck. Then I walked around on the starboard side, and when I got around there, there was a marine coming out of the *Arizona*. I think he had a pair of khaki shorts on and a skivvy shirt. But his hair had been scorched and burnt like these Indians that just had this row of hair down their head. That's the way he looked to me. Mooring lines were cracking and popping and cracking and popping. There were men on fire rolling all over the deck trying to put the fire out. We both stood there for a while and kind of looked around. He was dazed and I was dazed. He said: 'I guess we'd better get off of this thing.' A gangway was rigged from the ship to this mooring quay. He was in front. The mooring lines were still popping and cracking, but I got off. I just stepped off onto the quay, and the gangway fell in the water. That's how fast the ship was listing.

"By that time sailors off the USS *Solace*, a hospital ship, were coming aboard to help all the wounded that they possibly could. I kind of turned around and saw a second marine in the water. He was hollering for help, so I got down off of this quay and on the pilings, and there was a piece of line there. I threw that piece of line to him, and I pulled him over. I hollered at one of the corpsmen, and they said that they'd be right there. I told him to just hold onto that line, that they would be there. The only thing that I can remember that that man had on was his side arm. Now whether he had shoes on, I don't know. Whether his clothes were blowed off him or burned off him, I don't know. But that's all I could see—his sidearm. He had been standing guard on the bridge.

"Then I came back over to where the first marine was—the marine sergeant. There was a boat landing on the other side of this quay. He said: 'We'd better get down here because if those

things, the mooring lines, bust or break, they'll cut you in half!'
Well, we no more got down there and this big tugboat—seagoing
tug—came up trying to put the flames out. But they couldn't get
any waterpower. So they was backed up, and they started taking
on survivors. The marine and myself were the first two. The
marine just kind of hopped on, but I held my hand out, and a
sailor pulled me on. When he pulled me on, I found out then
that I couldn't walk. I was just laying on my back. So they
backed out, and they got in the channel. I think they picked up
maybe one or two more men. I can't recall—maybe one more
man. Anyhow, this tug was picking up survivors, and as they're
going across the channel, I was laying on my back, and I could
see three horizontal bombers.

"They got me aboard there and on the shore now, and they
had me in one of these wire baskets. I kind of looked over, and
I said: 'Well, the *Arizona* has already capsized.' The corpsman
said: 'No, that's the *Oklahoma* that's capsized.' He said: 'The
Arizona is just all in flame!' He said: 'Man, that is really burning!'

"Then they took me to the hospital. They had little houses
out here. They started with 'A,' but it seems like they had me
in Letter H hut. It had bunks, and they put you in a bunk and
asked you where you hurt and all of that kind of business, you
know, how you felt, if you wanted a drink of water. That was
the corpsman. Pretty soon a nurse came by, and she started
giving everybody a hypo, a morphine shot. Pretty soon the hut
got full.

"A doctor came in about that time, and he said: 'How's it
going?' She said: 'Well, everything's all right.' He said: 'Who
have you given a hypo to and who haven't you?' She started over
and put a red cross on their head. So everybody got another
hypo. That's two.

"They started shoving these beds together so they could put
more beds in there. I was right at a window, a little window. A
bomb must have hit pretty close to this hut because it shattered
glass all over me. So they got me out of the bunk and changed
the sheets real quick and everything, and put me back. Then
they took a sheet and nailed it over that window so that the wind
wouldn't come through.

"There were so many that was hurt worse than I. I can't remember, but I believe it was Wednesday before they saw me because I wasn't bleeding anyplace. I had a couple of bad burns here on my legs, and I had a busted hip. It seems like it was Wednesday morning when they took me to X-ray to X-ray my hip. They took about three different poses of this hip—flat, on your side, and I think they even took one from the back side. Then after they took me out of the X-ray, they took me back to this hut. Later on in the day, they moved me into the main building of the hospital at Pearl Harbor in a ward."

On December 18, Musick was sent with others back to the United States; he had developed a speech problem caused by the foul air and fumes he had breathed on December 7. At Mare Island Hospital, in San Pablo Bay, California, he was diagnosed as having a "paralyzed diaphragm." At his request he was transferred to Corona Naval Hospital, east of Los Angeles, to be near a brother. Musick stayed there until July 8, 1942, when he was "surveyed out of the service." At first he worked for a shipyard in Galveston but soon joined a rehabilitation program to learn to be a dental technician, a position he later held at the Veterans Administration Hospital in Temple, Texas. He married in July 1945 and retired from the civil service with a medical disability in 1958. He currently resides in Temple.

4
Seaman Martin Matthews
Ford Island and USS *Arizona*

Although Martin Matthews was permanently assigned to Ford Island Naval Air Station, he was visiting a friend on board the USS *Arizona* when Japan attacked Pearl Harbor. He had stayed the night and watched from the vessel and its mooring quays as the dramatic events of December 7 unfolded along Battleship Row. To make matters even more complicated, he was only fifteen years old at the time, having lied about his age to enlist in the Navy. His friend, Seaman First Class William Stafford, who was already a sailor, had talked him into joining. As luck would have it, Matthews wound up at the same military base as

Stafford, who died during the air raid at his post aboard the *Arizona*.

Matthews was born in Shelbyville, Kentucky, on October 14, 1926, and met Stafford while attending school in Dallas, Texas. Several years older than Matthews, the latter was home on leave in October 1941 and getting "all the attention from the girls by wearing a uniform." This convinced Matthews that "the Navy was the route I wanted to go." With his father's signature attesting that he was seventeen and with his mother's approval, he volunteered. He spent four weeks in boot camp in San Diego and was sent to the metalsmith school at Sand Point Naval Air Station, in Seattle. After four days he was reassigned to a similar school at Ford Island Naval Air Station; he never learned why the shift was made. He began his schooling, which was largely on-the-job training with the base's PBYs, on November 28.

Stafford and Matthews spent Saturday, December 6, sightseeing around Oahu, "eating and drinking a little that evening." When they boarded the *Arizona* that night, they "weren't inebriated, but [they] weren't sober either." The first portion of the interview begins at that point and concludes as the Japanese planes depart Pearl Harbor on the 7th.

"We went aboard that night. There was a different officer of the day aboard, but word had been left that Stafford was bringing a friend. He asked if I might spend the night, and the O.D. said, 'There's no reason for him not to.' I showed him my pass from the naval air station, and I spent the night there.

"Stafford's quarters were on the aft part of the ship, the boat deck or the boat well. I slept in a bunk in his compartment. We went to sleep because we were tired, and we got up fairly early the next morning about 6:00. I got up earlier than usual because of the excitement of being aboard a battleship.

"Sunday breakfast started at 6:00. We were wearing dress whites because we were going to do some sight-seeing. We finished chow about 6:30, and we spent the next twenty minutes or so on a tour of the ship. Then we were back on the aft boat well about 7:15 or 7:30. It's hard to remember the exact time, but it was approximately that.

"We were just talking in generalities, and I told him how

much I enjoyed it and that I was looking forward to coming back aboard ship. I even said: 'I wish I could get duty aboard a battleship,' not knowing any better at the time. We were going to go ashore again and spend some more liberty, since I didn't have to be back to Ford Island until approximately 10:00 that night.

"But then we heard noise over to our starboard side. You could see a bunch of planes coming in, but nobody paid any attention to them. Then you could hear what seemed like thundering in the background, which actually were bombs starting to drop, but none of us thought about bombs. We didn't know what a bomb was yet; I had never seen one in my life.

"But as the planes got closer, the thunder got closer, and then we started seeing clouds of smoke coming up from across the roads there, the roads or channels that the ships went in and out on. Then we saw fire and explosions where the bombs hit. Well, we knew that something was wrong, but we thought that maybe it was gunnery practice.

"We didn't know that the Japanese were actually attacking us; it wasn't until after the first wave went across that we knew. No bombs hit the *Arizona* during that first attack that I remember, but there was one bomb that hit a destroyer off of Ford Island. I didn't know at the time but I found out later that it was the *Shaw*. In fact, it broke her in half.* Then I think that's when General Quarters was sounded on the *Arizona*.

"Stafford said: 'I've got to go! I'll see you later!' I remember those words. I had no place to go; I didn't even know what General Quarters was. So I just stayed in the back part of the ship. Pandemonium broke loose; sailors were running everywhere. It was a state of confusion. Guns had been encased and not prepared at all for a possible battle; they were having difficulty uncovering them; many of the guns were plugged.

"We hadn't been hit yet as I remember. It could have been because there were a lot of explosions going on, but I don't

---

*The *Shaw* was in the floating dry dock at the Navy Yard on December 7. She was badly damaged and later repaired. Matthews must have seen another ship destroyed. The minelayer *Oglala* was the only vessel sunk that could possibly have resembled the *Shaw*.

remember it. It was fifteen or twenty minutes after that, which, if I remember right, would be in the neighborhood of 8:30, that she evidently was hit with a torpedo. I didn't know what a torpedo was, either, but I heard a thunderous explosion, and fire went up on the starboard side.

"It shook me; it shuddered the ship, but it didn't knock me over. I can remember several incidents, particularly on the aft battery there. The antiaircraft guns, which then, I remember, were 50-calibers—they didn't have the modern version—and I could see the gunners trying to get ammunition from the ammunition locker.

"The boatswain's mate in charge of the ammunition locker, even with all the bombing and strafing and planes overhead—it was obvious we were being attacked at this point—refused to release ammunition from the gun locker without the permission of the officer of the day. Of course, nobody knew where the hell the officer of the day was.

"Finally, one boatswain's mate, who was in charge of one gun crew, I remember well, told this chief, if he didn't get his ass out of the way, he was going to knock it out of the way. So he proceeded to do the same and hit this chief and knocked him out of the way and then broke the lock on the ammunition locker and took the ammunition from it to feed the guns to do some shooting. He used a marlinespike to break in.

"But shortly after that is when it got thick and heavy. The first bomb or two hit the *Arizona*. I think the second bomb that hit was close to the aft deck that I was on, and, needless to say, I was petrified. To put it in plain English, it scared the living hell out of me. The concussion from it did knock me down a couple of times, but my adrenaline was pumping about a thousand miles an hour, and sweat broke out all over me. I wasn't experienced with war; I hadn't been trained for it.

"I was trying to get under cover, but at my age and not prepared for this, I was scared to death. This was not what I went into the Navy for, and it was not what I wanted. Besides I had no place to go. I didn't have a General Quarters station; I wouldn't have known what to do if I went to one. I was too damned young to realize what was going on. I didn't even know that this was a war breaking out. I thought this was just some big mistake that was being made.

"But after the second or third bomb—I don't know which—that hit the *Arizona*, and after the second or third torpedo that hit—I can't remember to this day whether it was the explosions or sheer panic within me—I wound up over the side of the *Arizona* in the water. The *Arizona* was hit numerous times on the top deck and numerous times on the waterline with torpedos. This is my recollection, and I don't say it's absolutely correct.

"Like I say, to this day I ask myself whether it was the bomb explosions while I was on the top deck that knocked me over or whether it was the inner emotion that made me jump over. I would not be a bit abashed to admit if I jumped over, but I really don't remember. All I know is that the next thing I knew I was in the water. This is just a void, a blank, but I know after the second or third bomb, or it may have been the torpedoes, I was in the water.

"I was fully clothed. Of course, I lost my cap when I went in. Man's desire for self-preservation is great. I swam away from the *Arizona* to the nearest mooring buoy. I hung on there for the balance of the attack. The buoy was astern of the *Arizona* and approximately twenty, twenty-five, or thirty yards away. It was approximately eight feet across and probably ten or fifteen feet deep. It had a lot of algae on it, green algae, barnacles, and everything. But I managed to get on the far side, and I did hang on—out of fear only. I was out of the water from a little above my waist. I was safer there than if I had been on the *Arizona* for the entire battle.

"There were steel fragments in the air, fire, oil—God knows what all—pieces of timber, pieces of the boat deck, canvas, and even pieces of bodies. I remember lots of steel and bodies coming down. I saw a thigh and leg; I saw fingers; I saw hands; I saw elbows and arms. It's far too much for a young boy of fifteen years old to have seen. Of course, I never got hit by any of it. I didn't have a scratch when it was over with. I did have quite a bit of oil and sludge and diesel oil all over me. In fact, my white uniform didn't look white anymore; it was black.

"Most of the fire was confined to the actual ship area, which was fifteen or twenty yards away. If I was in danger of catching afire, I didn't realize it. I saw a lot of fire, but it wasn't coming toward me. There was fire on the beach, too. I would have gone ashore, except there was so much havoc going on with the bombing at the naval air station on Ford Island, which was about three quarters of a mile away.

"Now I was between a rock and a hard spot. I couldn't and I didn't want to go back to the *Arizona*, and from what was happening on Ford Island, I couldn't and didn't want to go there. So I was just more or less hanging on a thread for dear life.

"All I can remember about this time is that the Japanese kept coming in constantly, wave after wave, and it seemed like they were completely uncontested, unmolested. I saw maybe one or two Jap planes that might have been hit and shot down. They were very low. After their bombing and torpedo runs, they came in strafing, but none was toward my area. They weren't paying any attention to me. Mainly they were going after the ships or anything of military value.

"I tell you, it was complete pandemonium. Like I said, I was too young at the time to fully realize what was going on, but I can describe it now thirty years later. It isn't the same at fifteen, but I've had time to dwell on it. It was a comedy of errors from the word 'go!' The Navy was unprepared; none of the personnel had been trained for imminent attack. The ammunition wasn't readily available; damage control wasn't available; watertight hatches were never closed. Even though General Quarters sounded, most of the hatches never got closed. It was complete pandemonium.

"I saw very few of our planes that got in the air. Most of them that I saw, looking over at Ford Island, had been bombed and set afire or blown apart. The ones that did get into the air were the real old-style planes. I can't remember if they were shot down or otherwise.

"The *Arizona* finally started blowing up. There was ammunition, gun lockers, shells, steel fragments, and pyrotechnics coming from all parts of the ship. It was like a fireworks display. There was a series of explosions; it wasn't just one deafening roar. Things came to a final one where she seemed like the middle part just raised up in the water and kind of half buckled and then settled back down. Of course, she never sank, because the water at that time wasn't deep enough. Her bridge and mast-head were above the water; I remember that after that she finally settled. This was about the time when the attack was just about over. I decided to get the hell away from that mooring buoy.

"I thought it was time to try to head for shore. I had to swim approximately three quarters to one mile to shore. I swam around the oil-covered water and then started toward Ford Island. The last incident I remember then during the attack is when I swam up on the island, which was rocky around the beach area there. The marines were out on patrol, and everybody was trigger-happy because they thought of a possible invasion by the Japanese. Here I was, in a white uniform, but it was more or less black. I had oil and sludge all over me. You couldn't have recognized that I was a white man.

"I remember crawling ashore and running into a marine sentry who wasn't much older than I, a year or two at most. Fortunately, the guy looked at me before he was ready to shoot. He thought I was a Japanese trying to come ashore. Only I screamed and hollered: 'I'm Navy! I'm with the United States Navy! Don't shoot!' He didn't pull the trigger. But the rifle was aimed at me, and his finger was on the trigger."

In the remainder of the interview, Matthews comments on Ford Island Naval Air Station at the end of the raid and offers opinions regarding responsibility for the U.S. military's degree of unpreparedness. His view in this respect is one frequently voiced by the survivors.

"The attack was over when I got back. There was a lot of confusion still going on. Some people thought the attack was still going on. Most of the explosions still going on were from earlier hits the Japanese had made. Ships were still blowing up in the harbor; hangars were still blowing up; gasoline was still blowing up; planes on the ground were on fire and blowing up as their fuel tanks ruptured. There was confusion around there not only for hours but for days.

"I was told to stay in the beach area. There were other men there; some had been wounded. There were not enough pharmacist's mates, doctors, or anything for all the injured at the time. Nobody really knew what to do, where to do it, or why to do it. I didn't know what to do, so I just stayed in the beach area for the next two or three hours, until it came time to clean up.

"Then I went back to the station. There were many others that I was in school with at the time, and we proceeded to try to clean some of the sludge off. You couldn't use soap and water to get the sludge off me; I had to get it off with naphtha. Then we put some dungarees on, and we started trying to rescue people who might still be alive, to remove damaged aircraft from the runways, and do just about any and everything that needed to be done on Ford Island to put it back into operation.

"Everybody who had some official capacity was trying to give orders, but nobody really knew what kind of orders to give and why they should do it. Nobody was prepared for this; at least the ones I knew weren't. Maybe the top echelon were, but I certainly wasn't. We couldn't have done any better for the Japanese than if we'd told them when to attack: 'We're ready for you!' The planes were stacked wingtip to wingtip—they were just inviting them—when they should have been scattered about. If they had been, probably 50 percent less damage would have been done, but they were in a row. They were sitting ducks.

"We spent the rest of that day and late in the evening and the next day and for several days trying to remove the damage from the hangars, and we hauled the wrecked planes off and put out small brush fires that came up. Every now and then, we would come across somebody who was pinned in the wreckage and was still alive. In fact, one time—it was three days later—there was a plane on the end of the runway. We went down there and were going to remove it, and we found out there was a pilot in it who had been injured and trapped in it for three days. I wasn't by myself; there were several in the party. But basically we were trying to put some sense of reality back in the operation of Ford Island. I don't think there was a plane intact after it was all over. At least I don't remember any.

"I went through the first night and the middle part of the next day without sleep. In fact, I wasn't alone; very few people slept then. There were rumors, and then there were rumors. We were told numerous times that the Japanese had landed. Then that rumor would be quelled, and then they'd say the Japanese had landed on another island. Then we'd be informed of the rumor that the Japanese were going to attack again in the morning. Rumors were flying fast and furious. We found out later these weren't true, but we chose to believe them at the time. We didn't know any better.

"Our morale was pretty good. It's amazing that something like this can be a common denominator and bring people together. Everybody suddenly forgets their differences and works together. The morale was good even if we were disappointed in the Navy, were disappointed that we hadn't been prepared. I can't believe that an attack as massive as this could have gone undetected in advance. I believe in God, motherhood, and apple pie, you know, and I still wave the flag. But history should hold somebody in the United States responsible for what happened at Pearl Harbor and for all the lives that were needlessly lost there."

During World War II, Martin Matthews served in both the European and Pacific theaters, where he saw considerable action. His ship assignments included the *G. F. Elliot*, which was sunk; the *Alchiba*, which was torpedoed; the *Barnett*; the *Calhoun*, which also was sunk; the APL 10; the APL 11; the *Hunter Liggett*; and the *Orvetta*. He also served at several naval air stations. In addition to many campaign ribbons, he was awarded the Navy Commendation Medal. After his discharge on December 11, 1945, he attended Southern Methodist University and the University of Texas at Austin. He was self-employed for several years and currently works as a manufacturer's representative. Of Pearl Harbor he has "lots of memories, good and bad . . . I am thankful that I survived."

5
Boatswain's Mate Second Class Joseph George
USS *Vestal*

In 1935, Joseph George was a big, tough farm boy who joined the Navy "to show" his brother, who had failed to get in, that he could make it. George mustered in at Columbus, Georgia, in June and was sent to boot camp at Hampton Roads, Norfolk, Virginia, a recently recommissioned training center. Later that year he shipped out aboard the USS *Chaumont*, went through the Panama Canal, and arrived at San Pedro, California, where he was transferred to the USS *Vestal* (AR4).

George was born in Franklin, Georgia, in 1915. After finishing high school, he worked a ten-hour day for thirty-one dollars a month at a local cotton mill and also helped out on his father's farm. As he began his twenty-year naval career, he "had no glamorous ideas about the Navy." In fact, he did not do very well soon after he joined. "I was court-martialed quite a bit," he said, "for fighting." This was not the fighting that made him fairly well known in the fleet (he was three times all-Navy and once international Golden Gloves heavyweight champion) but the kind he practiced in the bars of San Pedro, Los Angeles, and Honolulu.

As a boatswain's mate, George was responsible for the *Vestal*'s general upkeep, and her role as a repair shop contributed to the difficulty of maintaining Navy spit and polish. Sent to Pearl Harbor in 1940 as part of Fleet Problem 22, an operation maneuver or tactical exercise at sea, the *Vestal* stayed anchored near or tied to Battleship Row. She never went to sea with the fleet and mainly concerned herself with battleships, although she was in the Cruiser Repair Division. She and the *Medusa* worked on all the capital ships at Pearl Harbor, except for those that received major repairs in the Navy Yard's dry dock.

On the day of the attack the *Vestal* was tied along the seaward side of the USS *Arizona*. Although George's battle station was first loader on the 3-inch/.50-caliber antiaircraft gun, he instead helped roll up the ship's awnings, which obstructed the four 5-inch broadside cannons, as ordered by Captain Cassin B. Young, who won a Medal of Honor as a result of his actions during the air raid. George also was commended by the Navy for his efforts on December 7, even though he had trouble remembering what he had done.

"On Friday, December 5, I fought in a smoker.* I participated in smokers at the recreation center inside the Navy Yard

---

*A smoker was a series of boxing matches where attending servicemen were given free cigars and cigarettes. It could be held aboard ship or ashore.

to entertain troops or sailors or whatever. The smoker was over, I guess, at 9:00 or 10:00 P.M., and the barrooms in Honolulu were still open until 2:00 A.M., and I went downtown with one of my buddies and got in a fight with him.

"He came up and hit me behind the head, and I just raised up swinging. I was half-out. He happened to be the captain's gig's coxswain. His name was Hudgins. He's a Texas boy. Well, I knocked him down. I beat him up, cut up his face. In the fight—the smoker I fought earlier—I was knocked out on my feet. If you get knocked out on your feet, you carry on, and you don't realize what's happening—you just keep fighting. I knocked out my opponent in the last round.

"Well, I was picked up by the Shore Patrol at the bar and brought back to the ship. Old Captain Young said: 'George, I'd like to take you over to a mast.' So I went to the captain's mast on Saturday morning. They didn't usually hold captain's mast on Saturday, but they did this Saturday just for me. The captain said: 'I wish I could take you on the forecastle and have all hands kick the shit out of you; but since I can't, I'm going to give you a summary court-martial.' If it hadn't been for the Japs, I'd have probably been a seaman in Leavenworth.

"Anyway, I was put on report and made a PAL—prisoner-at-large—and restricted. I had to muster at 7:00 at night and 10:00 at night. But our chief master-at-arms, Buck Dwane, excused me because I was a boatswain's mate second class at that time. He excused me because I slept in the forecastle—in the bunkhouse that was provided for the leading petty officers in the deck force. I was excused from the 10:00 muster. By the way, Dwane was the first guy I seen killed on December 7. A bomb fragment went right through his guts.

"So I spent Saturday night aboard the *Vestal*; I couldn't go ashore. Everything was routine, just as if nothing was going to occur. I went to bed early. I would say it was approximately 8:00 or 8:30, because I missed the 10:00 muster, [which] the chief gave me permission to miss.

"Well, the next day I had gotten up and went down and got me some breakfast. I had sunny-sides, cold french fries, and bacon, and I got me a Sunday morning newspaper, and I had returned back to my sack—bunk. They had three bunks in there.

I had just got back with the paper and laid down and was fixing to read it when somebody hollered: 'General Quarters!' I couldn't believe what I was hearing.

"I jumped up and the first thing I saw was a Japanese plane coming down. The first torpedo, I think, that was launched at Pearl Harbor that day down the channel was launched at the *Helena*, and the *Oglala* was tied up outboard of her. The torpedo went under her and exploded and sunk the little wooden-bottom ship, the *Oglala*. She blew up, tilted over, and sank.

"Well, I didn't believe such a thing could happen even though I had been reading about it. When the man came up hollering, 'General Quarters,' that plane's the first thing I saw when I went out to get a better view. We had awnings rigged over us, and I had to go all the way to the lifeline to see the sky or even the horizon. I'll tell you, you don't know how many thoughts went through my mind. My conscience scared me all the rest of the day.

"After General Quarters sounded, I went back down below and aroused everybody out of their sacks that I could and got them topside. That was my duty as a petty officer in the deck force. I aroused them and got them topside to their General Quarters stations. We didn't have no PA system on there, just word of mouth.

"Well, I'll tell you, the thing I could say about myself that day—the funniest thing, believe it or not—is that my conscience was my guide. I carried on without actually knowing very much of what I did the whole time. I was commended for helping save men's lives and fighting fires. All that time, from 7:55 or 8:00 when the attack came until—oh, hell, I didn't go to bed until midnight that night, I guess—I participated in a lot of things, but I'll be damned if I can remember all of what they were.

"One of the first things I did was to clear the guns so that they could fire, although the guns were surface guns. I helped throw back the awning on the forecastle. It covered the whole forecastle, and it had a beam of about 40 feet—about 40 feet by 100 feet, I guess. It was one awning, and you had your strong-back, which was like a roof on a house which the awning would come down each side of, and you had your ropes to tie it down with.

"I'd say it took at least fifteen minutes to furl the awning and then tie it to the strongbacks to clear the decks. In fact, I don't think we were so tidy with it that morning. Normally to furl an awning, you would furl it around the strongback, and then you would lash it off like you would a hammock—to clear the deck and make it look neat.

"I remember glass windows in the silvering shop, and there was a fire there. I kicked open the door because it was locked. I tried to put the fire out. Everything was burning. I didn't put it out; I smoldered it down some. Whether I got it out, I doubt it very seriously. The silvering shop was where they silvered things, silver-plated. Acid, see, was in there, and there was a lot of stuff that could recatch after I thought I had it out.

"I saw people over on the *Arizona* that were trying to get off, and there was fire all around. I threw a line over. One of the books written about Pearl Harbor mentions the unknown sailor on the *Vestal* throwing a line over to the *Arizona* sailor. I'm that unknown sailor that whoever wrote the book didn't find. The author didn't find the right guy to ask the questions to. I'm the guy!

"I was on the superstructure deck, which was up in the area where the silvering shop was. That part of the deck was about the only part that was even with the *Arizona*. At the particular place that these people were trying to get over, they were surrounded by fire on the *Arizona*. They were stranded, and they were trying to get off. I didn't wait to see how many got off. I secured the line on my ship as tight as I could. They forehanded themselves over [traveled hand over hand], and I went on about my business.

"No doubt when the *Arizona* blew up, we were hit by debris, because everything was on fire on the *Vestal* almost from stem to stern. That's when I traveled from bow to stern, and [along the way] I cut the lines on the bow. Who cut them on the stern, I don't know, but in the bow I did cut the lines. Our executive officer, named John Toole, jumped all over my butt about cutting the lines, but there was nobody over on the *Arizona* to cast the lines off. That's one time in my naval career that I ignored an officer when I got chewed out.

"I cut the lines because they had given orders to get the ship under way. There wasn't nobody on the *Arizona* to throw the lines off. We had bollard to bollard or bits to bits to tie up, and unless you cast them off the bollard over there and pulled them through the chocks, it wasn't going to get loose. The only man I saw alive on the *Arizona*, after I threw the line over to let them people off, was on fire and gasping for air. I cut the lines with a fire axe.

"Our stern was already down because we had one bomb that went all the way through the ship. We had this one bomb explode in the GCH, general cargo hatch, which was next to the magazine. They kept rags in there; they kept steel plates and steel beams. It was just a general cargo hatch for repair parts. It was next to the magazine, and it was on fire, and it was getting the magazine hot. They asked for volunteers to go down to salvage the ammunition, and I didn't volunteer for that job.

"The torpedoes that were launched at the *Arizona* all went under us. That's something I couldn't understand, either, because all those torpedoes were coming toward us, and nothing ever exploded because they were going under us and hitting the *Arizona*.

"As I said, I do not remember too much. I don't even remember the *Vestal* exploding, and that should be one thing that I should remember because the skipper was blown over the side, and the whole gun crew. A lot of people were blown over the side, as a matter of fact. The captain said he was blown over the side. I hate to say this, but I don't think he was.

"I'll tell you, he was like a lot of the rest of the people. He didn't think we had much of a chance of saving the ship. He went over the side himself to my estimation, but his Congressional Medal of Honor said, No, he was blown over the side. The explosion occurred on the aft part of our ship, so that would be about amidships for the *Arizona*, because that was a battleship and we were just a little repair ship. But I think he figured he had no chance of saving the ship—like most everybody else— so he jumped over the side, and he started to swim across that oil in the harbor, and he didn't figure he could swim that, so he came back aboard and saved the ship and got it under way.

"We went in the shallow part of the harbor where they usually had tin cans [destroyers] tied up. It was still burning as we went.

The stern was almost down. She was run aground to keep from sinking. Then, we were trying to get the antiaircraft gun working. I guess the doctors and medical officers were taking care of the injured. They were trying to get volunteers to go ashore to dig trenches, and I ignored that because I was going down with the ship if I had to go down—die. We had gotten word that the Japanese were landing on the islands, and we were supposed to go and dig trenches, and I declined to make myself available for that.

"Finally, the fires were all out, and they were putting a cofferdam on the rear, and all the repair forces were down there. They had shipfitters, and they put a cofferdam on it, and they pumped it out and refloated her. The stern was all the way down. They did it that night. I was pretty groggy and was trying to think things out. They were asking for volunteers, and I didn't volunteer. That night, I was so exhausted I slept. But I had a few nightmares and bad dreams."

Before he fell asleep, George, like many survivors, saw the Pearl Harbor defenders mistakenly fire on airplanes from the USS *Enterprise*. The next day he returned to his regular job of trying to clean the *Vestal*, a monumental task after the battle. Soon after refloating the ship, its crew began to perform repair duties on other vessels. Ultimately, the *Vestal* went into dry dock for a major overhaul. Soon afterward, in June 1942, George left the ship to return to the United States, where he was assigned to a seaplane tender. He served aboard the USS *McFarland* and the USS *Laws* and was at Okinawa when the war ended. He returned home through Pearl Harbor.

During his twenty years in the Navy, George served in Hawaii once more, in 1951. He had said: "I hope I never see Pearl Harbor again," but his wife wanted to return. He retired as a chief boatswain's mate in 1955 and then worked for the civil service at the naval air station in Alameda, California, for fifteen years and later for Remington Arms in Lonoke, Arkansas, before retiring again. An ebullient man, he said regarding this interview: "I hope I didn't exaggerate about myself. Somebody might say: 'That dirty stinker! Good Christ, he must have been very hipped up or hopped up or something!' " Joe George now lives in Cabot, Arkansas.

6
Seaman First Class William W. Fomby
USS *Oklahoma*

The weekend the Japanese attacked Pearl Harbor, William
Fomby was messcook, Fifth Division, broadside battery guns
on board the USS *Oklahoma* (BB37). He had been with the ship
since April 1941 and had begun striking, or studying, for gunner's mate. Since seamen had to pull mess duty before they
could advance to the petty officer ratings, the chief of Fomby's
gun crew had made him messcook so that he would have completed his duty when he became eligible for promotion to gunner's mate third class.

Fomby, who had joined the Navy on December 18, 1940, was
from Hamlin, Texas, a small town thirty-five miles north and
slightly east of Abilene. He was born there on December 22,
1919, and was unable to find a ''suitable job'' after high school;
therefore, when Congress passed the Selective Service Act, he
decided to volunteer. He chose a six-year enlistment in the Navy
over a shorter period in the Army because his brother-in-law,
who had served in World War I, told him that ''you've always
got your bed and your kitchen in the Navy, and you don't when
you're in the Army.''

Fomby believed that the United States would be at war sometime during his tour of duty, but he did not think war would
come in the Pacific. Thus, the young seaman was not apprehen-
sive when, after boot camp at San Diego, he was assigned to
the *Oklahoma* at Pearl Harbor. It took him several weeks to
reach Hawaii; he was sent by tanker to Mare Island outside San
Francisco and then on the naval transport *Henderson* to Honolulu. As was true for all new recruits, his first few weeks aboard
the *Oklahoma* he spent as a deckhand. He was then assigned to
the Fifth Division, where he worked and trained on the 5-inch/51-
caliber broadside guns.

On Saturday, December 6, he worked from around 4:30 A.M.
until about 7:00 P.M. breaking out the mess tables, getting food
from the galley, and then performing the reverse for breakfast,
dinner, and supper. That night he went to Honolulu, but, after
a few drinks, he returned to the ship to retire early, since Sunday

would start for him around 4:30 A.M. The first passage in his interview begins as his last day as messcook commenced.

"I got up quickly, as I always did. They call messcooks early. The master-at-arms came around and woke you up. Anyway, I got up and started getting the food and dishes and everything going. Well, after the fellows got through eating, and I was getting my dishes together, some old boy came in the gun casemate where we ate and said: 'Boy, they're having maneuvers this morning! Planes are diving all over the place!' I remember I was drying my hands on my apron, and I walked out there, and I looked.

"We had recently been towing a target sled for our dive-bombers, which had retractable landing gears on them. The plane was up there, and it was the same color and everything as our planes—a gray-looking plane—and he was diving. But one thing that I remember more vividly than anything else was that I wondered: 'What the hell is that guy doing, diving with his wheels down,' because our planes always had them folded up.

"He dropped his bomb. I saw the bomb drop when he released it—which was still nothing; I saw our own planes do that all the time when we were towing the sled for them. But I saw another one coming right behind him, and he had his wheels down, too. I don't know why that stuck in my mind, but I wondered: 'Well, why in the devil are they diving with their wheels down?' And about that time, the first bomb hit a hangar on Ford Island, and that durn thing went about five hundred feet in the air, and I thought: 'Oh, hell, somebody is sure going to catch hell for that!' About that time, they passed the word on the *Oklahoma* to man the antiaircraft batteries.

"Word for word, verbatim, they said: 'Man the antiaircraft batteries! This is a real air raid and no shit!' That's exactly the words that came over the loud speaker. My battle station, just in an air raid, was belowdecks—down in the magazine—sending the ammunition up to the antiaircraft guns. So I headed for the magazine. Most of the guys that were in the compartment below where I was messcooking were already at the magazine when I got there. Then they passed the word—and to my knowledge that was the last that was ever passed—to man the broadside guns.

"Well, now my battle station was on the broadside guns, and I went back up the ladders. In the course of my going up the ladders, why, we caught four or five—however many—torpedoes, and, by the time that I got back up to where I originally started, the ship had listed so far that I had to go hand over hand up the mess tables to get to the outside to where the gun barrels stuck out of the embrasure. By that time the ship was so far over that I walked part of the way over the bottom to get into the water.

"The ship weighed about thirty thousand tons, and when the torpedoes hit they shook everything on her. There was a tremendous explosion. Of course, at that time I didn't really realize what it was, but I knew something was blowing up on the ship. I knew that when you take something as big as a battleship and start the darned thing turning upside down—it would be like turning a motel upside down—everything in it would start to fly. That was a major hazard, for the big gun turrets and the shells that weighed two thousand pounds started breaking loose and mashing people and everything else.

"Of course, I wasn't on the inside of the ship when she got turned over, but, later on down the line, I served with some old boys that we cut out of the bottom of the ship on Tuesday, December 9. They had been in there, but they had enough air to breathe. Those old boys were really shook up, and I would have been, too. I believe if that would have happened to me, I'd have rather it just went ahead and got me. But we got those guys out. I served with a lot of guys who got off the *Arizona* and *Oklahoma*.

"Anyway, I was getting off the *Oklahoma*, going into the water. It was quite evident that there wasn't anything more that could be done for the ship, and there wasn't any word ever given, as far as I know, to abandon ship or anything like that, but there wasn't anything else to do. I got in the water, and there was a lot of oil and some fire and all that sort of thing. We had been tied alongside the *Maryland*, and the *Oklahoma* rolled away from the *Maryland* out toward the channel. It wasn't a long swim that I had to make to the *Maryland*.

"Of course, when you're in the water swimming, it seems

like a hell of a long ways, but it wasn't really. There was a lot of strafing, a lot of commotion going on in the water with the fire and oil. The planes, when they dropped the torpedoes and bombs, generally went back up and came back down strafing the ships and the people in the water. In a manner of speaking, all hell broke loose and continued there for quite a while.

"I had jumped in the water wearing the uniform of the day, the little shorts—you wore shorts and a T-shirt, and I had those on—but, when I got aboard the *Maryland*, a chief on the *Maryland* threw me a marine's uniform and told me to get it on because I had oil on me. He said: 'You'll burn up if we have a bomb or something explode and we get set afire.' So I put the uniform on, and I wore it for quite a while. I can't remember just how long, but it was several days.

"When I was swimming, there were so many things going on I can't even remember all of them. I saw a bomb hitting in the water by the *West Virginia* and planes strafing it. There were machine-gun bullets fired by a plane that were hitting the deck of the *Maryland*. When the bomb hit you could feel it! It was a jar—like somebody banged a couple of rocks together in the water, but it was magnified a good bit. It depended on how close you were to where the bomb hit.

"Another boy, named Nigg, was in the water with me. He was there when I went in. I don't know where he had come from, but he was in my division and had come through boot camp with me. I had known him a long time. Well, we climbed up an old fender that they had over the side of the ships to keep them from bumping together. There was one setting right in the edge of the water, and we got on that and climbed up the rope that supported it to get to the deck of the *Maryland*.

"When we got aboard the *Maryland*, as I said, I went inside the ship, and they had dragged out some clothes and stuff, and a chief grabbed the uniform and told me to put it on. I started to go up toward the antiaircraft battery, but he told me to stand down there because of that oil on me, so I did. He didn't want me around any gun flashes. Of course, all of this took time.

"This didn't happen in a short time. The firing by the antiaircraft guns kept going on for a while, but as I remembered the most severe part was caused by the torpedo planes. I think they did the worst part of the damage to the battleships. I would say that within the first ten or fifteen minutes of the attack is when all the dive-bombers hit and the torpedo planes came down the channel by Merry's Point and let their torpedoes go. Although I don't remember absolutely, I think there were at least four torpedoes that got the *Oklahoma*. I wasn't at Pearl when they got her afloat again, but the people that were told me that there were holes in it that you could drive a truck through—on the side where they got hit.''

In the rest of the interview, Fomby discusses what happened after the attack, from about noon on December 7 through May 1942. He also comments briefly on his other experiences during World War II.

"Sometime in the afternoon, I got sick. I drank a bunch of that oil and water when I was in the water, and saltwater and oil will make you awful sick. Well, we went to Ford Island and set up an aid station over there. We had mostly men wounded on Ford Island. The aid station was an officer's house, in a garage.

"Somebody came around and brought a rifle. How I came by it and when, I don't know for sure, but I wound up with an old rifle, which I kept with me. A guy just came along and handed you a rifle and some shells. You didn't have to sign for anything. A little bit later, somebody brought us an old van, and a boy named Fogelsong—he was off the *Oklahoma*, too—he drove the old van, and I was his armed guard.

"We stayed at the aid station that night, and they moved us the next day. One eventful thing that happened that night was when four or five fighter planes came in off one of the carriers, and we shot them all down. I saw part of it. I was inside the officer's house when it started. But I heard all the shooting, and I got out there, and some guy had my rifle banging away at them, too. There wasn't any organization or anything.

"I don't know for sure, but I was told that those planes were off the carrier *Enterprise*. I assumed like everybody else that the Japanese had come back. The planes should have come around and over Barber's Point when coming in. Instead, they came right across Honolulu. Well, the Army and everybody around

Honolulu opened fire on them. We had gotten addicted to shooting at everything that flew during the day, and I guess that it was automatic what we did.

"I understand they didn't fly the pattern they were supposed to, but they may not have gotten down, anyway, as disorganized and confused as everything was. At any rate, the Army opened up on them, and they came right across the Navy Yard, and, when they did, everything that could shoot started shooting at them. I think maybe one or two of them finally landed, but they weren't worth taking off in again.

"Well, anyway, the next thing we did was take the van over to the Navy Yard, up to the recreation center there. There was another aid station there. I'd say, until about Tuesday or somewhere along in there, we hauled wounded from there down to the hospital. I'll tell you one thing—and I've said this before—when you see all these people in bed sheets laying out stacked up like cordwood, it takes all the glamour out of war. You really realize that something bad is going on.

"Along about Tuesday or Wednesday, somewhere in there, I got word that the crew of the *Oklahoma*, what was left of us, was on the second floor of the submarine base, so I went over there and reported in. Incidentally, the Navy Department had notified my folks that I was missing and presumed dead because they didn't know where I was. Of course, I didn't know where they were. They later notified my folks that I had been located and was okay.

"Then I was sent out to the *Oklahoma*. We were trying to see if we could find anybody else alive in there. We cut through and liberated some good denatured [*sic*] alcohol out of the medical storeroom, and we used to have some mixed with powdered tomato juice or coffee when we came in every afternoon.

"Somewhere around Christmastide until about the first of May, I was in the harbor patrol. A bunch of sailors off the *Arizona* and the *Oklahoma* were sent down to Bishop's Point, and we had those old motorboats off the battleships that were sunk. We had depth charges and machine guns mounted on them, and we patrolled every night from sunset to sunup.

"I retrieved a lot of dead bodies when I was in the harbor patrol, because they'd come floating out of those ships, and we would find them floating out in the water. We were told not to handle them, so we would get a piece of rope or a piece of wire and pull them to the beach and anchor them there and then let the medical people take care of it.

"Sharks came into the harbor by the thousands.* We would be out there on patrol at night, and those big old fins would be coming alongside the boat. They came from everywhere.

"We had a lot of things going on out there in the harbor at night. The old timbers from the *Utah* were floating around in the harbor. The old PBYs would come in—they were seaplanes—and on one occasion one of those darned things landed and hit those darned timbers, and they took the whole front of the plane off at the wings. The pilot and the copilot went to the bottom, but we got into the plane. When it broke up, it flipped and stayed afloat long enough that we got in and got the other three guys out.

"I remained in the Hawaiian Islands until 1944. I stayed in the harbor patrol until the Battle of Midway, and then they transferred me to the Navy Yard. They had 108 .50-caliber machine guns and 20 40-millimeter antiaircraft guns. They organized what they called the Pearl Harbor Civilian Volunteer Force. It consisted of civilians that worked in the machine shops and the welding shops. Most of them were ex–World War I men. Each of those shops had sandbag emplacements on the roof with a .50-caliber machine gun. Some had as many as 4 guns on the roof. Those guys were the crews. They signed some paper whereby the governor of the territory of Hawaii declared them in the military to keep them from being shot as guerrillas in case the Japs took the islands.

"I took care of those guns during the balance of 1942 until early in 1943, when I was transferred to the naval air station at Ford Island. Then I went to French Frigate Shoal, a little man-made island out in the Pacific, and I stayed there six or seven months. Then they flew me back to Pearl and took my appendix out, and I went back to the harbor defense and security there in the Navy Yard until I came back to the States in 1944.

"As I said many times, I wouldn't have missed being or having participated in the Pearl Harbor attack for anything, but I

*There are no official reports that sharks entered the oil-covered waters of the harbor.

wouldn't ever want to do it again. Down the line, I look back and I think that maybe I did do something worthwhile there.''

Fomby's enlistment ended in December 1946, but he was held over until March 15, 1947, when he was mustered out. At the time, he was a gunner's mate first class, on duty in China. He had served on the USS *Goodrich* and the USS *Hanson*.

After attending Odessa College, in Texas, he went to work as a sales engineer in industrial and industrial-electrical equipment, spending twenty-seven years with the same corporation before retirement. He now lives in Odessa. Although happy to have made a contribution to the American victory in World War II, he regrets "that very few people remember or have ever heard of the USS *Oklahoma*."

7
Gunner's Mate Third Class George E. Waller
USS *Maryland*

George Waller enlisted in the Navy on October 7, 1937, and twelve weeks later, at the end of December, was assigned to the battleship *Maryland* (BB46). He spent one week in X Division, a holding section, and then was sent to the Fourth Division on the main deck, port side aft. After spending six months as part of the deck force, he joined gun turret number four. From the "bottom," the lower handling room, where the ammunition was stored, he worked his way "up to the pits," the guns' breech area, where he began striking for gunner's mate third class. Promotion came slowly in the peacetime Navy; he did not make third class until 1940.

Waller went to sea to avoid farming. Born in Keo, Arkansas, about fifteen miles southeast of Little Rock, he chose military service after high school graduation because he wanted to "get away," to do something on his own. He picked the Navy because he "liked the uniform"; he wore it for the next thirty-one years. He went through boot camp in San Diego, where, as was the case with several of the survivors quoted in this work, most southwesterners who entered the Navy went for basic training. A few months prior to the war, Waller transferred to V Division, where his primary duty was to assist in launching and recovering the battleship's floatplanes; he also helped in the ship's magazines, which V Division manned. Waller made the change because he believed promotions would come more rapidly at his new post.

The *Maryland* was part of the "Pineapple Fleet" assigned to the Hawaiian Islands in 1939. At first Waller liked being there, but after a while he grew tired of the local music, the frequent rains, the islands' smallness, and the crowds. "There were long lines wherever you went," he said. "Even in the parks you waited to sit down."

Occasionally, in the days before the attack, he and his shipmates discussed America's possible enemies, including Japan and its navy. "Scuttlebutt was," he said, "that if the Japanese attacked, they would never attack Pearl because they just didn't have enough to do it. If they did, however, they wouldn't last three weeks because we could beat them in that time." Like many U.S. military men, Waller underestimated the Japanese warrior. He considered his potential foe "very small, slant eyed, an individual that anybody could take if he wanted to—you could take three or four at a time."

The *Maryland* was part of the division that stayed in port during the first week of December 1941. When the attack came, she was anchored between Ford Island and the USS *Oklahoma*, which had entered port on Friday the 5th and tied up alongside her. On Saturday, Waller went to Honolulu, drank a few beers, and returned to his ship about 11:00 P.M. He ate a snack of crackers and sausages before bedding down on the boat deck. This was not his usual sleeping place; the night was warm, however, and he enjoyed the breeze that occasionally swept across the deck. At 6:00 A.M. sweepers who were cleaning the area awoke him. He stretched, collected his wits, and walked across to where coffee was being brewed. After drinking a cup, he returned to his cot near the pyrotechnic locker, lay down, and fell asleep again. The next time he awoke, the *Maryland* was under attack.

"I heard a lot of commotion; I could hear planes. I awoke and I could see a plane—it looked like it was only fifty feet off the water—coming from Merry's Point landing and flying directly over our ship. When it got up pretty close, I could see his big meatball underneath the wings, and I wondered: 'What in the world!' I knew the emblem, but I guess it wouldn't register that the Japs had the guts to do something like this. Then I could see machine guns shooting. I jumped up like everyone else.

"There was quite a bit of confusion, but within a short time we opened our ammunition lockers. I don't remember how we got the locks off. I know that later on we got keys and opened all the magazines and kept them open from then on.

"I'm not sure that General Quarters ever sounded. It may have. It seems to me like it sounded on the *California*, which was just ahead of us, and on the *Neosho*, the tanker directly in front of us. We were anxious to get out of there because the *Neosho* was loaded with high-octane gas.

"All hell broke loose then. The first torpedo plane dropped its torpedo, and we got it on the bow because it missed the *Oklahoma*.* The next one, the second, got her. Then there were others. The thing that really sticks in my mind was the *Oklahoma* beginning to roll. She had a big explosion, and a hatch came off and went up in the air. I can still see it—a seaman coming out of the hold and the hatch coming back down.

"We had been told all of our lives that you couldn't sink a battleship, and then to see one go upside down . . . it's . . . it's heartbreaking. I knew how many were on the ship. I had a lot of shipmates there—people I went ashore with—and I knew that they had gone down inside. Reaction on our ship was fantastic. We had people, however, go on to the *Oklahoma* and try to cut holes in its side to get people out before it had rolled all the way over. It rolled over slowly, but I got busy, and when I looked back it was over. In a battle like this you never see the whole picture.

"I remember little things. I remember Frankie. I don't know whether that was his name or last name, but that's what everybody called him. He was a little bitty short fellow, a petty

*No torpedoes hit the *Maryland*. She was struck by two armor-piercing bombs.

officer first class. He went over to the *Oklahoma* with hoses and a cutting torch and started to try to burn holes in the bottom. The planes were still attacking. It seemed like, when the planes came, he had to get back down on the side of the ship so they couldn't hit him. Then he'd go back up and start burning again.

"They tried hard to get people out. They just kept on; they were doing everything to get people out. In one area where they heard tapping, they began cutting and ran into cork, and cork smokes a lot when it starts burning. It suffocated the men there before they could get them out.

"My own ship went down in the bow. We had a pretty sizable hole there in the side. Since I was on the catapult there wasn't anything for me to do at my battle station. So I helped on the 5-inch gun, which was used against aircraft, and finally on the 1.1 antiaircraft battery—pom-poms. I helped with the ammunition. I'd hand the loader the ammunition. When the whole crew was assembled for the 5-incher, that's when I went on to the 1.1 battery.

"The Japanese were flying so low you could see them. It was like the old pictures, that's the way they looked. There they were, with a helmet—kind of a brownish-black helmet—pulled over with his goggles on.

"I also helped with the ammunition on the pom-poms. I don't know what else I did, but I know I began bleeding across the eye. I don't know how it happened. I did hurt my back, too, but I didn't go to sick bay. I was coming out of the 1.1's guntub, and I fell down. It must have been when we got hit. We got a small bomb in the forward part of the ship. I fell about twelve feet from the guntub to the boat deck.

"I remember seeing the big bombers, the horizontal kind, drop bombs. I saw the *West Virginia*, *Tennessee*, and *Arizona* get hit by these. I don't know if we did, but evidently we did. I also don't remember time. It seemed like it was dusk-dark. We were firing away, and, the next thing I knew, it was dusk-dark.

"After I fell, I went back to the pyrotechnic locker and sat down for a bit. Of course, I was scared to death. Everybody that I know of was scared to death. It might be your time; you didn't know. It seemed like the ocean was burning on the other side of the *Oklahoma*, and it was coming toward us from the bow and the stern because we were a little bigger than the *Oklahoma*.

"I do remember the *Arizona* blowing up. When the big bombers came over, that's when the fifteen-inch shells, bomb, or whatever hit her. I thought they were larger shells than that—some that the Japs couldn't use they put fins on. Anyway, it seemed like that all of a sudden the bay kind of made a little hop; the water started moving, and then there was a small explosion followed by a real big one. You could see all this black smoke.

"The *West Virginia* and *Tennessee* were both burning, and the *Arizona* was right behind them. The *Nevada* had gotten under way and had moved past us going out into the harbor. I don't believe she had gotten any hits until after she passed beyond us. I recall that she was shooting as she went by."

According to Waller, petty officers organized the *Maryland*'s defense, although the crew's training played a major role in what was accomplished. Once the battle ceased, he recovered sufficiently to lunch on crackers and Spam. His observations conclude with the battle's aftermath.

"The harbor was a big mess. My God, what a mess! Bodies were stacked up on Aiea Landing—getting them out of the bay. I wish I had taken a picture, but I didn't. I had a camera, and I didn't use it. There was oil everywhere. The oil was on the sides of the ships. People working on the sides were getting filthy. The big damage to our ship was a big hole on the port side of the bow. As well as I remember, I think we lost only two people.

"That night we fired again because some planes came in. We didn't know that they were our planes, and we cut loose on them. I was on the 5-inch gun this time. We fired until we got the word to cease fire. Nobody gave the word to fire; we just fired. I think we might have been the first ship to do so.

"I didn't sleep well at all that night. Catnapped, maybe. I heard rifle fire all along the beach. I heard they were killing Japs over there. Anybody that looked like a Jap didn't have a chance in the Navy Yard. Everybody thought the Japanese were going to invade.

"During the following days we stayed on alert, Condition Three, most of the time. We slept at our gun stations. Of course, I stayed at my station near the pyrotechnic locker. We were all happy when we got out of there. We went to the Bremerton Navy Yard, Puget Sound, to get a new bow put on.* So that we could get out of Pearl Harbor, the *Oklahoma*, which was laying against us, was blasted away. Then there was room enough with the *Neosho* gone so that we could pull out at the front with the tugs and our own power.

"Morale was high after the attack. The attitude was both anger and revenge. 'Let's go get them! Let's do this job! We can do it! Let's get it over with!' That was our feeling. After the battle we talked about it a little. We said: 'Boy, that scared the living so-and-so out of me!' After we settled down we were still a little bit afraid, but we had a job to do."

Waller was assigned to the USS *Indiana* after Pearl Harbor and stayed with her during much of the conflict. A career sailor, he reenlisted many times after World War II, mustering out finally as a chief warrant officer, with thirty-one years of service, in 1968. He earned a bachelor's degree in business administration at the University of Central Arkansas in Conway and taught high school math for seven years. He is now retired and resides in his hometown.

8
Seaman Jack Kelley
USS *Tennessee*

Jack Kelley joined the Navy for many of the same reasons that prompted other young men in the depression years to enlist—the service offered a job and a chance for advancement and travel. But he also had a private incentive: His father had been a sailor in World War I.

Jack was born on October 7, 1921, on the family farm near Anson, Jones County, Texas, and graduated from high school in Hamlin. In August 1940 he enlisted and was sent to boot

*There is no record that the *Maryland* received a new bow.

camp in San Diego. Three weeks before his training was scheduled to end, he was assigned to the battleship *Tennessee* (BB43).
The Navy was bringing its vessels up to "fighting standards"
and needed more men. Like every other apprentice seaman,
Kelley was in the deck force at first; later he was made a powder
handler for gun turret number four in the Fourth Division, which
comprised seventy-three men and three 14-inch guns. Number
four turret was the farthest aft.

The routine of Kelley's days before the attack was similar to
that followed by most American sailors in peacetime: a lot of
naval practice during the week and generous liberty on weekends. Kelley was a sightseer, sportsman, and hardworking seaman striking for gunner's mate. Life had become so
commonplace that he could only speculate on what he had done
the night before the air raid. He either went to a movie, played
poker or acey-deucey, or wrote letters home. He had much less
trouble, though, remembering what happened the next day.

"I remember that we, the Fourth Division softball team, were
playing some other division on the ship, and we were getting
ready to go over to the island. At the time this all started, I
happened to be in the head, the toilet. Wasn't that a great place
to be? But that's where I was! The head was a little past midships
toward the bow, where we lived. Facing from the bow to the
stern, our living quarters were about two thirds of the way back
to the aft, and the head was on farther forward.

"I didn't know what happened. I thought we had been rammed
or something. But we got two bomb hits, and evidently what
caused the big commotion was the bomb that had hit on the top
of the number two turret. I'd say we were fifty feet from the
number two turret. Anyway, whatever it was, it caused the ship
to really give a bounce. It shook us, and was like the ship dropped
about two feet and then bounced back up. Water flew all over
the place. Everybody was saying: 'What in the hell is going on?'
I didn't know it was an attack. We were tearing outside to see
what was going on, because most of us thought that some other
ship had rammed us or something.

"About the time that we got out on topside, why, they sounded
General Quarters. I'd say I had gone about, oh, two or three

hundred feet down the starboard side when General Quarters sounded. My battle station was below decks, the aft end of the ship, but I did go out on topside to the turret to go down. And when I came out on topside, why, the hangars over on Ford Island were already burning. I could see smoke billowing out and planes and such on fire on the ground. There were Japanese planes buzzing around. I just got a glimpse of several before I went into my General Quarters station. It was evident that we were being attacked as soon as we got out topside and looked around.

"I didn't know specifically what happened, oh, for an hour or more, I guess. There was quite a bit of jabbering to start with. Some of the crew didn't know we were being attacked, and after you got that settled, why, you settled down to silence, wondering and waiting. Everybody had their own thoughts. You just sat down there wondering what was going on, because you didn't see anything and nobody passed much word around because it's strictly business that goes over the phones, and they weren't worrying about informing all of us about what was going on.

"I guess, if we had been at sea, we would have worried about sinking, but everybody knew—even I knew—that the water there wasn't very deep. And if the ship sank, it wouldn't matter one way or the other unless water came in from the bottom and trapped you someway where you couldn't get out. I guess that the concern of most people was if any of that stuff they were dropping was going to get into the magazine. You have a few thoughts that it might happen to you like it happened to the *Arizona*. Of course, we didn't know it could happen to the *Arizona*, but that sort of things goes through your mind—you sort of know what's possible.

"Occasionally, you could feel little shudders or trembles or however you want to say it. I mean, you're sitting down, and you sort of feel it shudder, and you know that something is going on but you don't know what. That was about as big a commotion as we felt. We knew the ship wouldn't get under way. We were tied up so that at least two other ships, maybe three, would have to get under way before we could commence to move. Well, if you had tugs to pull you out, you could, but, of course, with that going on, there was not going to be many tugs running around.

"I guess the reason they kept us down there that long was that they may have thought there would be some landing or ships or something coming within range. Of course, that was some goofy thinking, but, about an hour later, why, they took most of us from the lower magazines to up topside because oil, spilled out from the *Arizona*, was blowing toward us and it was all on fire, and the ship was burning from the aft end to about, oh, a third of the way up the decking on top. All the paint was burning, so they sent us up to man the fire hoses, to put out the fire or to keep it sort of beat off.

"I went up to the quarterdeck. That was my duty station. We manned fire hoses to keep from burning up, because the officers' quarters were already burning inside, and all the decking was burning off. I don't suppose they called very many people up until they decided the ship was going to burn up; I don't know why they kept us down there as long as they did.

"The oil from the *Arizona* kept coming in our direction, and there was a sea of fire around us. The old paint on the ship— fifty coats of paint on it—was burning, and the deck was burning. Once you got the deck put out and the paint on the side of the ship out, you could hang over the rail and keep the fire knocked down. Of course, every few minutes a plane would come over strafing and chipping splinters out of the deck, and we would throw our hose down and run under the overhang of the turret until it passed.

"There were several strafings that hit on the deck that we were on, probably a half dozen. I mean, we would throw down the fire hoses and get out of the way. You could see them coming in, and you could tell if they were coming your way. When the splinters go chipping out of the deck, nobody has to tell you to get out of the way. You hunt some place. In my division there wasn't anybody that got hit. Now, they may have been strafing other parts of the ship that I didn't see, but we were probably strafed a half-dozen times.

"We stayed on keeping the fire put down, contained, or however you want to put it, until the entire attack was over. We still had fires nearly all day, and the *Arizona* burned for several more days. Well, every time the wind would blow a little bit, why, the fire would lick back across to where we were tied up. Somebody had to stay to keep the fire down then.

"Whenever I came up on topside the air was full of black smoke, bursting shells, and all that. Of course, I guess the heavy part of the attack was already over by the time I got up there, but there were still quite a few planes bombing and such. There was still quite a bit of firing going on. The regular crews manned their guns, so I didn't have anything to do with firing. I didn't fire a shot; I didn't even help in firing a gun. All I did was sit and wait and squirt a little water.

"When I came topside, that was one of the times I would say I was most depressed in my life. When we went to General Quarters, here was this array of battleships setting out there looking fine and trim, and, when I came up and ran out on topside, why, the *West Virginia* was settling on the bottom beside us, and I looked behind, and the *Arizona* was just one big ball of fire, and up ahead to the left the *Oklahoma* had turned upside down with the screws sticking up in the air. It made me wonder where we ever got the idea that we were so secure.

"Like I said, a bomb had hit our number two turret, and one had gone through our number three turret as well. I never did know why it didn't cause more damage on the inside than it did. It penetrated the top of the turret, which is pretty thick metal, and there were only three casualties. But, like I said, freaky things happen. You would think that, if the bomb that went in was big enough to penetrate the turret and explode, it would kill everybody inside. But there were only three casualties in there."

Kelley's opinion was that his role during the battle was not especially exciting. Of course, it was. Still, what happened to him later is at least as interesting and, for students of the attack, even more important in judging the effect of battle on the individual sailor.

"You did odd things then. The Third Division was on the starboard side, and we were on the port. I knew a lot of guys over there, and one guy that I knew real well was killed in the number three turret. After it settled down, crewmen went up there and took mattress covers and picked all the body pieces that were in the part that blew up, and they brought them down and just set them over in the corner of the Third Division. Well, they didn't set up a regular mess table that day. They made up a chow line over there, and everybody went by to get eats and did eat with those three or four mattress covers sitting in the corner. It didn't bother you as much as you would think it would. I mean, you would think that all of us couldn't eat. But I don't know, you sort of gear yourself up to the circumstances or something.

"There were always funny stories—I say 'funny,' I mean odd stories that come along. There was a Japanese plane shot down, and it fell on Ford Island just a little ways from where we were tied up. There was an old boy that had come back from over there. He had gone over to this plane, and he came back with a picture—an aerial photograph of Pearl Harbor—and we were all looking at it.

"The *Oglala*, which was an old supply ship actually serving as a heavy minelayer,* came in either Friday evening late or Saturday morning. It had come in after we were already tied up. But I remember watching that old supply ship come in and tie up almost even with the stern of the *Arizona* but on the other side of the channel. That old supply ship was in the aerial photograph.

"They said there was no planes that came over, but how in the hell had the Japs got that photograph? I don't know. Our shipmate had no place to get an aerial photograph. He said he got it out of that plane, and, if he didn't, I don't know where he would have gotten it. But I saw it with my own two eyes, and I've often wondered why there was never any mention made of any reconnaissance plane. Even in all these so-called war movies there is never any mention of that.

"Later, maybe on Monday, I was in a small boat crew in a motor launch that was to go around every morning, and, when bodies came to the top, why, we would pick them up and carry them over to the Aiea Landing to be identified and such as that. Not very many came to the surface for several days. It got to

*The *Oglala* was not previously a supply ship.

where they were getting a little bit ripe whenever they were coming to the top. It was mostly people blown off the *Arizona* that were in the water and had sunk. They would come up around the sides of the ships or the quays over against Ford Island.

"Then we would just gather them up as they came up. We were getting a half dozen or so. It got to where, if we pulled them into the boat, they would bust open and run all over the bottom of the boat. So we would just tie a little piece of rope around their leg or their arm or whatever you could get hold of and get you a string of them and tow them over rather than trying to pull them into the boat. That was one of the most gory things I did. Of course, that was after it was all over with, and we weren't the only ones doing it.

"Since I was in a boat crew running up and down the harbor, I got a little better view than the average person of the damned near total destruction. You could see all the sunken ships and damage and such that was.

"Well, in fact, the chaplain off the *Tennessee* wanted to go over to the *Arizona*. I don't recall if it was the next day or the following day, but it was after they got the fires put out on her. So the crew I was in carried him over to the *Arizona*, and we just tied the boat up to a broadside barrel that was up above the waterline. We pulled up and crawled over onto the boat deck.

"I wished I hadn't gone aboard after I went aboard because there were pieces of burnt bodies and little dabs of clothing, helmets, and, well, just half-charred bodies all over the place. They gave off quite an offensive odor. But he wanted to go aboard, so we carried him over. I prowled around and picked up two or three things laying around—junk to anybody else. There was an old marine belt buckle and a spoon. I guess they were serving coffee or something. I picked up two or three little old items. I sure wished I would have stayed in the boat.

"He was a Protestant, the best I remember, and he said prayers, but he didn't have services of any kind. He just walked around and looked and said a prayer and then went back to the ship. I guess he just wanted to be over there.

"I don't suppose anybody would stay there very long, unless their job was to clean it up and identify the dead. There was a similar need to clean up on the *West Virginia*. They came over wanting volunteers to swim back in the living quarters on the *West Virginia*. There was about so much space between the overhead and the water, and they were going to swim back there and pull bodies out. They got a good bunch of volunteers, but I didn't feel like that I wanted to volunteer. I wanted no part of it. It's not that I was squeamish about death, but fooling around back there in that oily water to get somebody that was already dead didn't seem like a practical thing to do.

"You never forget about things like this. It was an unpleasant experience, and, well, I don't know what's made me remember. I guess it is part of the total thing of being that close to so many dead people. You'd never been around that, and at least it stuck with you. I guess there are just things you can remember pretty clearly—things that were not so important, that you've not thought about for thirty-five years. We felt pretty helpless then. I don't know whether you call the word depressing or what. I guess we were all glad to get out of there."

The *Tennessee* was eventually pulled from Battleship Row to the Navy Yard, where it underwent enough repairs to enable it to sail to Bremerton, Washington, for a total overhaul. Seaman Kelley remained in the Navy until December 1946, when, having risen to the rank of chief boatswain's mate, he was discharged. He spent his civilian years first as a farmer and later as a construction worker. Retired, he now lives in Bedford, Texas.

9
Shipfitter Third Class Louis Grabinski
USS *West Virginia*

To the crew of the battleship *West Virginia* (BB48), Louis Grabinski was "Ski." The nickname was almost inevitable at that time for a Pole whose name ended in *ski*. The stereotype of a blond, strapping fellow failed in the case of Grabinski, for he was small and skinny, weighing only 128 pounds when he enlisted. In fact, his size almost kept him out of the Navy. When the recruiters found he was several pounds below the requirement, they sent him off to eat bananas and drink water, a quick way to gain weight. When he came back, he barely passed.

Grabinski was born in Erie, Pennsylvania, on August 25, 1920. He ran away from home several times, starting when he was twelve, before finishing the tenth grade at Erie Tech in 1940. One of ten children, he had found during the depression that "the world was cruel." He grew tired of eating potatoes, soup, and dark bread with lard and salt and hoped to find better chow as a sailor. Having been reared in a Lake Erie port, he had heard tales of Navy mess, and he thought that the life of a seaman would be "pretty good" for him. On the day of his twentieth birthday, he enlisted in the Navy. He hopped a freight for Buffalo, New York, where he was mustered in.

After boot camp in Newport, Rhode Island, he was sent by train to Long Beach, California. The ride dazzled him, but, when he saw his new assignment, the *West Virginia*, he said: "God almighty! What a ship! There was nothing that big on Lake Erie." On the *Weevee*, as seamen called the ship, he was assigned as a deckhand to the starboard bow, First Division. One of his main duties was to holystone the deck, or use a brick-shaped pumice stone with a hole in the middle in which a handle could be inserted to rub down the teakwood surface. Saltwater acted as the lubricant, and afterward the deck had to be swabbed dry. Grabinski also polished the brightwork (fixtures of brass and other metals susceptible to corrosion by the sea air) and scraped and then helped paint ladders, hatches, bulkheads, and other parts of the vessel.

When he soon grew tired of the assignment and asked to be transferred, he was sent to the scullery, much to his chagrin. He nevertheless applied himself, and, when the dishwasher's water pipes fouled, he found a wrench in the shipfitter's storeroom and fixed them. The rudimentary plumbing he had learned at Erie Tech now paid off. His work came to the attention of the chief petty officer who ran the shipfitter's section, and, with the chief's influence, which could be immense aboard ship, he ultimately was assigned to the R Division, shipfitter's shop.

Before the year was over, he was a shipfitter third class and had found a home in the Navy. He liked the food, the pay, the recreation, the opportunities, and, most of all, the liberty. Like the popular notion of a sailor, he drank hard, fought hard, and played hard, especially on Canal, River, and Hotel streets, the red-light district in Honolulu, where he got "jumps."

On the weekend of the attack, however, Grabinski was too busy to worry about booze, fights, or sex. The *West Virginia* returned to Pearl Harbor from maneuvers with other ships in its division on Friday, December 5. He had two weeks of mail awaiting him, and he spent most of his free hours reading copies of the *Erie Times*, a subscription to which his sister had given him. He even read it during the watch he pulled for Sunday morning, when he discovered that a former girlfriend had just married.

Grabinski's experience on Saturday night differed from that of most sailors interviewed. Things were rowdy on the *Weevee*: It was "very noisy, with drunks and fighting. The master-at-arms had to get them quieted down." Awakened "more so than ever," Grabinski used a pillow to muffle the noise until he arose at 3:30 A.M. to relieve the earlier watch.

"After I made my first round, I went to the boat deck. It was a nice, beautiful, cool night. That's when I started thinking. Well, the girlfriend got married on me; I told her not to wait. I thought: 'Boy, this is the best thing that has ever happened to me. Here I am; I'm in Hawaii on a big battleship, a ship I'm very proud of. I'm progressing, already a shipfitter third class.' I had the best in life that I could have had at that time. I had money in my pocket. I could go ashore and get a 'piece of ass' if I wanted to. I could get drunk. I was enjoying life. I thought: 'I'm going to stay in the Navy for twenty years!' I made the decision there. The Navy's been good to me and good for me. I became a petty officer, and I've loved it.

"Well, everything went along peacefully. The routine of the ship commenced. Reveille went; our breakfast went. All the decks were cleared of mess tables. The ship was set up for the day at least until dinnertime. I did notice that there was hardly nobody around, but on Sunday that's the way it usually was. That indicated to me that a hell of a lot of people were ashore.

"I went into the shipfitter's shop and was having a cup of coffee. There was a first class shipfitter by the name of Ray; he was sleeping on his mattress on a worktable. The phone rang, and a guy from the laundry said: 'We got the R Division laundry done. Do you want to pick it up?' I said: 'Okay, I'll be right over.' I was going to be coming off of watch.

"So I went over and got the bag of laundry. I had just come back dragging that bag when all of a sudden the word went: 'Away fire and rescue party!' So I dropped the laundry bag. I was on the port side already, but I didn't have my white hat on. So I went to my locker, because I had to have my white hat for the muster on the quarterdeck. I got my hat and went on the main deck, past the supply office. As I got through the opening of the compartment, the word came: 'General Quarters! General Quarters! Man your battle stations!' I was where I could see a plane bank. I was surprised like everyone else: 'What the hell's going on?' I thought. 'Away fire and rescue and now GQ!'

"What was happening was they were bombing Ford Island. I didn't see it because I was facing aft on the port side of the main deck. Like I said, I saw this plane bank, and I saw a meatball. But it still didn't strike me as to what was happening. Because of habit I got to my station. I just dropped down a ladder to the second deck, and I was down to the third deck, at my repair station—repair three—within minutes.

"As soon as I got there, I opened up the repair lockers, got the battle lantern out, and got the tools out. This is what I'd been trained to do, and I got ready. I was even thinking about the cards, but for some reason I didn't get the cards out to play with somebody. I was there, and nobody else came down for quite a while. They were slow in coming. By that time, the lights went out; the ventilators went off. It was pitch dark. Well, I started turning the battle lanterns on. People were drifting down, creeping around.

"I said: 'What the hell's happening?' This first class shipfitter by the name of Rucker said: 'The goddamned Japs are hitting us!' He was the first one to say it. Then he said: 'What the hell are we going to do?' There was nothing we could do. We were trying to hook up the phones, but they were dead, too. There was nobody to give us orders; the repair officer in charge wasn't there. We were on the third deck not knowing, except we knew it was the Japs, because Rucker kept saying: 'Goddamn them son-of-a-bitching Japs hit us!'

"We couldn't feel we were hit, because we were aft, away from it. We lost power, so our engineering spaces must have been hit. But we didn't feel anything at that time. We were sort of milling around, wondering what we were going to do, when it felt like an explosion. It felt like our steering sort of went out. The ship sort of gave a lunge, and it just bounced back. It might have been an explosion somewhere to cause us to sort of raise up.

"Then Rucker said: 'Well, goddamn, we've got to do something!' He said: 'Ski, get the lantern, and we'll start flooding.' See, our ship was starting to list. It was listing to port, so Rucker said: 'We better start flooding.' I'd say there were six to eight men in there, and he sort of took charge. He said: 'Ski, you come with me.' Having been his striker, he knew me, and he said: 'You get the lanterns,' and he took a couple of wrenches, and we started to work our way down the third deck, where all the controls were.

"Rucker was one of the men I had a very high respect for. I hoped to be like him. Whatever he said, I was ready to do, because he knew what he was doing. He had been around the voids, cofferdams, and all this flooding before. Once in a practice run we did this, so he knew all about it. I wouldn't have been able to do it if I had had to, but then I wouldn't have tried, because that meant opening up the valves to get water in the bottom.

"Well, we were down there, and we were working by ourselves. It was a slow procedure, because it was dark. As they were moving, I would move along with the lantern. I stood back a little ways so they would have more light. I wasn't working on the valve; he and somebody else were. We worked forward—I don't know how far forward—but it seemed like we were there quite a while. We came upon another group. Rucker talked to them; they had already got everything forward. So Rucker said: 'We're going back to the repair party,' and we headed back.

"So we got back, and again there was no officer. Rucker said: 'Well, hell, there ain't nothing we can do here! Let's get the hell out of here.' There was no water on the third deck, but, as we came up to the second deck, it was completely flooded because of the list. The ports were open, and the water rushed in there. The third deck was closed off where we were. That's why no water got in there. Well, we found a ladder that got us past the water and up to the main deck or quarterdeck. Now we were outside.

"About a half hour to an hour or less had passed. I looked over, and the *Arizona* is all afire, and it didn't look like a ship. It was just a hulk, all blown up, and the oil was all afire, black smoke all over. There was a bunch of us coming from below-decks and milling around, because this was the only safe area to be in. There was no other place to go.

"We were several hundred feet from the *Arizona*. She was at the next quay; she was inboard. There was a repair ship tied to her earlier, but it was gone. I thought it was sunk. It was the *Vestal*. 'God!' I wondered. 'What the hell happened here?' I wasn't scared or anything; it was just amazing what the hell happened. You still couldn't recollect what really was happening.

"All of a sudden, there was one plane flying by up high, a bomber, just one plane. The next thing, we looked up and saw a bomb or a projectile. It hit our scout plane on the number three turret, about fifty feet away. The debris was flying around and set the plane afire. We scattered; we laid down. It seemed like everybody did it automatically; they didn't want to get any shrapnel. We were trained to lay down; we all hit the deck.

"Some people were jumping in the water. I thought: 'We should get the hell out of here!' So I was looking around, getting ready to go, and a sailor bumps me and says: 'Don't leave me! I've got some oil in my eyes! I can't see good.' I said: 'Okay, don't worry about it; I'm not going.' I said: 'We can't go in the water in your condition.'

"I saw some lines to the *Tennessee*. I said: 'Come on with me! Hang on to my back there! Just grab hold of me! I'll walk slowly with you.' So we went up the ladder to the boat deck, over the lines, and got on the *Tennessee*. I got on first, and then I dragged him. I said: 'We'll bounce on together,' so we bounced over on a line and got on the *Tennessee*. We sat on the line and bounced over.

"There was no communication to abandon ship. The word was: 'Let's get the hell out of here!' There was nothing we could do; that was a dead ship. We were getting out of there because, if another bomb or something comes in, we're hopeless. The way out was either in the water or sit on the line and bounce over. There was quite a strain on the line, because it was holding the ships together.

"We got over these, and I went to the first-aid station; they had them throughout the ship. There was a pharmacist's mate in the area. I brought the sailor there, and there were other people laying on the deck. They were wounded. So I asked the pharmacist's mate: 'What can I do? Can I help?' He said: 'Yeah, here's some stuff. Put it in his eyes. We'll try and clear them out.' Well, I did that, just bathed them and tried to get the oil out. Finally, he was able to sort of take care of himself, and I left him and helped out around there.

"There were a lot of burned people. They were black and had oil all over them. You could see blisters on them. I was trying to put some petroleum jelly on them and trying to cover them with gauze. But that wasn't helping; it seemed to be taking their skin off. It seemed like it was better to just leave the skin open instead of putting something over it. They wanted to tear the gauze off, or if they had a skivvy shirt, they wanted to tear that goddamned thing off, because they were blistered, burnt. I was around there for quite a while.

"That's when they passed the word over the speaker—ship's communication—that the *West Virginia* sailors were to muster on Ford Island. So I got off the *Tennessee*. I left that area and went toward Ford Island. Several of us were getting hungry, so we wandered into some houses. They had dependents' housing there. We went into the kitchen and got something to eat before we went on. We figured we wouldn't get anything to eat there.

"All the houses were abandoned; there was nobody in them. So we went in and got some bread; there was some meat, like bologna, and we got a few pieces of fruit and some milk. Then we went over to the building where they were rounding up people, over to the mess hall. We got over there, and they started feeding us. We stayed there that night."

* * *

Grabinski spent the night following the attack in a state typical of many Pearl Harbor survivors—that is, he was unnerved by constant gunfire. He later helped in salvage operations and stood guard duty aboard the sunken battleship.

"During the night we were sitting around, and, all of a sudden, all hell broke loose. The antiaircraft started firing. Well, there were some planes in the air and tracers flying around. I said: 'Uh-oh!' We dived under the tables—the mess-hall tables. This sailor near me says: 'I guess we'll all be pulling rickshaws here pretty soon.' I said: 'They must be coming in!' We were helpless; there was nothing we could do but just lay under the table and hope we didn't get hurt. All the ships that were able opened up on the planes. Then things settled down.

"I was thinking: 'How the hell could the Japs do this?' I guess the expression is: 'Jesus Christ! How are we going to get out of this? The Japs are probably going to land. What are we going to do? We're sailors! Our ships are sunk! What are we going to do? What are they going to do with us?' We thought they were landing. They hit us, and they crippled us. We figured: 'They're going to be coming in,' because of the planes. We didn't know at the time that they were our own planes, but later we found out that they were our own, from the carrier *Enterprise*. At the time we figured it was a second attack, and they were going to land. They had every opportunity. We were helpless. If they had come in, hell, there was nothing we could do except go in the bushes and try to hide from them. There were no guns for us or anything else like that. We weren't trained for this.

"Well, we stayed in the mess hall on Ford Island until the next day, and then they ferried us over to the mainland and put us in the Bloch Center arena, where they had 'The Battle of the Bands' on Saturday the 6th. We slept there the next day. That second day I was assigned to ride the ferry for four hours between the mainland and Ford Island. So I had a bird's-eye view of everything. All the ships, it was unbelievable. Jesus! 'How the hell are we going to get out of this?' I asked. 'This will take forever to fix up.'

"Rucker was looking after me. He found out that they were going to have a salvage detail for the *West Virginia*—all *West*

Virginia men only—because they knew the ship. He said: 'Ski, they're going to assign fifty guys to the salvage detail. I'm getting you on it with me.' I said: 'Good! Yes, I'll go with you.' I wanted to be his protégé, you know. Okay, they got fifty of us. They tried to get anyone that was a diver or a shipfitter, people who would be good for a salvage detail. This was the third day.

"That night I was to be the security watch on the *West Virginia*. I was on the ship all by myself. This time I was on the starboard side sitting with a rifle and reminiscing again: 'What the hell's going to happen now?' A few days earlier I thought what a good deal this was, and now I'm wondering: 'Jesus! What's going to happen? War and everything! A lot of guys will be drafted, and I'm way ahead of them.' I was thinking all of that when, during the quiet of the night, there was a bang, bang, bang! Bang, bang, bang! I figured there were men trapped down there. But then I learned the crew off the *Tennessee* was crossing over to the ship and looting it—lockers and everything—looking for valuables, money, anything.

"My instructions were: 'If you see anybody coming across, open up the chamber and just close it and click it so they can hear it.' You ain't got no ammunition anyway. You're not to shoot them but to frighten them away. So I wouldn't shoot at anybody, because I'd have killed the son of a bitch that was coming over.

"When I came on duty just before nightfall, I went to check my locker, and everything was out of it. I could only salvage my clothes. They looted everything on the main deck; all the lockers were looted. The clothes were pulled out, a photo album, and everything was in that oil. They had a reason for not giving us ammunition. If I had had a clip, I'd have killed the first two I saw coming over. I honestly would have shot them. But after I clicked, I said: 'Turn around or I'll blow your heads off.' They heard the click, and they turned around and left.

"Then I heard the pounding again. I didn't have a flashlight. I wondered where it was coming from. It sounded forward, so I figured it's trapped men down there. See, we were sunk all the way to the main deck. The pounding kept going on. I didn't even doze off; I didn't even sleep. Usually, it would be easy for me because it was dark. But I didn't even close my eyes. I thought: 'Maybe the ship is going to blow up.' You know, they said the ship could blow up. Maybe the ammunition would blow up.

"Well, I reported that noise in the morning. They said: 'Somebody must be trapped below, but there's nothing we can do about it. We'll check on it.' Several more times when I was aboard, again alone, I heard that same noise. They were still pounding. I reported it again. They didn't do anything about that pounding that I know of. The others talked about it, too.''

On December 29, Louis Grabinski was reassigned from the *West Virginia* to the Pearl Harbor submarine base, where ship-fitters were needed. When they later began reassembling the *Weevee*'s crew, Grabinski was frozen in his new assignment; he began learning to operate radar, which was just being placed on submarines. In mid-1942 the *West Virginia* was raised. He went to watch, as he describes: "You could have driven big trucks in her center. Most of the damage was done in the center, in the engineering spaces. The port side had holes through the decks — the destruction was unbelievable—from the torpedoes and bombs.''

Grabinski never rejoined his battleship. In late 1942 it left Hawaii for the West Coast. "On the day she left, tears came in my eyes. I bawled. My ship was leaving, and here I was still stuck. I thought, 'What the hell am I doing?' '' He stayed at the submarine base, where he made chief petty officer at age twenty-three, after only three years and three months in the Navy. He stayed in the service for the next seventeen years, retiring in 1959.

Only thirty-nine at the time, Grabinski moved to Long Beach, where he worked two years for the Todd Shipyard before moving to the U.S. Navy Yard there. Eleven years later he retired for a second time. He spent one year working for Litton Systems in Pascagoula, Mississippi, building destroyers and carriers, and then spent another year back with Todd. He retired for the final time in 1974. An exuberant man, he said: "I've been retired ever since, and I'm enjoying life completely.'' Louis Grabinski died on April 28, 1989.

10
Fireman Dan Wentrcek
USS *Nevada*

The only Japanese national that Dan Wentrcek had known before shipping to Pearl Harbor was a professor at Southwestern University in Georgetown, Texas. He met him the day he left for boot camp at San Diego in July 1941. Dan, his mother, and his brother and sister were in the sister's backyard when she told her Japanese neighbor that Dan was leaving for naval duty on the West Coast. "Hmm," said the professor, "you'll be sorry!" When Dan thought about this later, he was sure that "the professor knew all along what was going to take place! He didn't tell me good-bye, good luck, or anything. He just said: 'You'll be sorry!' " Regardless of whether the Japanese man knew about the approaching assault on Pearl Harbor, he was right about Wentrcek's being sorry. On December 7 the latter lost shipmates and worldly possessions when his ship, the USS *Nevada* (BB36), tried to clear the harbor and was forced to run aground during attack by enemy aircraft.

Wentrcek was born in Granger, Texas, on December 11, 1922. By mid-1941 he had found that jobs were scarce in central Texas even for a high school graduate, and the lure of "steady pay, good food, good quarters, and things of that nature" was strong. Moreover, he had a friend and several relatives who had served in the Navy, and they excited his interest. He paid attention to world affairs and suspected that the United States was heading for war, although he thought that it would come only in Europe.

After six weeks' training in San Diego, he waived a seven-day leave and a chance to attend a naval trade school, choosing rather "to go to sea." On the advice of Chief Petty Officer Sullivan, his training company commander, he secured duty aboard the *Nevada*, joining her on September 10. The battleship sailed for the Hawaiian Islands that night. He received on-the-job training in the engineering division as a boiler fireman.

Duty in Pearl Harbor was ideal. Wentrcek liked the chow, which was served home style at tables. His quarters were at the forward end of the crew's area near those of the officers and, by Navy standards, were spacious; bunks were only three tiered at the time. Morale was high and work was light. In port, firemen were on duty for twenty-four hours and off for twenty-four hours, while "Cinderella liberty," or liberty ending at midnight, was frequent. Returning to ship at midnight did not bother Wentrcek, who avoided Honolulu's night spots, especially those on Hotel and Canal streets. The city was "wall to wall with sailors," but Wentrcek was more like a tourist than a seaman. He watched others, the "suckers," being tattooed, and he window shopped, bought souvenirs, bowled, ate hamburgers, walked along Waikiki Beach, and visited other memorable places on the island.

The *Nevada* went on maneuvers about once a month for two weeks at a time, usually for gunnery practice, firing on the target vessel *Utah*. The *Nevada* and a number of other ships had just returned from a two-week cruise on the Friday before the attack. Routine was broken slightly by the *Nevada*'s tying up alongside the *Arizona*. This gave the crews visiting privileges, and some of the *Arizona*'s sailors came over to the neighboring ship. "We had a movie together," Wentrcek said, "and I'll never forget it. *One Foot in Heaven* was its name."

On Saturday the *Nevada* backed off, and, with the ship having been cleaned, holiday routine was declared. This meant liberty, and so Wentrcek went ashore. He later regretted that the fleet apparently let its guard down that weekend. "We steamed into harbor, and it was, 'Happy days are here again.' This was the attitude of everybody. Everything was wide open. Nothing was closed or shut off or anything like that." Wentrcek returned to the ship to stand watch on the Sunday morning 4:00 to 8:00 shift. The interview begins with his relief's arriving early.

"It's customary whenever you have to stand auxilliary watch that you get relieved early. I got relieved about 7:30 or thereabouts. Your relief eats breakfast and comes on down, rather than relieving you first to let you eat and then have to come back. This way you're through when he comes. This was just one of our routines that we had amongst ourselves. So he came down and relieved me, and I was going to clean up and go ashore.

"I don't know what I had planned to go ashore for that Sunday, but I wanted to spend it over on the beach. I didn't even stop to eat breakfast. Breakfast was something like chipped beef on toast or something like that that I didn't care for too much. So I just went on into the shower. I left my clothes back on the bunk, took me a clean pair of shorts, my soap and razor, and went into the shower. I was there when General Quarters sounded.

"Air Attack first was sounded. There's a difference in the bugle call for Air Attack and just regular General Quarters. Air Attack was the first alarm, and then we went into the General Quarters alarm, and I don't know what else. The bugler was putting it through the PA system. He was with the officer of the deck, and he had his orders to sound the alarm.

"There were two or three other guys in the shower who said: 'Aw, of all the damned times to have a drill!' And then somebody said: 'Well, that's a crazy time! A lot of guys are not here!' So we thought: 'Well, it's some kind of drill. Some guy with a little authority is pulling something.' This was our attitude.

"Rather than running back to my bunk between the shower and our compartments—where I had my clothes laid out—there was a hatch going down to the engineering space and down to the boiler rooms. So, after putting my shorts on, I just scooted down there to my battle station. About that time we had a hit of some kind, and I realized something wasn't kosher. It just felt like the whole ship was raised up. I was standing there on what we called 'the floor plates,' and they bounced up. If you've ever heard a real hard car crash, this is similar to it. I thought: 'My God, what's going on?'

"We couldn't hear down in the boiler room with no speaker system, but the headman there had on earphones. He said it was a Japanese attack; the planes had Japanese markings on them. I know that we got that word.

"I guess before I got to the boiler room and probably before we got this hit, the bridge had called down to start cutting in burners, give them everything they had. Things happened so fast that it seemed to me that hours passed. All we were trying to do was to give them all the steam we could. During this process I had to change these burner tips.

"Whenever we were in port, we had a tip on our burners—

very small orifices to burn a small amount of fuel—since we didn't need much fuel going through there. I believe we had three or four different sizes that we used for more capacity or consumption. I know they said we were to put in the biggest ones that we had to get all the steam we could immediately.

"Things were popping, and I was right over in front of that boiler where I had to do this—put these tips in. They were hot with hot oil, and I put them in a vice, unscrewed the tip, put a new burner tip in, and put them back in there and lit them off. Of course, they lit off from others that were burning. I guess I did it all right.

"I changed these burners, but I was afraid because we had another crash of some kind. We had always been warned, even when we were firing our big guns, not to stand in front of that boiler. We had what was called 'flashback'—the flames, influenced by a vacuum, would come out and then back because of the concussion. Here I was, changing these tips right in front of the boiler, next to the bulkhead. Anyway, I got them in there and fired up, and I got back away from there. I was moving pretty dadgummed fast.

"A kid that had come aboard ship recently was in one of the other boiler rooms. He had gone through training in a different company. He got burnt very badly because he got caught in a flashback. But that flame—when we'd get a hit—would come clear back to the bulkhead and go behind the boilers. Bombs or torpedoes would cause flashback.

"Well, at last we had everything opened up, and we were standing off to the side. It seemed like we did this in just minutes—very few minutes. We had gotten under way. I've been told that we were under way in fourteen minutes. Normally, it took about four tugs to get us under way, yet we got under way with our own power. But then the ship began to list. I think it was the result of the first torpedo. I remember very distinctly that the list was making it difficult for the water tender. I remember him saying: 'Man, I can't see that water gauge!' I think he probably just opened the thing up and let the water go, you know.

"I know we were moving. I remember feeling the motion of the ship, and somewhere along in there we got a hit just above us. It was right forward of the stack, and it came down and kind of deflected—I think they said it was a five-hundred-pound bomb that hit—and instead of coming on into the stack, it deflected away from it. When this happened, it blew out some tubes in our boilers, and we started filling up with steam and then had a heck of a fire up above us, and our blowers were bringing in this smoke and we couldn't see.

"Well, I was scared as hell! To be honest about it, we were all scared. When a bomb hits, it's a feeling or a sound you'll never forget. It is just a rending of metal and a concussion that's huge—just like something was picking the ship out of the water and bobbing it around or something. I was on a ship that was torpedoed afterwards, and it's the same thing. It's a sensation you can't really describe.

"Our headman told main control: 'We've got to come out of here!' They told us: 'All right.' So we had an emergency valve there. He just pulled it, and that shut all the fuel off to our boiler. Now, the ship was running on four of our six boilers. One of our boiler rooms was being overhauled, and it was all torn down.

"So, like I say, we shut off our fires and started out, and we came to an airtight door—what we called 'an air lock,' with two doors. It's called the air-lock chamber because it was under pressure. We got out of there and started up the ladder. The deck above us was the armor deck—that's a three-inch steel deck—and there's a hatch up there. Whenever you go into battle stations, the repair crews close all these hatches. We got there, and a guy by the name of Kelsey was with me. He said: 'We got to close this steam line off, 'cause our boiler is out, and it's going to bleed the others!' So there was a big valve there, and we closed it off, and then we saw this hatch was dogged down, and I remember we couldn't open one of the dadgummed dogs. I think there were six dogs that held this hatch down.*

"We got all the other dogs loose and then took the big crow's-foot wrench we used to close the steam valve off and reached down and hit that dadgummed dog that wouldn't open. It came open, and we came out of there. But we had the eeriest feeling.

---

*In nautical parlance, a dog is any of several devices, such as a latch, used to hold a door or hatch in place when shut.

We were on the starboard side, and we had listed a lot. We had water above us. When we opened that hatch here comes the water. That is a dadgummed eerie feeling. It was about ankle deep in the passageway.

"Well, then we went into the other passageway running fore and aft of the ship, opened that one, and there was no water in there. We felt better then, and we could see guys down there. We went down there. It seemed like it wasn't very long before other boiler rooms started taking water and had to be shut down.

"We huddled down in this area in these passageways for a while. Of course, they were trying to maintain some steam to keep some electrical power going because you had to have electricity for the guns. All your broadside stuff, the 5-inch guns, and the lights had to have electricity. Somebody got a case of gallon cans of apricots, and they broke them out. It might have been noon. Like I say, I lost all track of time.

"We hadn't secured from General Quarters yet. Then they said: 'Well, let's try to put number six boiler room together.' Well, I was glad to get something to do. I think by the time we started putting this boiler room together, we were beached. They ran the *Nevada* aground purposely up on a ledge. At Hospital Point, I believe. Then they ran a bunch of lines and cables over to the trees to hold the ship. They said we were up on a ledge, and they didn't want her to slide down off it. So we worked in the boiler room. If I remember right, it was about 2:00 in the morning, Monday morning, that we had the boiler room ready to go.

"They asked: 'Are you ready to fire it?' We said: 'All right.' Well, we couldn't pump any fresh water because our water was all contaminated with salt water. We fired it up, but we couldn't control it. With salt water you can't control your steam. It foams. We tried to make it work for a little while, and then finally they said: 'It's hopeless. Shut her down.' So we came out of there, and it was morning by then. It was daylight when we went topside and looked around.

"I had been up briefly on Sunday afternoon and found an old pair of dungarees to put on. My own locker was on the side that listed, and everything was underwater. So then on Monday morning, sometime after daylight, I came topside to look around.

Everything was still burning, and it was smoky. I felt sick, and I guess I really was. I remember there was a kind of drizzle falling and that smoke and everything hanging there, smoke belching out of the *Arizona*. I looked over the harbor and had a very weird feeling. I stayed on board until Monday afternoon, when they took us over to the Fleet Landing.

"The water was covered with oil and debris. A boat came alongside—a crew boat—and took us over, and, of course, we had to go back along Battleship Row to the landing. We had to watch out for the timber, floating pieces, chunks of wood, and that kind of stuff. Oil was everywhere, and things were still smoldering.

"We stayed over there. They fed us. That's one time I ate chipped beef and toast, and it tasted really good. I've never turned it down since. They wanted us to relax. We slept in the bowling alley that night. Have you ever tried to sleep on a bowling lane?

"We went back the next day and tried to clean up topside. In a couple of days, then, they took a group of us for burial details on Aiea Landing. We worked over there as they would pick up bodies where they were salvaging. They'd find them floating in the water, and they'd bring them over, or they'd bring body pieces, and pharmacist's mates would take fingerprints if the bodies were unidentifiable.

"As they brought bodies in, we had a bunch of pine boxes that'd been made up that we would put them in. They would give the box a number. A lot of times they had a bunch of pieces. We'd just put them in a box. Then we loaded the boxes on a truck, and we would take them over to the cemetery. They had bulldozed out trenches, and we buried the bodies or parts every evening. Three denominations held services. We were there and would sound taps and then cover them over and stick up a wooden stake with a number for whatever identity we could give that would correspond to the number. I think I worked at Aiea for seven or eight days."

Eventually, Fireman Wentrcek was assigned to the heavy cruiser *Chester*. He spent the remainder of the war on it and, with other crew members, made "quite a record" for the ship. He was "proud to have been a part" of the military at Pearl Harbor on December 7, because he "loved the Navy." He had "no regrets" except that he and his shipmates were let down that day: "I think we had warning. I think we had ample warning. They just didn't take heed. They were trying to keep from having conflict of some kind, I guess. Of course, we'll never know. But I think we had enough warning ahead of time to be more prepared. We could have saved a lot of our fleet rather than steaming them in there on Friday like we did and just letting our hair down and forgetting it all. I think that was the big blunder!"

After the war, Wentrcek farmed and then sold farm equipment. He later became a maintenance worker at the University of North Texas, in Denton, retiring in 1986. He now lives in Granite Shoals, Texas, near Austin. Voicing a sentiment common to Pearl Harbor survivors, he said: "The attack has made me realize that America must always maintain a strong national defense and never again let her guard down."

11
Machinist's Mate Second Class Leon Bennett
USS *Neosho*

Leon Bennett boarded the USS *Neosho* (AO23) the day after it was commissioned at Norfolk, Virginia, and remained with her until she was sunk during the Battle of the Coral Sea in May 1942. The ship had been built as a civilian oil tanker but was taken over by the Navy in 1941. At the time of the Pearl Harbor attack, she was carrying petroleum supplies on a regular basis from the West Coast of the United States to Hawaii.

Bennett had previously served on the USS *Gillis*, a four-stack destroyer that had taken him along the Yangtze River and to Shanghai, the Philippines, and finally the Hawaiian Islands. Born on October 24, 1918, in Kennard, Texas, he worked for several years before joining the Navy in November 1939. His decision to enlist was caused by the outbreak of war in Europe and his opinion that the United States would soon enter the conflict. He chose the sea because he "didn't like the walking part of the Army—the mud, water, and slush." He had heard "too many soldiers from World War I talking about it."

After four months of boot camp at the San Diego Naval Training Center, he got into trouble while on liberty downtown and, as a result, was assigned to the Asiatic Service. The first portion of the interview concerns what happened to him in San Diego and his six-month tour in and around Shanghai.

"Well, on liberty I ran into a boy who had been going to Rice University. He was a football star down there—Donald Yeager. He wasn't old enough to buy beer, so I was buying him beer, and he got upset and knocked out a plate-glass window on Broadway in San Diego. Consequently, we wound up in the brig back on base. He was luckier than I was. The captain that he went before was an old ex-Rice man; they belonged to the same fraternity. They sent Yeager to North Island and made a pilot out of him. When I went up before the captain's mast, I told him I came in the Navy to fight, and I didn't come in to march and hang around a base. Well, the captain saw to it that I got out of there. They shipped me to China.

"I was on the *Gillis*. It was an old four-stacker, an old tin can. It was on river patrol. We just went up and down the river. It was a rough Navy over there. I don't think they ever tamed them. Of course, I didn't stay long enough to get as flaky as they were. Most of the sailors didn't want to ever come back.

"When they got transferred out, someone would buy their Chinese wife, and when you bought their wife, you inherited a family. I mean, you took care of everybody. You gave five or ten dollars in gold, and that took care of the whole family. And she took care of your ironing and all your other necessities!

"People liked to stay over there because the pay was low in the Navy, and there you could take five dollars in gold and live high, where back in the States it didn't go far.

"I was on a boxing team for a while, and I thought it was pretty good. I liked those steaks, and all I had to do was skip rope and punch a bag around a little. I won my first four bouts, and then I ran into the guy who was the welterweight champion of the Asiatic Fleet. I told my coach: 'Hell, I don't want to fight that cat!' I said: 'He'll beat me to death!' He said: 'Oh, you can take him; you can take him!' So I got in and did pretty good. I knocked him down a couple times in the first round. About the second round, he came up, and I didn't know where he came from. He paralyzed me, and that ended my boxing career. I mean, I lay there. I knew everything, but I couldn't move.

"China duty was fine at first, but before we left, it got to where we had to carry side arms when we went ashore. I mean, people would crawl over you, jump on you. Especially the beggars, they would attack you right on the street. So they finally wouldn't let us go ashore unless we were armed, when they sent us over on detail for supplies or something like that.

"I was there six months. They moved a bunch of us out of there at the time because trouble was brewing. They were beginning to evacuate Americans that were on the mainland of China. They just brought us out, pulled us back."

Bennett first shipped to Manila, but soon he was sent to Hawaii and finally to Norfolk to join the *Neosho*. The tanker arrived in Pearl Harbor at 8:00 P.M. on the Saturday before the attack. It carried a mixed load: aviation gas for Ford Island Naval Air Station in the forward part of the ship and fuel oil for other vessels in the after part. It was lightly armed with one 3-inch cannon and several .30- and .50-caliber machine guns. The remainder of the interview begins with the entry into the harbor and concludes with the days following the attack.

"We came in on the night of the 6th, and we had a darkened ship. Of course, we knew that there was an alert out and that we might go to war with Japan. As we came in that night, two of those midget submarines* were in under the belly of the ship, and we bumped them. We thought we had run aground; you know, we were heavily loaded. So they opened the net [that guarded the harbor entrance]—they had had it closed—and as we came in we bumped those things.

"Anthony and I were down in the engine room—the main engine room—standing throttle watch. We thought maybe we were running aground. I said: 'God Almighty, Anthony, we've hit something! Somebody can't drive up there or something!' He said: 'Well, I guess we are loaded a little heavier than usual.'

---

*See also Ellis interview, pp. 2-9.

But actually the next day they figured out that that was how the subs got in, because we were the last ship to come in that night. The subs were ready to come in right under us, and they came on in.

"We went over to Aiea Landing and pumped out all the fuel oil that night. I had pumping duty, too, so I had to stand and watch the pumping. Then we moved over to Ford Island on Battleship Row and tied up at a little pier that ran out from there. I pumped aviation gas from around 4:00 A.M. until around 8:00. I had secured everything, and I walked out on the dock to smoke a cigarette because the smoking lamp was still out. That's when it all took place—while I was standing at the dock.

"I saw planes coming in, and they were diving on the hangars and stuff like that. I said: 'I wonder what those bastards are doing drilling this morning!' I thought they were regular Navy or Air Corps* maneuvers and that they were dropping sandbags; that was what they always dropped. I just couldn't believe, you know, that they were Jap planes and that they could get that close in or get a task force that close. Then all of a sudden smoke boiled up and BOOM! BOOM! BOOM! I looked up and one fishtailed, and I could see the plane's rising-sun insignia. I said: 'Oh, hell! This is it!'

"I guess I watched about five minutes maybe, and by the time I got back on board, why, the torpedo planes were coming in, and they were machine-gunning the decks. They were chipping paint right behind me while I was running across the deck, you know, to get to the midship pump room. General Quarters sounded as I was running to my battle station there; I ran the steam-smothering system in case we got hit. So that the tanker wouldn't blow up and catch fire, I would turn on the steam-smothering system. It was real important to get to that steam valve to smother that stuff down so it wouldn't explode.

"Well, there were dive-bombers and torpedo bombers. One flight was taking care of the hangars, and the planes in the other flight, the ships. The torpedo bombers were coming in over a little mountain, right down through the harbor. Well, you could

---

*The U.S. Army Air Corps became the Army Air Forces on June 20, 1941; however, most of the interviewees used the older title.

chuck potatoes at them, they were so low; and some guys, the cooks on the fantail, were chucking potatoes at them. They would just rear back and throw, because they were coming that close. They were coming directly in, and there was no way you could avoid them.

"Luckily, either a destroyer, or somebody on that 3-inch peashooter that we had, lobbed a shell over and hit a torpedo right on the nose, and the Jap plane disintegrated. It was coming right at my General Quarters station, right at midship, and I said: 'Oh, God! I'm in for it!' About that time, you could see the shell lob over and hit. It blew up right before he was going to drop the torpedo. Otherwise, we would have been hit and probably blown up. From Japanese intelligence we learned that they thought we were an aircraft carrier because we were sitting so high in the water.*

"They were so low you could see them grinning, you know. I mean, really, they were laughing, all smiles; they were having a field day, a ball. It was a regular ball for them. They were coming in deliberately, taking their time, because nothing much was going on—no firing. They really had a field day. It was a beautiful morning, just right. You couldn't ask for better weather; it was just perfect.

"Well, I opened up my valve, and I went out there and watched. You know, I had smothered down the steam system. That was my main job—to turn it on—and I was an observer from then on. There was a little deckhouse there, a little shed, protected, right in the middle of the tanker. The hatch was open, and I stood right by it. I had a ringside seat, so to speak.

"Well, we were tied up at that pier that extends out in front of the *Arizona* Memorial today. We were tied to that. Right behind our ship was the *Oklahoma*, and right behind it was the *Arizona*, and I watched them both turn over. I mean, I watched the *Oklahoma* roll over and the *Arizona* blow up.

"The Japs came down at a low altitude. I don't guess they were fifty feet high, and they came in two at a time. They were right close together. I saw them release the torpedoes; I saw

---

*No evidence has been found that Japanese pilots mistook the *Neosho* for a carrier.

them go into the *Oklahoma*. There was a terrific explosion. You could see it jump out of the water. You know, I thought for a battleship that was something unusual. I never dreamed torpedoes could do that much damage, really. You could drive a truck through the hole. Well, it was hard to believe unless you were there to see what they did in an hour and thirty minutes, actually.

"Well, the *Oklahoma* just did a slow roll, and the guys were jumping off into the water. They were abandoning ship. And, of course, the water had caught on fire, and it was drifting on down the harbor out toward the sea. The survivors were swimming around, and a bunch of boats were trying to pick them up. We lowered some whaleboats and were picking them up. Some got burnt real bad, and the ones that got killed—they were pulling them out and stacking them up, and the medics were working over them, you know.

"The *Arizona* got hit with torpedoes,* but what really got her was a dive-bomber that came in and dropped what looked like two bombs right down the stack. It hit an ammunition storage area, and, heck, it just exploded. I mean, WHAM! and everything. Whenever the ammunition magazines blew up, well, that was it. I mean, in just a few minutes it was down.

"Debris off the *Arizona* hit us. I got a piece of shrapnel. The only wound I got through the whole war—a little shrapnel cut. I think I stuck a Band-Aid on it or wrapped it up, and that was all. I was really lucky.

"They beached the *Nevada*. I saw her pull out, and then all of a sudden, when they were way ahead of us, I saw them beach her. I mean, they ran her aground so that it wouldn't sink. It was trying to get out of the harbor but was peppered by Jap planes that followed it all the way. And, of course, after they had dropped their bombs, then they sent what looked like five or six waves machine-gunning and strafing, that's all.

"Other than seeing them bomb the hangars and stuff on Ford Island, that's all I could see. I mean, I think they hit every hangar over there, because I could see the smoke and the bombs exploding and stuff like that. I said: 'We're in a hell of a shape!' I

*No torpedoes are known to have struck the *Arizona*.

thought the cat's eye was out for us unless we could get out of this thing.

"A thing that kept going through the back of my mind was: 'Oh, hell! They are going to land!' There was no way we could have kept a landing force from invading and taking over. We were so disorganized; not only the Navy but the Army and Marines were all totally disorganized. They were even shooting their own planes down. I was afraid they could capture the whole fleet.

"After the attack, the first thing I had to do was take back all the aviation gasoline we had pumped over. It took us about three and a half hours to do that. Then we moved over and got the fuel oil back. We had orders to meet the *Lexington* and join in trying to make contact with the enemy.

"By about dusk-dark we left there. We had filled the oiler back up with what we had and eased back on out. They opened the net and let us go. We had a destroyer with us, but I don't remember which can it was. Anyway, it was our escort out to catch the fleet. We caught the *Enterprise*, some cruisers, and destroyers. I think maybe the *Blue*, the *Ward*, and two or three others that had gotten out there, too. There were not very many ships. That next day, we fueled the whole fleet, and then we floated around out there for about six weeks before we came back.

"We were hunting them. I don't think there was ever any doubt in our minds that we could whip them and that we would eventually whip them. I mean, I never had any doubt. I had confidence in the Navy and naval personnel. You had to be a good man to get in the Navy at that time. You had to pass intelligence tests and be perfect physically, or they'd kick you out.

"After the attack we were a little low at first, but we had a bunch of boys who could play the guitar, and we sang at night. I can't say our morale was ever really down again—not on that particular ship. I understand others had morale problems, but not us."

The *Neosho* stayed with the flotilla described above until the Battle of the Coral Sea, when she was sunk. Machinist's Mate Bennett spent the remainder of the war in the Pacific, taking part in most of the major naval engagements. He was transferred to destroyers, again to the USS *Gillis* and later to the USS *Bush*. He was at Guadalcanal and the New Hebrides and then served in the Aleutian Islands. He had planned to be a career sailor, but the war changed all of that. He left the military in 1945, became a Pepsi Cola distributor, switched to the agricultural equipment business, and built the highly prosperous Bennett Equipment Company in Crockett, Texas, where he currently resides.

12
Musician First Class Warren G. Harding
USS *California*

The night before Pearl Harbor was attacked, Navy bandsman Warren G. Harding witnessed a shower of meteors and remembered his grandfather's telling him as a boy that "every time you see a meteor fall, someone close to you is going to die." As he stood on the fantail of the USS *California* (BB44), he thought: "My God! How many people do I know that are going to die soon?" The next morning, in the midst of battle, he recalled the meteor shower and said to himself: "Isn't it weird!"

Musician First Class Harding, who was a member of the U.S. Navy Band Sixteen, was born on March 6, 1921, in Greensburg, Indiana, about forty-five miles southeast of Indianapolis. He spent an adolescence normal for a Hoosier youth during the Great Depression. When he graduated from high school in 1939, jobs were hard to find, and, with the help of a family friend, he arranged an audition with the Navy bandmaster in Washington, DC, and was accepted.

After spending two weeks in an abbreviated boot camp at Norfolk, Virginia, Harding returned to the nation's capital to spend the next eighteen months at the Navy School of Music, where he received "highly disciplined" instruction as a bandsman and trombone player. On June 23, 1941, he was sent to Pearl Harbor to join Band Sixteen, which was being completed for duty aboard the USS *California*. During the ensuing weeks he spent what he later called "the best five months of my life."

As a first class petty officer he received seventy-four dollars a month, "not much, but enough."

Harding's reason for enlisting in the Navy was not so simple as wanting a job. He knew that war was coming and preferred to join the same branch in which his father had served. He also had a good friend who already had volunteered and was aboard the USS *Arizona*. In fact, on the day of the attack, Harding was going to join his friend for a picnic in Honolulu. He had spent an eventful Saturday and needed the relaxation.

On Saturday, December 6, he had been part of the fleet landing, a general military review involving about six thousand marines and sailors on the parade grounds at Hickam Field. He had then gone with his unit to the Bloch Center and played in a fleetwide competition, "The Battle of the Bands," against the *Arizona*'s band. His group won. On December 7 all of the *Arizona*'s bandsmen were killed.

Harding's interview begins with his failure to catch the 7:30 A.M. liberty launch because he was delayed by a shipmate who was to accompany him on the picnic. The first passage ends with the *California*'s being abandoned except for the area occupied by Harding and his repair crew. His battle station was repair fore port, or on the left forward section of the vessel, where he was to relay communications between repair central and his crew.

"As I got out to the quarterdeck, the liberty launch was just pulling away. I'd missed it. It's a good thing, because every one of those men was killed. They were strafed and killed because it took over half an hour to get to Fleet Landing from where the *California* was.

"So I leaned against the rail and waited. About fifteen minutes until eight, the duty band got ready to play colors. They went back to the fantail and started forming. It was 7:55, and the prep flag had just gone up. The prep flag is a blue flag with a white square in the middle of it, and that goes up five minutes before colors.

"I looked over to the right because I heard this drone, a ROAR-R-R-R-R. It was a plane diving. I thought: 'My goodness, this is Sunday! Who practices dive-bombing on Sunday?'

I'm looking up in the air, and immediately I spotted that red ball. I said: 'That's a Zero!' I'd been aircraft identifying, and I knew immediately it was a Zero.

"I saw it and recognized the red ball, and just like that I saw the bomb being released. It burst on the runway on Ford Island. I thought: 'We got it!' My attitude had been built up to us being in war for the last four or five weeks, especially the last four days. I thought: 'My God, we got it.' So I headed, automatically, to my battle station. That's all I thought—get to my battle station.

"I went below—it was four decks below, repair forc port—and I grabbed the headphones. I'm sitting there with the headphones on when we hear the boatswain's mate piping and the marine bugler blowing General Quarters. Then the master-at-arms gets on the PA system and says: 'Everybody get to your battle stations! This is no shit! They're bombing Ford Island! Get to your battle stations!' And he blew his pipe again, and the bugler came out with his bugle and sounded battle stations again.

"Then there was a little bit of quiet, just a hair, and then all at once I heard POW, the first explosion. It was an extraordinary feeling. When you fire a broadside on a battleship, it feels like the battleship is picked up in the water, then it kind of shakes and then settles back down. That's just the way the torpedo felt. Everybody looked at each other, and somebody said: 'Why are they firing a broadside? They're only airplanes! You can't hit airplanes with a broadside!' Down there where we were, we had no way of knowing we had been hit. Shortly after, another torpedo hit, and it was the same as before. It picked that ship up and just shook it, and then it settled back down.

"We never lost power, we were never without light and air. After a bit we noticed that the watertight door on the aft side of our compartment was sprung a little bit. Since it was sprung and we were getting oil and some water in that door, we knew that things were in bad shape back there. We also knew we were in trouble, because we developed about a 10- to 15-degree port list.

"After we got the hit forward, we were right between two torpedo hits. When I saw the USS *California* in dry dock, after they pulled her up out of the mud a couple of years later and brought her to the dry dock, I couldn't believe my eyes. I almost fainted. You could have driven a Mack truck through either one of the torpedo holes, and I was in the place right between them. I couldn't believe it because we weren't really in trouble except for the fact that we were getting some water and oil in the compartment.

"About 8:25 we took a bomb down the midships hatch. We knew we had been hit, but we didn't know what it was. I didn't tell anybody, but they had begun to abandon ship. Repair central notified all repair stations: 'Abandon Ship'; but they said: 'Repair fore port, maintain your watertight integrity.' That was my order.

"My thoughts were mixed. I thought: 'Here I am, a Navy man. My orders are to maintain watertight integrity,' and I said: 'Maintain watertight integrity.' So then after a while the fumes began to collect a little. So the shipfitter who was in charge of the repair station said: 'Let's check the compartment forward and see whether or not there's anything in there because we're getting stuff in here.' So he checked forward, and there was no problem. So they opened the forward compartment, and there was an air duct or wind scoop. So the shipfitter said: 'Look, at least we'll have fresh air up here, so let's all move in there.'

"By that time, they'd abandoned ship two different times. After the third time that they abandoned ship, repair central said: 'Repair fore port, are you still in your repair station?' I said: 'We've moved forward one compartment. It's clean and there's fresh air here.' He said: 'We're preparing to abandon ship, and you're the only ones now that we haven't accounted for, but we know where you are, and we'll come back and get you as soon as we possibly can. But we're abandoning ship now. Stay where you are and maintain watertight integrity.' I never did tell anybody about this. This is something I've kept to myself all this time. They didn't know."

Six other men were trapped with Harding in the compartment. They were shipfitters, electricians, and one other bandsman, Gus Manley, who played the bass horn. One of his favorite pastimes was eating, and he was called "Jug Butt" and "JB" by the crew. As Harding goes on to describe, Manley suffered more than the others from the confinement, which lasted about six hours. During the period that they were trapped, the men joked, sang, and reflected seriously on their lives. One suspects that under these conditions many other sailors acted similarly.

"Manley passed out because of the smoke fumes in the first compartment, and we carried him into the other one. There was fresh air, and we put him right under the air scoop so that he finally came back a little bit, but he was sick.

"Finally, I said: 'I don't get anything from central. I don't get any signal at all. Apparently they have abandoned ship.' That's the first time I'd given them any indication. Nobody panicked because I don't think we realized the full impact of what had happened. We couldn't believe our ship was sinking. We could still breathe good, fresh air, and we could see the lights were on. There were no bullets flying around, no shrapnel. But the ship kept sinking down.

"Then we started getting some water and oil from up forward. It just kept filling. Time went on. Some guys went to sleep. There was a guitar and an electrician who knew how to play. He started strumming, and we started singing. We sang and we sang. Hours passed. Finally we ran out of songs and just sat there.

"Then somebody said: 'You know what? I don't think we're going to get out of here.' Somebody else said: 'Well, in case we don't, it'll probably go easy. I understand that when you get fumes, the carbon monoxide puts you out. You don't feel anything, and it won't be painful.' And somebody said: 'Yes, that's pretty good!' There was a lot of joking.

"I was very young at that time. I was twenty years old. My dominant thought was: 'Okay, in case we go it'll probably be easy, so I don't have to worry about that. But I haven't really lived yet. I still haven't made love to a woman.' I made up my mind that, in case we ever got out, I'd never pass up a chance, and I didn't. I had lived a pretty clean life—I was always scared where sex was concerned—but, after that, it does something for your confidence. So I think I ran around with a hard-on for the rest of my life.

"Then somebody said: 'You know, in case we do get caught,

somebody ought to know what happened to us.' Somebody had a pencil, and one by one we wrote our wills on the bulkheads. Some guys wrote messages to their wives. A couple wrote letters to their girlfriends. We got tired of doing things, and the guys were laying around sleeping. You're laying in water. Your head's above the water, but your feet and legs are in the water.

"We just kind of laid around and laid around, and finally somebody said: 'You think we ought to try and get out of here?' I remember saying: 'Well, they told us to maintain watertight security, so you know what orders are.' The shipfitter said: 'Maybe nobody even knows we're down here.' I said: 'Yes, when I talked to central last, they said they had a record that we were down here, and they'd get somebody to come in and get us out whenever it was logical for the watertight integrity to be relieved.'

"The shipfitter said: 'Who's the smallest one in here?' There was a little electrician's mate who probably wasn't more than five feet one inch. He said: 'Well, I guess I'm the smallest.' The shipfitter said: 'Do you think that you could get into that air duct and work yourself up to the boat deck and get out and tell somebody that we're aboard and maybe find some way to get us out?' The electrician answered: 'I'll try.' So he crawled into the damned thing and inched himself up through the duct and got out. He yelled at us from up there. He said: 'I'm out! I made it! I'll be back as soon as I can!'

"There was another long, long wait. We got to the point where everybody wanted out. We'd had enough of this. We've got this nervous energy building up. We're wondering whether or not we'll ever get out. People started talking to each other about 'in case you get out and I don't, you do this,' and we started writing down addresses and how to get to mothers and fathers, loved ones, things like that.

"There was never any overindulgence in any religious activity, no born-again Christians, hallelujahing, or anything like that whatsoever. There was just good, sound thinking and conversation. Then, about 3:00 that afternoon, we heard a knock. Everybody sat up. It wasn't much sound, but any sound was electrifying. The shipfitter said: 'Do you think somebody's come back aboard to get us?' I said: 'Let's knock back.' So he hit on the watertight door, three times, and boom, boom, boom, came back. Everybody roared: 'YEA!' and we started helping them open up. This was the aft door that we thought we couldn't get through.

"They opened it up, and some more water came in, maybe two feet. We could have gone through that door anytime. It tested water and oil, so we didn't go through. We thought it was full of water and oil. We walked through, went up the ladder, and we got out. We carried Manley out. He was still sick. Boy, that wasn't easy, because he was a big man. He weighed about 260 pounds! It took four of us to get him up the ladder. But there wasn't anybody hurt.

"I walked out on the deck, and it seemed like every bone in my body just melted. I didn't have any strength. I couldn't believe what I saw. Right in front of me was the quartermaster that I had known, and both of his legs had been blown off. All around me were pieces of flesh and dying people. There was one head all by itself laying over on the side. Smoke and fire were still on the water around the *California*. There were dead bodies in the water and bodies hanging over the gun turrets. I had nightmares of this for twenty years after that. I'd wake up in the middle of the night, screaming.

"I must have laid there for three hours. After a while I got up my strength and went over to the starboard side. I crawled down and swam to shore. There was oil all over me, but I was alive. I crawled under a small building up on piers and just laid there until it started to get dusk. Then I heard a guy yelling: 'Anybody out there, come in and get some clothing.' So I went over. I took off my oil-soaked pants and skivvy shirt. I left my shorts on. They gave me a sheepskin coat, two bandoliers of .30-caliber ammunition, and no gun to shoot it with.

"They said: 'We're going to be heading for the hills.' Somebody handed me two hand grenades. I said: 'What do I do with them? He said: 'Never mind! Don't pull this!' That's all the instruction I had. Well, we went into a hangar. Everybody huddled in the corners. As soon as it got dark, we heard the damnedest bunch of shooting you ever heard in your life. We crawled over to where we could see outside, and it was just like a big wall of fire, with all the tracer bullets and everything else.

"All at once I heard BANG, on Ford Island. It was one of our own planes we shot down. I don't know how many we shot down, but I saw at least one of our own planes get shot down. It's a shame, but that's what happened. There was no sleep at all that night. The next day we went back and started digging bodies out of the *California*. The most horrible part of the whole thing was in the area where the forward torpedo had hit. It had opened up a lot of the oil supply and had literally boiled the oil. The people that were in there were literally boiled in oil, and we could only get them out in pieces.

"I helped with the bunch that had been cooked in oil, and then I slipped off to check my trombone to see if it was all right. A clothes locker had fallen over on the trombone and had protected it. There was a dent in it, but I still have the trombone today. I haven't played it in almost thirty years, but it's in my bedroom, on a stand. I keep it shined. I shine it every December 7 and when I go back tonight, it'll get its shine.* It still has the same dent. Things like that will get you emotionally."

Warren G. Harding ended his interview in tears. Since his discharge from the service following World War II, he has worked in the real estate business in Florida. He travels extensively across the country, presenting seminars on how to profit through real estate investment and ownership.

*The interview was conducted on December 7, 1980.

Chapter III

The Navy Yard and Ford Island

Construction on shore installations at Pearl Harbor began in 1901, three years after the U.S. Congress annexed the Hawaiian Islands by joint resolution. The original dry dock was started then but was not handed over to the Navy until ten years later. The Navy Yard was built between the Southeast Loch to the north and Hospital Point and Hickam Field on the south. During the 1920s and early 1930s it was expanded, and, as trouble developed with Japan after 1939, many of its facilities were upgraded.

Ford Island, which sits in the middle of the lochs that form Pearl Harbor, was named for Dr. Seth Porter Ford, who, by marrying Carolina Jackson in 1886, became owner of the island. Among its earlier names was Mokuumeume, or Island of Strife. The U.S. Army assumed control of Ford Island in 1917 and established on the west side an airfield named for Lieutenant Frank Luke, a World War I ace. As more naval activity centered on Pearl Harbor, the Ford Island Naval Air Station was created in January 1923. Dredging operations added to its size, and it became home to Pan American Airlines' *China Clipper*. Many of the structures on the island at the time of the attack were built in 1939. Not only did the PBY unit Pat Wing (Patrol Wing) Two operate from the station, but it also was the repair and supply base for most other Pacific Fleet planes.

At 7:55 A.M., when the prep-for-colors signal was being hoisted, Japanese dive-bombers appeared over Ford Island. Nine planes are estimated to have engaged in the attack on the naval air station and on aircraft parked near hangar number six at the southeast corner of the island. The hangar took about five bomb hits, which made a crater twenty feet wide and caused two thirds of the structure to burn to the steel girders.

Within minutes of the attack's beginning, thirty-three of the Navy's best patrol planes, about one half of the seventy aircraft present, were demolished or badly damaged. The launching ramp also suffered, as did hangar number thirty-eight. A delayed-action bomb aimed at the *California* missed the ship and disrupted water and electrical service to the Ford Island Dispensary. Buildings were hit by bomb fragments and debris from Battleship Row, but none was dealt serious harm.

The island's water supply was curtailed when the *Arizona* settled on the six-inch main. For the most part, however, the naval air station did not sustain the degree of devastation visited on other major airfields. Machine-gun emplacements were hastily set up, but, as Seaman Virgle ("Archie") Wilkerson said, the return fire they provided was "pitifully weak."

The attack on the Navy Yard docks began at 7:58 A.M., when a plane coming from the southwest launched a torpedo that passed under the *Oglala* and hit the light cruiser *Helena*. Both ships were berthed not at their normal moorings but at the "ten-ten dock," which was 1,010 feet long and normally reserved for the Pacific Fleet commander's flagship, the USS *Pennsylvania*. The *Pennsylvania*, however, was in dry dock number one on December 7, undergoing regularly scheduled maintenance.

The blast of the torpedo against the *Helena* ruptured the much thinner hull of the *Oglala*, causing her fireroom to flood. Around 8:00 a bomb burst between the ships and caused further damage. Unable to operate the ship's pumps effectively, the crew could not stop the flooding. As the attack continued, the *Oglala* came under heavy strafing, but a tugboat was able to pull her free of the *Helena* and allow her to be tied to the dock. Nevertheless, the inrush of water was too great, and the order to abandon ship was given. At 10:00 A.M. the *Oglala* listed, capsized, and sank.

Meanwhile, the *Helena*'s crew was able to close all necessary hatches and keep the flooding minor. When the torpedo had hit, nearly midships on the starboard side, an engine room and a boiler room began to fill with water. Some of the ship's wiring also was fouled, but engineers were able to cut in the forward diesel generator and supply power to all gun mounts. The *Helena*'s return fire was effective enough to minimize the damage of future attacks.

The *Pennsylvania*, in dry dock number one with the destroyers *Cassin* and *Downes*, was attacked during the initial phase but sustained little damage. Despite having the power cable from the Navy Yard cut by a bomb early on, the battleship's crew mounted antiaircraft fire "fast, quietly and efficiently," according to Gunner's Mate Third Class Frank Townsend. Men aboard the destroyers also returned fire from machine guns, and by 8:20 those crews were able to restore parts that had been removed from their larger guns for repair and bring the weapons into action.

Around 9:00 the situation began to worsen for the ships in dry dock number one. An incendiary bomb hit between the *Cassin* and *Downes*, and at 9:07 Lieutenant Shohei Yamada led his entire squadron of dive-bombers in an attack on the *Pennsylvania*, which was then hit on the starboard side of the boat deck. Although sixteen men died, damage to the ship was light: several guns and a casemate were wrecked, as were the crew's galley and some compartments.

Mistakenly, the ship's captain, C. M. Cooke, in an effort to put out the fires, ordered the dry dock flooded. As water and oil flowed in, the oil ignited, heating the destroyers' magazines and torpedo warheads and causing them to explode. Shock waves from the blasts toppled the *Cassin*, which rolled onto the *Downes*. The hulls of both ships were badly burned, but their engines and interiors were salvageable.

The destroyer *Shaw*, which was nearby in the floating dry dock, had its bow blown off, but, like most of the other vessels, she was repaired and fought again. Other ships at the Navy Yard piers received little attention from the Japanese. Slowly their

guns were manned, and they inflicted some damage on the attackers. A fragmentation bomb exploded near the heavy cruiser
New Orleans, puncturing her with many small holes and injur-
ing some of the men. The light cruiser *Honolulu* also sustained
damage. Possibly the horizontal bombers that crisscrossed the
area after 8:40 caused some of the harm that befell the Navy
Yard. On the whole, however, the yard fared better than might
have been expected, and, most important, the oil tank farm was
not touched.

Neither the Fourteenth Naval District Headquarters nor the
Marine Barracks figured in the plan of attack. They were, however, subject to errant strafing by Japanese Zeros and, during
the horizontal bombing, suffered from flying debris and shrapnel. Most of the strafing occurred early in the first phase of the
attack, with the bombing later, around 8:30. As was to be expected, marines organized themselves quickly and began returning fire with rifles and machine guns, but their volleys,
although launched with fury, had little effect.

13
Seaman Virgle ("Archie") Wilkerson
Ford Island Naval Air Station

Archie Wilkerson spent twenty-six years in the U.S. Navy before retiring in 1967, but none was more exciting than his first.
A high school dropout from Ardmore, Oklahoma, he joined the
Navy on March 29, 1941, when he was seventeen years old. He
enlisted through a program called "the minority cruise," which
meant he would be discharged on January 16, 1945, when he
reached twenty-one years of age, rather than serve a regular six-
year tour.

After seven weeks of boot camp in San Diego, he was sent to
aviation machinist's mate school in Chicago because he was
handy with tools; back in Ardmore he had worked on an old
automobile owned by the family. He spent sixteen weeks at the
school before being shipped to Ford Island Naval Air Station in
the latter half of November 1941, when he was assigned to a
PBY unit, VP-23 of Pat Wing Two. He was a seaman second
class at the time and, like all new men, had to learn every task

that he was assigned. His first duty was with a beaching crew, a group that helped secure PBYs after they landed. He then was detailed to compartment cleaning, a job that involved largely janitorial work. One month after the war began, he became a flight mechanic on a PBY.

On Saturday, December 6, Wilkerson helped sweep down the compartment, the second floor of a three-story barracks, and then went to the gedunk, or Navy exchange store. He read, talked, and generally loafed around until 10:30, when he went to bed. The next morning he arose at 6:00 sharp, shaved, bathed, ate breakfast, and returned to the second floor's rear lanai, where he was when the first bombs were dropped.

"I was out on the back lanai, looking out through the screen. There were maybe a dozen guys lying in their bunks, dressed but reading a magazine or talking. I heard some aircraft go over. This was not uncommon on weekends. Sometimes pilots from Hickam would come up, and two or three Navy pilots would get up, and they'd dogfight on Sunday morning. You could tell from the sound when an aircraft was in a dive or in stress. These were, but that wasn't uncommon either, because we thought that they were just dogfighting.

"When we heard the first bomb drop, our reaction was that a plane had crashed. We looked down toward the hangars, and one of the planes was pulling up. I said to an older sailor, a first class radioman who was laying on his bunk: 'Hell, that's a Jap plane!' When we went through A school in Chicago, we had a lot of recognition of ships and aircraft, and we had to study flags, radio, and blinkers. But he said: 'Oh, hell! They wouldn't be here!' and I said: 'What the hell is that red circle on the side of that?' And when I said that, he came out of his bunk.

"There were big buildings between us and the hangars. I don't remember whether the first bomb hit the seaplane hangar, or whether it was one of those that fell on the ramp, but it was in that area. I think that it was the first bomb that fell on Pearl Harbor. We could feel the vibrations.

"Well, everybody started helter-skelter, grabbing stuff out of their lockers that they needed. Some of them went to the hangar. My job was at the barracks—to control fires or whatever—so I didn't go to the hangar. I didn't really have a job to do there, and I didn't want to stay in an enclosed building, so I got out in a few minutes. I went across the street to the Administration Building. It was two stories, and I went up and out on the roof of it. There were three or four officers and several enlisted men up there.

"Planes were everywhere. There was smoke, explosions, and strafing going on. When you're young, you don't think about hazards. I stayed about five minutes. The roof was an excellent observation platform. You could see the entire harbor. You could throw a stone onto the deck of the *California* from the Administration Building. The building was right on the waterfront.

"The *California* was already sinking, already down quite a bit. I remember there was a warrant officer on it, and he was running along kicking men off of the ship. They had already sounded Abandon Ship, and he was getting them off of there, trying to get them to go down the lines, jump in the water, and swim to the beach. Of course, the bay was three-quarters covered with oil already. In certain places it was on fire. The water was burning. I can understand why some of them were a little reluctant to go into the oil. Still, the fire hadn't reached the *California* yet. The ship itself was afire; it had fires on it, and heavy smoke was coming out of it. But the fire hadn't got to the water. What the warrant officer was trying to do was get them off of there. Some were confused, probably shell-shocked, and he was trying to get them to the beach.

"The *Shaw*, which was a destroyer in dry dock over in the Navy Yard, just across the bay, blew up. I don't know whether it was a bomb or whether it was a torpedo dropped in—right in the dry dock—but it actually blew the bow off of it plumb back to the gun turrets. It was a pretty sizable explosion and fire. The *Oglala*, which was a minelayer moored close to the dry dock, took two or three fish [torpedoes] and rolled over. There was also a cruiser, the USS *Helena*, over there that took some hits.

"There was one of the destroyers trying to go out of the harbor. It got under way probably five minutes after the battle started. There were motor launches and whaleboats, lifeboats, in the harbor picking up survivors and trying to go from one side to the other for various reasons. The *Oklahoma* had already started to list. I don't think that the *West Virginia* was damaged very much. The *Arizona* was already afire.

"Of course, the *California* was afire and settling. Most of the cruisers were way down at the end of the island. Most of the battlewagons were tied up right along the side of Ford Island where our barracks were. On the other side of the island was the *Utah*. The *Utah* was a target ship at that time. The common belief is that the Japanese thought it was an aircraft carrier because it had decking all over some of the main part of the deck to protect it. The aircraft used to drop water-filled bombs on it for practice.

"In the first attack the Japanese came in from over Pearl City, which was on the Luke Field side, north of the island. The mainland, south from our side, was where the barracks, the Navy Yard, and submarine base were. They came in low, down through the cut in the mountains. The dive-bombers were first, and the torpedo planes came in second. You could actually see the guys in the planes—their heads. They were skilled aviators. They proved that from the damage they did. I don't think they knew that they could possibly have come on in and taken the Hawaiian Islands. They weren't equipped for it; they didn't attack believing that. But we thought they were going to come on.

"There was practically no resistance by American forces in the first attack simply because of the amount of time that it took to man the guns and get the ammunition lockers unlocked. It was common practice to keep the ammunition lockers locked, and it took time to get them opened and get the guns loaded and started firing.

"Just before I went up on the roof, a truck pulled out, and they said they had another one on its way. So two or three of us went up on the roof and looked until another truck came. Then we came down and got in the truck and went on an ammunition detail. They said that they needed volunteers. I should have gone to the hangar with my own squadron, but my age and inexperience caused me to go up on the roof.

"I got on the truck and went over to the Luke Field side, the old side of Ford Island. They had some ammunition hangars and bomb dumps there. We went over to pick up a bunch of small arms ammunition. The second attack started while we were on the other side of the field. We started to run into a bomb dump for shelter, and the marine there said: 'You don't want to go in here!'

"The *Utah* had started to settle just then, and there were personnel off it coming into the ammunition hangars. They were pretty much in a daze. The explosions and noise and everything, I guess it was preying on them pretty heavy, because they were scared. I'd call them quick, you know. The least little thing would excite them.

"Most of them had some oil on them, and their clothes were dirty. Most were in whites, because, on Saturdays and Sundays in the holiday routine, the uniform of the day was whites. They were in shorts, white shorts and T-shirts, and a few had their hats.

"Then we went into the ammunition hangar. I call it an ammunition hangar. It was a building 50 feet by 150 feet. They had rows of small arms ammunition in boxes, and we had to load up the truck with that. We picked up those boxes of ammunition and ran with them like they were a brick. I imagine they weighed about 75 to 100 pounds.

"When the attack started, for a minute they were going to stay there. I don't know whether a bomb hit the hangar, or whether it hit close to it, but about half the roof disappeared. There was debris flying everywhere. We left. I went out and jumped into the truck, and the truck took off with the ammunition to the new side of Ford Island. We brought it back to the Administration Building. They needed small arms ammunition over there. They had rifles in the supply building, but no ammunition.

"During the second attack there was quite a bit of resistance, quite a bit of fire coming from the ships and our aircraft down on the ramps. A bunch of sailors manned the guns that were in the aircraft and fired back from the aircraft sitting there. Some of the planes were damaged and not flyable, but we got two planes off during the second attack.

"As soon as we unloaded the ammunition, they had rifles there, so I took one of them. I had a .30-06 Springfield. I took a bandolier of ammunition, and then I went to the hangar. We did various details. The second attack was over, and we didn't know if they were going to come back.

"My hangar was in good shape. The hangar that Squadrons Twenty-one and Twenty-two were in was destroyed. The VOS squadrons—that's a term that they used for cruiser and battleship planes*—their hangar took one bomb, and it did very little damage. They lost a bunch of aircraft out on the ramp. Several of them blew up. There was a Dutch PBY there. It was brand-new. They had gone to San Diego and picked it up and were ferrying it back to Java. One of the hangar doors lifted up and fell right on top of that PBY and pretty well demolished it. We eventually salvaged eight of our planes.

"There was a lot of running around and confusion. They were still checking aircraft, trying to determine whether some of them could fly or not. Two of them had already gone down the ramp and were in the process of taking off. We had one plane in the hangar. It was on skids. We had taken the beaching gear off so we could work on the side of the plane. Later in the day we got under that airplane and physically lifted it. There must have been fifty of us or better under it with just our backs up against the hull. We raised it enough to set the beaching gear under it and move the skids out from under it. We got it out of the hangar.

"There were sirens constantly going off, false alarms, all throughout the afternoon and evening. After dark, I spent the night sleeping part of the time under the wing of a plane. It rained that night, and I had a slicker. I had wrapped the rifle up in the slicker to keep from getting it wet.

"About 9:00 or 10:00 that night, there were planes off the *Enterprise* that came in. It may have been earlier, but it was dark. We had a limited amount of communications. The information we got was that we were to watch the tower. If we got a red light, we should fire; if we got a green light, we should let them go through. What I think happened is that the planes were supposed to come in over Barber's Point Lighthouse and make their recognition turn and proceed straight to Ford Island. What they did is come in toward Hickam. When they saw their

---

*V referred to an aircraft division on a warship; OS stood for Observation Scout.

mistake, instead of turning around and going back out and finding the lighthouse and then making their recognition turn, they made a turn toward Ford Island; and, when they did that, it brought them right up the channel coming into Pearl Harbor. The red light went on, and all hell broke loose.

"You could have read a newspaper by the tracer bullets. The air was completely filled with gunfire and sirens. I fired. I don't know whether I did any good or not. Two or three rounds were all I tried to fire. Two of the planes went back to the *Enterprise*. But two of them were shot down—one over the Pearl City channel and one over the channel between us and the Navy Yard or the submarine base. The one that went into Pearl City crashed into a house, and that pilot was killed. But the pilot that went into the bay, he bailed out.

"A third plane flew over to Ewa, which is Barber's Point now, and he dropped his gear and flaps. We heard that he said his aircraft was damaged so bad that he didn't think he could make it back to the ship. He got as low as he could and came in over the treetops at Ewa as he started to cross the channel there. He must not have been twenty feet off the water. They picked him up and started shooting at him when he was coming across the channel. They had two searchlight trucks that were sitting on the end of the runway, shining down the runway. They knew planes were coming in, but they didn't know the exact time. The minute he dropped in over the searchlights, everybody quit shooting at him because we recognized the aircraft. The other two went back to the *Enterprise*.

"But all through the night, there would be somebody who would clear their guns. Whether it was an accident or intentional, the guys would fire a short burst, and the others would shoot at his tracers. He'd return two short bursts. Then, I guess a half-dozen times, all hell would break loose. Sometimes it would get to be a short episode of gunfire, and then it would stop. But there was one star out there that, if it had been close enough, they'd have gotten it for sure, because they shot at it all night.

"There was a ditch about six feet deep that was alongside VP-24's hangar. They were laying some kind of pipeline. The ditch had been there for several days. I suppose during the first and second attacks, it probably saved fifty men's lives because they used the ditch. Half of the people who were out on the ramps and the hangars got in the ditch. I spent the night right there by it. Every time gunfire would start, why, we'd all hit the ditch.''

Following the sleepless night he spent on alert, Wilkerson joined others in clearing Ford Island Naval Air Station of debris and rebuilding the structures and planes that Japanese pilots had destroyed. Within the week, six PBYs were engaged in patrol duty. One of the pat wing squadrons was sent to the Philippines, and some members of his group were temporarily assigned to San Diego, but Wilkerson stayed in Hawaii. Within one month life had returned nearly to normal, and he was "eating three full meals a day in the mess hall" and flying with one of the PBY crews.

Wilkerson spent the remainder of the war at Canadian and American military bases in Guam, Newfoundland, and Puerto Rico. In September 1942 he received a battlefield promotion to aviation machinist's mate second class "for heroic conduct in action against an enemy of the United States of America." Since he retired on January 31, 1967, at the naval air station in Memphis, Tennessee, Wilkerson has been involved in the real estate business in Denton, Texas. He said that his feelings about Pearl Harbor "can be summed up by saying: 'One day I found out I didn't sign up for a free ride!' ''

14
Fire Controlman Third Class James McClelland
USS *Helena*

James McClelland was pleased that the USS *Helena* (CL50) tied up at the ten-ten dock when she returned from gunnery practice on Friday, December 5, 1941, for it meant that, instead of taking the liberty launch to shore the next day, he could walk across the gangway to the pier. Yet, if the *Helena* had gone to its usual berth at a mooring buoy out in the harbor, on Sunday she might not have taken a torpedo midships, and McClelland might not have been seriously injured.

The *Helena* was a new light cruiser commissioned in late

1939. McClelland, who finished boot camp at Newport, Rhode Island, at this time, was among her original crew. He boarded the vessel at the Brooklyn Navy Yard. She had the latest equipment, including air-conditioning; on the other hand, according to the crew, she had some terrible cooks. Yet morale was high, from the shakedown cruise to South America, to the assignment to Pearl Harbor in the summer of 1940, and up until December 7, 1941.

McClelland was born in Detroit, Michigan, on August 17, 1921, and joined the Navy in June 1939; it took him six months to get in. He had taken many physicals and had several background checks before he became one of two chosen from over thirty men who were trying to enlist. Unlike many of the others, who thought of the Navy as a means to economic security, McClelland joined to ''see the world and obtain an education.''

After the usual period as a deckhand and messcook, he became a striker in the fire control and, ultimately, director-trainer in the main battery forward. Should his position be disabled, there was a second director-trainer in the main battery aft, a precaution that was necessary because these men aimed the three forward turrets and the two turrets aft, where the ship's fifteen 6-inch guns were located. They were assisted by pointers and given traverse and elevation settings as guides.

Unlike most of his shipmates, McClelland expected conflict with Japan by late 1941. He had followed America's difficulties in the Far East and was aware of the sinking of the U.S. gunboat *Panay* by Japanese pilots in late 1937. During boot camp an old chief boatswain's mate had told him not to worry about Hitler's Germany, that the big trouble would be with Japan. And, one week before Pearl Harbor, the *Helena* had gone to battle stations in chasing unidentified vessels in unauthorized waters near Oahu. McClelland was fairly sure they were Japanese submarines.

The interview captures some of the agony of seamen who were badly wounded at Pearl Harbor. It begins just prior to the attack.

''I recall having a pretty good liberty that Saturday and getting up Sunday morning with a hangover, but I wasn't totally sick or anything of that nature. I don't think I was in really bad shape.

"I went to chow rather late, but I managed to get in before the door was shut and had breakfast—the mess hall was on the third deck—and then I went back to my compartment, which was forward, to get a cigarette out of my locker. I found that I didn't have any, so I walked across the compartment to a friend who had some. I recall lighting up when General Quarters sounded. It was getting close to 8:00.

"I thought: 'Damn! They're having another drill!' Drill had come so frequently that I accepted it as another damned drill. I was off in the usual hurry. I don't recall who announced the raid, but they said: 'Japanese planes are attacking! Use service ammunition!' Then I really took off. But I didn't go very far.

"When General Quarters sounded, I was in a position where it was best to go aft; the quickest way to go to my battle station was to go aft. If I had been on the other side of the compartment, my side, I would have gone forward and up. But having crossed the compartment, I went aft. That was a mistake.

"There was a terrific explosion toward midships, in the forward engine room. I didn't know it was a torpedo hitting. I thought we were hit with a bomb, because the flames seemed to come down and the ship heaved in the water. I heard some screaming, and I knew we had been hit bad, and somebody was hurt bad. The passageway was filled with flames. I didn't realize at the time that I had been burnt. I was still trying to get to my battle station.

"My T-shirt was burnt off; all I had was the rim of the collar and sleeves and front part of it. My legs were severely burned. I recall looking down at my shoes, and my shoestrings were burnt off, and my socks were partially gone. I was burnt mostly in the back. I think that was because I had just passed a hatchway to the engine room, and I think that flames probably came up through the hatch. Of course, it followed all the open areas, you know. I think that having just passed the hatch, I caught the flames as I went through.

"I knew I was hurt, but I didn't feel I hurt that bad. The lights were out, and it was pitch black, so I felt that, by going forward, I could get out through the forward hatch. It seemed that everybody in the passageway felt the same way, because we all seemed to turn at once and go forward. There was no panic. We all seemed to know the way was blocked, and we all seemed to turn at once. Everybody'd say: 'Here's a hatch! Step high!' Everybody was helping the guy next to him, you know.

"Light was shining down through a hatch, and it lighted the area so that we could find the ladder. I got up to the second deck, and our first lieutenant was standing on the second deck at the hatch, directing traffic, so to speak. When I got there, he said: 'Get back to the sick bay!' I think all the drill and training just seemed to take over, and I tried to go around him, and he stopped me and said: 'You'd better take a look at yourself and get down to sick bay!' I did.

"I had skin hanging down from my arms. Of course, I couldn't see all of it; I wasn't really looking. But I could see that I was burnt pretty bad, so I did go back to sick bay then. I did feel a little weak, but I was more concerned and shocked at the sight of people coming into the sick bay. There were very severely wounded people coming in. It was a very depressing sight. Some were badly cut and bleeding profusely.

"The corpsmen were overwhelmed with the number of patients that they had to take care of. They were trying to give some first aid to everyone and also trying to determine who needed it the most.

"When I came in, a corpsman said: 'Sit down and wait; we'll get to you.' I could already see that my legs were badly burned, so I sat on the edge of the chair. I could see other people—how bad they were. That seemed to concern me more than anything else.

"I thought: 'I want to see what happened to my face,' so I started making my way over to a mirror. The corpsman said: 'Where are you going?' I said: 'I want to take a look at myself.' He said: 'You'd better not. Go back and sit down.' I said: 'No, I'm going to have a look.' That was a shock. My face was black. My hair was burnt off. I was a pretty sorry sight.

"Well, I was in pain, but not to the point where I was incapacitated. Pretty soon I began to have chills—uncontrolled chills—and then they began to administer aid to me. They wrapped me in blankets, and my condition began to go down rapidly. They ran out of room, of course, in the sick bay, so they took a compartment in the next deck below, and they put us in there. I went down and got into a bunk down there, and then I began to feel pretty rotten, pretty bad.

"Donald Brown, who broke his leg in football, came by and wanted to know if he could do anything. I told him I could use a cigarette. Of course, this cigarette that I had got brought a great deal of relief! I took deep drags on it. They also gave me a shot of morphine, but I think the cigarette did more than the morphine!

"I could feel the ship firing on aircraft. I felt a huge explosion, which I knew was a close hit. I wasn't concerned that the ship might go down. We were tied to the dock. I was going to rely on my shipmates; in fact, I had complete trust in them. I wasn't concerned. My main concern was that I was not able to do anything about the attack. It was a very frustrating feeling. I really wanted to be up there on deck.

"Of course, I was very concerned about my brother at this time. He was on the ship, too. I was trying to find out what happened to him, but no one knew. I knew he was on watch at the time, but there was no one who could tell me about him. Then a corpsman came in and gave me a shot of morphine.

"Time ceased to matter for a period there. It was someone's decision to get us to the hospital, so all those who could walk got up and walked. We made our way topside. I recall going through the mess hall. It was in terrible-looking shape. I recall meeting a gunner's mate—a friend of mine—and I can recall the expression on his face as he saw me. He looked extremely surprised at the condition I was in, I guess. I thought: 'You know, it's not that bad.'

"They had taken the cars and trucks of yard workmen, any vehicle that was on the dock, to transport people to the hospital. I recall meeting another friend of mine—another fire controlman at the gangway—and he left just ahead of me. His name was Mayo. He got into a pickup truck. I think another fellow and I got into a coupe, and we started for the hospital.

"There was still some strafing taking place. I don't recall being concerned at the time about it. But in getting to the hospital, I recall someone saying that Mayo was killed on the way over. He said Mayo was still sitting there in the seat. I think it was by strafing. I don't recall that we were strafed.

"It was almost complete chaos at the naval hospital, too. The wards were filling up so rapidly, and the nurses were directing the injured into the wards and so on. They were doing their best for each one that would come in, but they had to cover so much, you know, so they had difficulties in looking after everyone.

"They put me in bed. I think there was very little they were able to do other than to cut off my wristwatch, ring, get my clothes off, and get me under the covers. That's about all I recall at the time. I was in a considerable amount of pain, and I think I was less concerned about what was going on around me or unable to comprehend all that was going on around me. For some reason or other, I didn't want to lay down. I don't know why I was fearful of laying down, but the nurse finally made me lay down. Now I recall that something seemed to be between my head and the pillow, you know, and here it was two huge blisters on the back of my head. That, I recall.

"I stayed in the hospital seven months total. I recall a doctor's evaluation shortly after things got organized and under control, and it listed my condition as extremely serious. But it seemed to me like I was going to be out in a week or two. I felt like I was only going to be here another week or two.

"The burns on my face seemed to heal up rather rapidly. My lips and ears were the two tender spots that seemed to take quite a bit longer to heal, and they remained tender for a long time. I couldn't use my arms or my hands, and I had to be fed. I couldn't shave. Of course, I knew I was a mess with the burns and the beard, and trying to get help with everything. I still have some scars on my back and my arms and legs.

"Men from the *Helena* would come over, and they would check on us every now and then, and I would have them look for my brother. Well, they found him in the hospital there, and he had a broken hip and a broken leg, but I couldn't see him, of course. Every time someone would come over to see either me or him, why, we would have them check on the other. So, while we couldn't see each other, we kept in contact this way.

"I think my parents knew within a few days. I later saw a telegram that my mother received shortly after the attack, informing her that we had both been injured or wounded. They didn't express how badly or whatever—just that we were wounded. Of course, she was extremely concerned about us. I can recall writing letters and trying to explain to her that everything was fine and we were all right and wondering why I wasn't hearing from her. Weeks went by, and I hadn't heard from her because there was such a disruption of the flow of mail. I didn't understand it at the time.

"I came back to the United States in January on a troop convoy. I came back on the *Henderson*; it was an old World War I transport that they used to bring us back. I recall some long nights out there when I couldn't sleep.

"Just about a year ago [1977] was the first time I had been back to Pearl Harbor. I was a little disappointed in what I saw. Pearl Harbor is no longer the strong naval base it used to be. It is a mere shadow of what it was."

McClelland spent the remainder of the war in the United States on limited duty. After being discharged in August 1945, he went to New York, where he studied art for two years, and then he moved to Columbus, Ohio, to continue his education for another year. After a career as a commercial artist, he joined the Peace Corps in 1980 and served in Belize. He is now retired and living in Corpus Christi, Texas.

15
Seaman First Class A. J. Dunn
USS *Oglala*

Born and reared in the port of Corpus Christi, Texas, A. J. Dunn had "always wanted to go to sea." He said that he always had the sea in his heart and once intended to make the Navy a career. But, he added, "the war changed things, and when my six-year hitch was up, well, I got out."

Dunn was born on October 23, 1922, and was almost eighteen when he joined the Navy in October 1940. After boot camp in San Diego, he shipped to Pearl Harbor on the USS *Neosho*, an oiler that carried quite a few new seamen to the Hawaiian Islands. Once there, he was assigned to the USS *Oglala* (CM4), a converted transport that had been a heavy minelayer since World War I, when it had worked the cold waters of the North

Sea. Dunn did not like the idea of being aboard the *Oglala* and was shocked to discover that, once a man was on a minelayer, Navy practice was to keep him there for at least four years. His dream of serving in China in the Asiatic Fleet seemed ruined. "It was a romantic desire," he said, "something you always read in storybooks, and it sounded like it would be really exciting."

Nevertheless, he settled into the routine of the *Oglala*. When at sea laying mines he was a helmsman; while in port, where the ship was most of the time, he was bow hook on a motor launch used to check the minefields that the crew had helped lay around Oahu, especially near the entrance to Pearl Harbor. As bow hook he handled the lines of the launch, while the engineer steered it, and others checked the location and number of the mines. His battle station was first loader on the vessel's one big gun, a 3-inch cannon located forward and used mainly as an antiaircraft weapon.

Seaman Dunn's interview begins with his activities a few weeks before the attack.

"The only time that we ever went anywhere outside of the islands was the one time we picked up a load of mines at Mare Island, San Francisco. This was just two or three weeks before the actual attack. We had a full 360-mine load and had just unloaded it over at the ammunition dump and had tied up to ten-ten dock before the attack.

"Before the actual attack, I had got a five-day pass, and I was in Honolulu up until Sunday, December 7. I had got up real early on Sunday. I had stayed over at the YMCA. My main purpose for this five-day pass was to get all my Christmas shopping done, which I had. I completed it, and I was supposed to go back on Sunday morning and go over to the *Arizona* and meet W. J. Sherrill, who was a personal friend of mine, and we were going to go back to Waikiki.

"So I grabbed a cab, and we were en route to Pearl Harbor. I was going aboard the *Arizona* to meet Sherrill. I was in the cab when it started. Of course, everyone was excited, including the taxicab driver. Every radio in town seemed like it was turned up all of a sudden. It was coming from every direction: 'All personnel, return to your ships and stations! This is not a drill! This is an emergency!'

"The driver got real shook up. He got us to Pearl in record time. I never remember making that trip in such a short time. The cab was full of men, and we were wearing whites. As soon as we got to the gate, instead of the usual procedure, he just slowed up, and everybody dismounted from the cab. He never stopped to collect his fees or anything else; he was just gone, because at that time there were shells hitting all around the gate area.

"The *Oglala* was several blocks from the gate. Ten-ten dock was located right close to the fleet area and the dry docks. I immediately headed in that direction, and I found myself running down the street with a group, and everybody was in whites. I got a flash of a plane making a dive at us, and I knew what he could see with all these guys running along in their whites, and so everybody hit the ditch. It was just a little shallow ditch alongside of the road, but it was as close to the ground as we could get. By that time shells were bouncing around—all around us.

"The plane was quite low. You could see the pilot and everything. It was just real visible. I saw the big rising-sun insignia on the wings, and that was enough for me. I didn't really pay close attention; I was looking for a hole and found the roadside ditch.

"Immediately, there was a chief in this group, and he grabs me and several others and says: 'Follow me! We're going to the dry dock! There's two destroyers afire—the *Cassin* and the *Downes*—and we're going to help fight it.' We went along with him to the dry dock, and we were on the fire hoses not very long—fifteen or twenty minutes—when someone told us to get out of there. Everything on the ships was ablaze, and I could see they had depth charges and torpedoes, both, topside. So I had just cleared the area and just went around this building when one of them exploded, and there was debris of all sorts falling like rain.

"Things were still pretty well chaos and confused at this point. I recall the *Arizona* blowing up about this time. It was just a tremendous explosion. It kind of rattled your teeth a little bit.

Then I immediately started toward where the *Oglala* was tied up. I was running down the street, and some yard workmen kept hollering: 'Come on in here and get out of the way!'

"They were standing in one of the buildings—maintenance buildings—and I looked up at the top, and the roof was glass—mostly glass—so I just continued on my way. This was a little later down the line, when the Japs were still strafing and dropping bombs. I don't believe they were dropping any torpedoes at that time. I think they had already dropped their loads, but we were still getting blasted, and there were fires and explosions going on from that first wave of the attack. All I can remember is that I had one thing on my mind, to move out of there someway, somehow.

"I arrived at ten-ten dock, and by that time the *Oglala* had already rolled over on its side. Although the *Oglala* was tied up outboard of the *Helena*, a Japanese torpedo went under the *Oglala* and hit the *Helena*. But the explosion ripped apart plates on the *Oglala*. The *Helena* remained afloat because her crew shut their watertight doors. After that they just moved her up the dock. So that's where the story of the *Oglala* being sunk from fright came from.*

"The *Oglala* was on her side at this time, and it kept going until it was completely bottom-up. I've seen some pictures with the bottom up. But I didn't stay around there that long. There were several of the ship's company around and several officers. I noticed this destroyer pulling away from the dock, and me and a friend of mine decided we would take leave of that place, and we ran and jumped aboard this destroyer that was backing away from the dock. She was the destroyer *Mugford*.

"We went straight out, and we passed Battleship Row as we went. The *Nevada* at that time had already backed down on the beach, and they were pretty much afire from the bombs that they had taken. We went on to sea, and, just as soon as we cleared the harbor, why, the old routine that everyone had in their minds was: 'Clear ship for action!' Everything went over

*A story that made the rounds afterward was that the *Oglala*, being an old vessel, actually sank from fright when the *Helena* was hit. The *Oglala* lacked watertight doors and bulkheads.

the side; all the mooring lines and mess tables and what-have-you went over the side immediately.

"I had no more than gone aboard than they sent me and my shipmate below to send up ammunition to one of the 5-inch guns. Neither one of us had really seen an automatic ammunition hoist before, but I guess we learned how to operate it in two or three minutes' time.

"Considering everything, I believe everything was coming off just like they had been trained to do, except, in our instance, we were doing something we weren't trained to do, but apparently we were getting ammunition up there.

"After we got out of the magazine—the ammunition hoist—they assigned us as lookouts and what-have-you as regular seamen duties. At this time, all I owned was the pair of white trousers I had on and a skivvy shirt. My jumper and my hat got lost somewhere. I was issued a life jacket, so I had a life jacket and a pair of white trousers and a skivvy shirt for about seven days. That's kind of hard to wash.

"We were out seven days and six or seven nights before we came back into Pearl. We joined up with a small task force consisting of a couple of the old cruisers which, I understand, were near the islands. They weren't in Pearl, but they were near there. Several destroyers—I forget how many—were in this task force which was supposed to have been looking for the Japanese attack force. But we were looking in the south, and I understand that the Japs were to the north. It probably was a good thing we didn't run into their force, no better equipped and armed than we were.

"Of course, things were happening and happening pretty fast. We did sink a submarine that was actually confirmed later on. This was not too far out of the mouth of Pearl. We dropped depth charges, and this is the first time I'd been aboard a destroyer when they did drop depth charges. I was below decks, and it sounded more like we took the hit when the depth charges went off.

"Every time they would sound General Quarters, I would end up down below decks in a magazine somewhere. This didn't make me too happy. I'd liked to have been up on deck where I could see what was going on. We had several submarine alerts.

Probably several of them were true, besides the one time we actually sank one. When I went aboard the destroyer, I thought: 'Well, I'm getting out of here before they land troops!' You know, everybody seemed to think: 'Well, they are going to take the place over, and we're wanting to get out!'

"During the attack, everyone seemed to do the duties that they were trained to do, and this is the only thing you were thinking of. You were probably so scared, you know, that you were just doing what you were taught to do, and that's what everyone seemed to be doing. I'm sure they were probably all as scared as I was, but they did things automatically because that was the way they were taught.

"After the attack, most of them were saying: 'Well, let's go get them!' This was the type of mood they were all in. I think it would be more of anger. They probably would have gone if they had a chance to go after them right then. And after the seven days that I spent at sea and got back in, well, of course, there was still this thought that it could happen at any time again, and everyone was on their toes.''

In the months following the attack, Dunn first served aboard the cruiser *New Orleans* but was transferred to the new battleship *Indiana* just prior to her commissioning. During the next two years he fought as a gunner's mate in the Marshall, Gilbert, and Philippine islands campaigns. When the war ended, he was with the fleet that entered Tokyo Bay, serving on the attack transport APA 136. He separated from the service in December 1946.

Dunn spent two years in vocational school learning to be an auto mechanic, a job he held for a while. He next became an insurance salesman but achieved financial success ultimately in real estate and investments in his hometown of Corpus Christi.

16
Electrician's Mate Third Class Jack J. White
USS *New Orleans*

Because some of the officers aboard the USS *New Orleans* (CA32) suspected that their ship had been sabotaged during an overhaul at the Bremerton Navy Yard from August to November

1941, the vessel was tied to one of the piers in the Pearl Harbor Navy Yard on December 7. According to Jack White, scuttlebutt had it that Navy intelligence was going to inspect the ship to see whether its problems during the voyage from Puget Sound to Hawaii were the results of negligence or of purposeful acts. During the trip to Pearl Harbor the crew had found that the newly installed radar would not work because the wiring was bad in many of the ship's junction boxes. They also discovered that iron filings had somehow been left or placed in the propeller shaft, and they were suspicious of the breakdown of one of the main turbines, one that had just been reworked. After the attack, however, their doubts seemed moot, and an investigation was not pursued.

White had joined the Navy in November 1939 but was not inducted until the next February. At the time, he was a student at North Texas State Teachers College in Denton. Born in Fort Worth on August 20, 1921, he was eighteen when he enlisted and was interested in seeing the world. He said that "like a lot of people born inland," he had "a certain feeling or romantic idea about the sea, the ocean." Thus he chose the Navy. He was fortunate and competent enough to meet the high standards of intelligence and physical fitness that the peacetime Navy had set for recruits. He volunteered for duty on a heavy cruiser at the end of electrician's school in San Diego. Since he was from Texas, he asked for the USS *Houston*, but he got the *New Orleans*, which was stationed in Hawaii and only temporarily in port at San Diego.

Like many seamen at Pearl Harbor, he expected war but not one that would begin there. About six months before the attack the Navy, as a precaution, had begun issuing gas masks to sailors going on liberty. The *New Orleans* also had cut back on the amount of liberty granted. Moreover, when operating at sea at night, she sailed darkened, as required by wartime conditions. Later, White understandably was frustrated that, after "anticipating and preparing for the attack, the fleet was caught completely by surprise, unprepared."

Although White was an electrician aboard ship in peacetime, his battle station was with the 5-inch antiaircraft guns. These weapons could be fired in three ways: electrically from the ship's power, electrically by battery power, or manually. If something went wrong with the power supply, he was to try to repair it and get the guns firing electrically again. His position during battle was topside, on the well deck near eight 5-inch guns. Until needed, he was to stand out of the way.

Since the Navy Yard was located on the mainland (as Oahu was called), east by southeast of Ford Island, White, on the stern of the *New Orleans*, could clearly observe Battleship Row. From other places on the ship, vision was hindered by the oil tanker *Ramapo*, on the starboard side, and the USS *San Francisco*, on the port side. A large crane used to hoist materials to and from ships also blocked the view.

White watched Japanese aircraft cross East Loch on their way to Battleship Row. He said: "It's kind of a helpless and frustrating thing to see planes coming in and flying so low, ignoring you, and you can't do a thing. You can't fire your 5-inch batteries. Immediately after the attack began, small arms were all we could mount, and they don't stop torpedo planes." When the *New Orleans* was tied up to the dock, her crew had stowed the ammunition in the magazines and thus did not have it available when the Japanese first hit. The ship also lacked electrical power.

On the evening before the attack, White went to Honolulu, but he had been in the islands long enough that liberty there "wasn't a pleasure anymore." He came back to the ship at 9:00 P.M., played acey-deucey, and turned in at 11:00. He slept in the E Division, second deck, crew's quarters, forward, and was in bed and asleep when the raid commenced.

"When the general alarm sounded, I acted like many others, I'm sure. I said: 'My God! What is General Quarters doing going off at 8:00 on Sunday morning?' I was thinking: 'There must be something wrong. Surely it isn't what it seems; it isn't General Quarters.' Although we were not dressing at double time, the way we would under anticipated drill, we were at least dressing, when it came over the loudspeaker that it was actually General Quarters, that there wasn't a mistake, that it wasn't a drill. So when we heard the imperative voice, then we started doing things and acting accordingly.

"I dressed and ran topside. There wasn't panic, but, when a

ship is tied up at a dock, some of the battle stations that you would normally have weren't actual battle stations. Thus, I think there were a lot of people topside who had no business being there, and they wouldn't have been there if we had been at sea or anchored in the harbor. But they were there, and so were the gun crews.

"The Marines manned the two forward 5-inch batteries, and the Navy manned the four 5-inch batteries toward midship. The first thing we did was put on helmets and life preservers. But there was no ammunition. All the circuits to the ammunition hoists had been cut off. But finally—I don't know how long it took—they did get ammunition up to the 5-inch guns.

"I was so excited and nervous I was shaking, and I imagine I was scared, but probably more excited than scared, because I did get topside when the planes were coming in, and I saw the planes. The reality hadn't yet sunk in, not until I saw and heard explosions on the battleships being hit.

"I remember at first there were some horizontal bombers. They were relatively high, and they came through dropping bombs. The only thing we had to shoot at them was our 5-inchers, but we didn't have any ammunition available. So they passed over, dropped bombs, and we didn't fire a shot. The next thing that came to my attention, then, were the torpedo bombers that came in. I guess they were making their final approach. They must not have been fifty yards astern of our ship, coming into Battleship Row. So this was kind of hair-raising to see—a plane coming in that close and totally ignoring you.

"The pilot could have banked at a small angle and opened up with a machine gun, and probably a lot of us who were standing there gawking and gazing at him would have been killed. I had gone back to the stern of the ship, trying to get the full impact of what was going on. And, sure enough, here were the torpedo planes coming in and laying their torpedoes. Again, this was kind of surprising. You could see the torpedoes launched and then the explosions of the battleships.

"Some of the older hands had said that a torpedo attack in Pearl Harbor couldn't ever happen. According to Navy tradition and documents, torpedoes from a plane had to be launched in 50 or 75 feet of water. There had to be that much water. But, nonetheless, the Japanese were launching them in quite a bit less and being effective.

"Finally, we got maybe one or two 20-millimeters operating at the stern of the ship. The ones up forward or at midship couldn't fire at the torpedo bombers because their line of fire was restricted by the other ships. So, frankly, we were sitting there, a capital ship with nothing but small arms fire to be effective on the Japanese Air Force that was bombing and torpedoing the hell out of our battleships.

"When I ran back to the stern, I stayed long enough to see one plane. It was not fifty yards from us. I could see the pilot's head in the plane, he was that close. That was enough. I went back to midship then. They were still trying to get ammunition up to the 5-inch guns. We finally got all the men on the batteries, and they started testing the guns. They found out they didn't have any power, no electrical power.

"When we had tied up to the dock, we got power from shore, and, down in the main engine room at the electrical distribution panels, we cut off all power circuits that weren't required so that we could save overloading the power coming from the dock. The main switchboard had cut out the power to all gun mounts. When you're taking power, there's no one on duty in the engine room. You don't have any generators running.

"I was trying to get a crew to go down to the battery lockers and bring batteries up. When you're at battle stations, you just can't organize a crew of people to go down and get batteries. They have their own battle stations. I was trying to get some volunteers. I finally got a couple of other electricians. The batteries weighed around forty or fifty pounds apiece. They were under the first deck of the 5-inch guns that were along the well deck, and they were in the officers' quarters of the ship in the sealed overhead. There was a compartment that you went in and took out the batteries and connected them up. So this was what we were trying to do when the secondary battery officer said: 'Forget it! We'll fire manually!'

"After the torpedo attack—I don't know how long that lasted—there was a second wave of horizontal bombers, and our gunners did actually get to fire the 5-inch batteries. Oh, boy! I think they made up for the initial wave because these big shell casings from the 5-inch ammunition were just strewn all over the deck from their firing. The ammunition was brought to the guns by hand. Later on, they did energize the main circuits to the ammunition hoists.

"The biggest scare that I had was when I thought the ship was hit, when they had gotten too many ammunition cases around the guns, and they were trying to get rid of them. They started pushing and shoving them, and a bunch came rattling down one of the ladders. Oh, it made a terrible noise. My back was to it, and I didn't realize what was happening. I'm sure several others didn't know either at that point, and we thought that we were hit.

"When there was a lull, I went down to my chief electrician, whose battle station was down in the interior communications room, which is about three or four decks below in the bow of the ship. I told him about what had happened and about the frustration that I and everyone felt. He said: 'Well, just don't worry about it. Do the best you can.' And he said: 'For God's sake, be careful and stay under cover! Don't get hit!'

"So I went back up on topside, and this is when the second wave of horizontals came. We had a near miss on the starboard bow. A piece of shrapnel from a bomb hit the ship. One of the pieces hit on the starboard side near the forecastle and knocked a hole in the deck, which was the only damage that was done to us during the attack.

"Of course, the first thought was to get under way and not be caught like dead ducks, dead in the water. Someone did give a command, I believe, or at least someone undertook to cut or disconnect the cables from the ship. But, my God!—we didn't have our fireroom fired up or anything. It takes a couple of hours at a minimum to get up steam.

"All of us who didn't have a demanding job wanted something to do. All that I did was pass a few pieces of 5-inch ammunition. I had something peculiar come over me. I didn't want to watch the ships, the smoke and everything. I don't know. I felt kind of ashamed to see all of the destruction that was going on and not be able to do anything about it after working and training for two years. Here I felt my entire military life had been pointing up to this one moment. And, when it came, what did I contribute? Not a damned thing except for passing a few pieces of ammunition. I wanted to do more. I felt that I had been deprived of my opportunity to do more. I'm sure that this wasn't an isolated feeling on my part. There were others.

"We had an old master-at-arms, Jacobs. Everyone called him 'Jake'—Mike Jacobs. He was one of the men firing a .45. But I saw him in a crying rage, shooting and hollering: 'They can't do this!' Battle affects different people differently. You never know how you're going to react until it actually happens. I guess the whole thing didn't last forty-five minutes or an hour, as far as I remember."

Like many of the survivors, White mentioned the aircraft from the USS *Enterprise* that had been shot down by Americans, and he questioned the wisdom of those responsible for dispatching the planes. He, too, could not remember eating, claiming that nervous excitement at the time of battle clouded his recollection. He was proud of the way his shipmates responded to the attack. The interview concludes with events of the day after the attack.

"We left Pearl the next morning. I think it was with a light cruiser—the USS *Phoenix* or the USS *Honolulu*—and two or three destroyers. We pulled out of the harbor. We were supposed to scout a sector south of Oahu down toward Christmas Island and Palmyra Island. As I remember, we didn't know when we left where we were going or what we were going to do. Here we were, just two ships, a heavy cruiser with 8-inch guns and this light cruiser with 6-inch guns, and two or three destroyers. I thought: 'My gosh, what if we do run into the Japanese fleet? What will we do?' Fortunately, or maybe unfortunately, we didn't see anything. I guess we stayed out for a week or ten days in that sector. The only thing we ever found was a piece of floating debris or garbage or something.

"We heard later that there had been a destroyer that had sunk a Japanese sub. I think that they were taking supplies to Christmas Island, and they had run into a large Japanese sub. I think it raised everyone's spirits. We thought: 'Well, at least someone found something and got to fire a shot!'

"I'm sure that we had submarine scares and several other types of scares—even a lonely seagull out flying. We had just experienced the worst devastation that any major American fleet had undergone. We didn't know what we were looking for; we didn't know what to expect. I don't remember how many times we were called to General Quarters for submarines being located with our sounding gear or for an airplane or something else that might have been seen.

"I think the full impact of what happened struck me when we came back. I was on watch. I saw all of those ships. The *Oklahoma* had capsized and was bottom-up, and oil and debris were still all over the harbor. This brought home the destruction. It looked just like a desolate graveyard. It was disheartening. I think at that time I started having a doubt of, 'Well, what are we in for? What is in store for the country and the Navy? Does anyone, even the Japanese, know what they have done?'

"We didn't stay long in Pearl Harbor. We were ordered back to San Francisco. What was to have been repaired in Pearl, we had to go to Mare Island to get done. I remember after we were ordered to San Francisco that several times, on the ship's loudspeaker, the captain and the executive officer came on and told everyone: 'Don't talk about what has happened. The people don't know, and the enemy, we don't feel, knows what has been done—the damage at Pearl Harbor.' Since we were one of the first ships that came back from there, they didn't want any rumors to be spread.

"When we got back to Mare Island, I went ashore, and there was a *Life* magazine that had a picture of the *Oklahoma* capsized and a picture of another battleship. So at least they knew that there had been some destruction."

Jack White stayed with the *New Orleans* through the battles at Midway and the Coral Sea and then transferred to the Small Craft Training Center, Terminal Island, California. He later was reassigned to sea duty with Admiral William F. Halsey's Third Fleet and was at Tokyo Bay when Japan surrendered in 1945. Although White returned to Pearl Harbor three times during the war, he never saw the shrine made from the *Arizona*, an omission he has lamented. He wrongly doubted that his views of the attack would be of interest to anyone but himself.

In 1946 he attended the University of Texas on the GI Bill and graduated with a business degree. He worked in purchasing in Austin and then returned to the University of North Texas to be its purchasing agent. He has since retired. Of December 7, 1941, he recently wrote: "I still have ambivalent feelings about being at Pearl Harbor. It wasn't a battle we won—but neither was the Alamo."

17
Machinist's Mate Second Class
James R. Kanaman
USS *Tracy*

Two reasons more often than any others seem to have persuaded young men to enter the service in the 1930s: the scarcity of jobs during the Great Depression and the influence of friends. Perhaps James Kanaman spoke best for his generation when he said: "The pay wasn't great, but there was some pay." And later, when commenting on the impression hometown boys already in the Navy made on him, he added: "All sailors are recruiting most of the time." In any event, several in his neighborhood of Frisco, Texas, helped recruit him.

Kanaman was born on October 23, 1919, in McKinney, a small town about thirty miles northeast of Dallas on U.S. Highway 75. Reared in nearby Frisco, he graduated from high school in 1938 and, in normal times, would have attended Texas A&M University. But money was tight, and, instead of going to college, he went to work at a filling station in Dallas. Although he felt fortunate to have a job, his ambitions went beyond pumping gasoline and greasing cars. He joined the Navy on January 16, 1939, "hoping to find a better chance."

Kanaman was one of the few Texans who went to boot camp at Norfolk, Virginia, rather than San Diego. He believed that he was sent there as part of a group of new recruits who would be assigned to the Pacific Fleet, which was scheduled to be on the East Coast to take part in the 1939 World's Fair in New York City. As expected, he was added to the fleet as a fireman on the

USS *New Mexico*, but, rather than go on to New York, all the ships were ordered back to the Pacific.

After one year aboard the *New Mexico*, where he began his training as a machinist's mate, Kanaman sought a transfer to the "China Station." Instead, he was assigned to the USS *Tracy*, a World War I "four-piper tin can," which had been converted to a destroyer-minelayer. Early in the war she also served as an escort vessel for the aircraft carrier *Enterprise*. Kanaman joined the *Tracy* at Pearl Harbor in March 1940.

On the *New Mexico* and the *Tracy* he met men with whom he would have served had he been sent to China, men of the fabled "Asiatic Station." Like other young seamen, he was impressed, although not favorably, by these veterans. His comments are presented below as representative of what a number of Pearl Harbor survivors felt about their mates who had served in the Far East.

"They were a colorful lot, those old Asiatic sailors. The first one I ever ran into was on the *New Mexico*. He'd just come off the Asiatic Station after being there six years, and they wouldn't let him ship over there any longer. He wasn't an old fellow. I'd say he was twenty-seven or twenty-eight years old. Of course, he was a lot older than I was at the time. He still had a couple of months to do when they sent him aboard the *New Mexico* to finish out his time.

"Finally, when he got discharged, the officer of the deck had to sign his papers, like they always do when you leave. This guy was an electrician, a second class, and he didn't wait for the officer of the deck to sign. He just walked over and threw his seabag over the side. We were at anchor; we weren't alongside a dock. I don't know what he had in the seabag, but anyway it sank when he threw it over the side. Then the O.D. said: 'Well, you got to have a seabag before I can sign your orders.' They held him aboard and made him draw a seabag full of clothes. I think it cost $117. That was a lot of money in 1939. They made him stencil, roll, and pack the clothes. Then he had a bag layout, and, after all of that, they let him leave the ship.

"Some of them had the Asiatic stares! They'd look off into the distance, and you'd wonder what they were thinking about.

Most of them were heavily tattooed. I know we had one on the *Tracy*. His name was Sudh. He even had hinges tattooed at his elbows, spider webs. He was just tattooed all over. He was the most tattooed man I ever saw, and he was still getting tattooed. He had started getting those while he was in the Asiatic Station. I guess they were cheap. I never did care for tattoos, but, if you can say a tattoo is good, well, he had some good pictures. They were really well done. I don't have a tattoo; I never did get one.

"Anyway Sudh had the Asiatic stares, and I guess in more liberal times like now you'd call him a 'hop head.' Of course, people then, if they enjoyed dope, why, they kept it to themselves because they'd kick you out of the Navy just that quick, you know, if you got to playing with dope. They're more liberal now, and I think they allow some marijuana, or they turn their back on it. I don't know which it is—allowed or turn their back.

"A lot of the men that came out of the Asiatic Station, after being there a long time, they were either on opium, codeine, coke, hashish, or something, you know. And they were a very picturesque bunch of men. I don't know how they could survive.

"If they went out into civilian life, it'd be difficult. But most of them stayed in the Navy prior to World War II. They'd come back and put in their two years here, and then usually they could get back over there with a little influence. If you'd get to the right people, they'd send you back there because most normal people, I guess, didn't really want a tour over in the Asiatic Station. Now the Philippines weren't as severe as the China Station, you know. They used to call the Yangtze patrol, the Yellow River, that area, the China Station.

"The movie *Sand Pebbles* was a good movie if a person wants to get a fair idea of how the China Station was back in the thirties.* Of course, I've been around over in China, but I was never there for a tour of duty like these guys used to put in, anywhere from two to six years there. But it was an experience to know those people.

The Sand Pebbles (1966) was based on a book of the same name by Richard MacKenna, a Navy chief.

"Most of them were kind of quiet. They'd talk to you if you went over and had a few beers with them. Then they might get to telling stories.

"I knew one old boy, a quartermaster, who'd been over there, and he had him a Chinese girl. He'd bought her. In other words, she was his. He had to leave the China Station, and he came back to the United States. I think he was at Pearl for two years, and then he got back on the China Station. Someway this girl knew when he hit back on the China Station. She'd been working as a sporting girl, and she came and gave him all the money that she'd made while he was gone. She was still his property. That's when you could just buy a Chinaman like a slave. And that's actually what they were; they were yours, and you could do whatever you wanted. If you wanted to cut their heads off, I guess it was all right."

On the weekend of Pearl Harbor, Kanaman stayed on board the *Tracy*, which had been in the Navy Yard undergoing a periodic overhaul for about one week. Immediately prior to this time, the *Tracy* and two other vessels had been sent to the coast of Hawaii, just off the port of Hilo, where a Japanese tanker had anchored and was sitting for "no apparent reason." Ordered to avoid any incident, the U.S. ship stayed for several days, until the Japanese hoisted anchor and sailed away. Kanaman believed that it was the "mother ship for the small two-man submarines that later attacked Pearl Harbor," but the midget vessels in fact were carried on the decks of I-class submarines.

As the senior mechanic, Kanaman was busy on December 6 because the *Tracy*'s main engines had been removed and the machinery torn down. He followed a normal routine, going to bed early and rising around 7:00 on Sunday morning.

"The initial attack was right at colors, say within a few minutes of 8:00, one way or the other. An old boy from Texas, Riley, a boatswain's mate third class, was making colors when this plane kind of ran over the area, loosely strafing everything. Well, Riley just hung the flag and was running up the deck hollering like the devil. He had to holler down the hatch, and everybody thought he was crazy. We were just sitting around, taking it easy. We'd eaten breakfast, and it seems to me like we were still drinking coffee.

"Well, we came up and started looking. General Quarters finally sounded, after we were topside, but, sitting in port like that, General Quarters just didn't ever go off. I imagine the duty commander, Mr. Ross, an engineering officer, was in a state of confusion. He was the youngest officer, a nice fellow.

"But they got the Klaxon sounded, and General Quarters went. We were already topside looking and trying to figure out what in the devil was happening. You know, you're just amazed. You can't believe it; you're kind of spellbound.

"Well, we saw these durned planes. We thought at first that it was some kind of dummy maneuver, you know. That was the first thing that entered your mind—like the time in the early days of frogmen, when they'd come aboard your ship, and you were supposed to be watching for them. They were very new then. In fact, I don't think they even called them frogmen. I think the terminology was 'underwater demolition men' or something like that. They would slip aboard and pretend to blow up your ship, and you were supposed to catch them. We thought it was some kind of maneuver like that, but, when all the flames started busting out on Battleship Row, why, you knew durned well that it wasn't a maneuver.

"Battleship Row was located off of Ford Island, and the repair base, where we were, was southeast of it. We were so the *Rigel* was on the side of us and the *Helena* was back of us.* We could look straight at Battleship Row. We had a clear and unobstructed view of the *Arizona* and the *Oklahoma*. The *Pennsylvania* was in dry dock near us. We were close to the ten-ten dock. The *California* and the *West Virginia* and some others were up farther. We didn't have an unobstructed view of them. But you could see all the flames and fire busting loose, you know, and then we decided: 'Well, man, this is crazy as the devil here!'

"We could see the fire and smoke, and it seemed like in several minutes the *Arizona* sank. Of course, the *Oklahoma* rolled over, sideways. The *California* was sinking, but it didn't

*Kanaman confuses the *Helena* and the *New Orleans*, which was directly behind the *Tracy*.

sink completely, you know. The *Nevada* got under way, and it got out and was beached. Everything was in just a tremendous state of turmoil, and there was a vast amount of fire. Sailors were jumping off of ships. They were burning, so I guess they had to jump.

"The oil was thick on the water. But I guess why so many were saved from it was because it seemed like the fire was burning off of the water, and the sailors could get some air. The boats were going right into that damned fire, lots of boats, and they were picking up sailors.

"When you saw this, you thought everything was lost. In other words, that was a tremendous blow to absorb. Of course, we still had a lot of ships. We were fortunate that we didn't have any carriers there. But then your battleship was the ultimate. When we lost all of the battleships, what in the devil were we going to do? We had had it. But it later proved out better that it wasn't the carriers that we lost.

"It seemed like we stood and watched a lifetime, but actually I imagine it was just minutes before it finally got through to us that this was no drill. Then we started running and getting some guns, and the officers on the *Cummings* said they needed some men, and men went over there. After that, the first wave of the attack didn't last more than ten minutes or so.

"Well, we went up and broke into some lockers. I had already got a fire axe somewhere, and I went up and knocked a lock off the armory and got some guns. We got an old Lewis machine gun—me and a guy named Sekot. Some guys got Brownings, but we got the Lewis gun and put it on a stanchion out there. Not a regular stanchion. We just had a rope and tied up to it where we could just swivel the gun around. You know, the Lewis had drums that you had to put your shells in.

"After the initial attack, there was a lull. Then they came back and really hit us. That's when they got into our area. They dropped a bomb between us and the *Rigel*, but they didn't hit anything. There wasn't much space between us—fifty feet or something like that. There was a little shrapnel and water blew. We didn't lose anybody; I don't think the *Rigel* lost anybody at that particular instant.

"During the first wave, there weren't many guns firing. Nobody was ready to fire them. During the second wave, there still weren't too many guns firing, but there were some. The thing about it was that it was nothing like the movies, with all this whistling and everything. You don't have that. I don't know why they put that in the movies. I guess it's for the effect, but you don't have all that whistling and stuff. Just silence until the guns, actual guns, go off, and the bombs bust.

"Well, Sekot and I were sitting there ready for bear. And they came in and were hitting the base. There were strafers and bombers. I don't believe there were any torpedo planes in the second attack. At least, I didn't see any. The torpedo planes all hit on the first wave.

"Then this one plane came over and dropped a bomb. Well, the *Rigel* had machine guns out and was shooting. The *Helena* was behind us and shooting, and we were shooting. There were so many shooting at it that we don't know who shot it down. It went down over by the hospital. It didn't seem like the plane had much height on it at all. You could see the pilot. He was looking straight at you, and it looked like he was grinning, but it might have been an illusion. The plane wasn't over one hundred feet high, and it was a clear day.

"I imagine what happened was that so many shot at the plane that someone hit it in a vital point or killed the pilot. Anyhow, we were ready for another. It's surprising how mean you can get when something like that happens to you. You get bloodthirsty; you want revenge. But that was the only plane we shot at. Sekot and I used a whole drum—about three hundred rounds, something like that. Of course, we were inexperienced. Later in the war we knew how to shoot. You learn to lead planes, but then we just started shooting when they came in sight. We were real proud of getting one anyway."

After the battle, Kanaman waited with other members of his crew to go to Barber's Point and fight as infantrymen against what many assumed would be a landing of Japanese troops. When the invasion failed to materialize, he was sent to the *California* to help keep it from sinking. In the concluding passage he discusses his role on board the *California* and then comments on a civilian pilot who flew over Pearl Harbor the day of the attack.

* * *

"They grabbed a bunch of us off the *Tracy* and said they needed men out on the *California*. I said: 'Well, let's go.' Well, it was as black as it could be when we got down there, and that was my first real close involvement with a lot of death. I was working on the second deck where the torpedoes had hit. There was a guy sitting up by the hammock netting maybe with a pair of shorts on and a skivvy shirt. And he'd been burnt black—just as black as night. And we put him in blankets. We put all of them in blankets, and the skin would just pull off of them when you tried to carry them in blankets to the tugs that were alongside. They'd slip, you know.

"We got the men off, and then we carried anything off to lessen the weight. One thing that sticks in my mind is a big bag of money—quarters, dimes, nickels, half-dollars. We were getting this over to the tug, and it was so heavy it took about four or five of us just to drag the durned thing. I guess it was from the ship's service.

"This was in the morning of the 8th, about 4:00, give or take some hours. It was still dark. That's when they had these American planes come in to Pearl, and the deck guns on the *California* cut in and started shooting. I was down on the second deck, and all I had was a flashlight to see with. I was down there, and the *California* was sinking, and I knew of men trapped on the *Oklahoma*. I like to have broke my neck getting out of there, but I got on deck. It was dark, and you could see the shell bursts. They finally got a message in, but everyone was jumpy and started shooting at anything.

"There was a lot that happened that has gotten a little dim over the years, of course. It has been quite a few years since then. I'd like for somebody to write a book about some of these things. Did you ever read about the plane that was up there on December 7—the civilian plane?

"I knew the pilot. Tommy Thomason; they called him 'Tailspin Tommy.' He had been on the *Tracy*. I knew him well. In fact, I was over to his house after Pearl. He was working for Mrs. Gamble at the commercial airport, and he was up on a flight, you know, training. He had spent eight years in the Navy trying to get into aviation, and he just absolutely couldn't. He had a commercial pilot's license, and he'd paid for all of his aviation training himself. He could really tell about what happened. He was up in a plane. He could see it all.

"I talked to him after Pearl. At first, he couldn't believe what was happening. You know, the planes never did try to shoot him down; they just flew around him. He said there were a dozen of them that could have shot him down. Old Tommy Thomason, he was from Arkansas. In fact, we used to call him 'Arkie,' but after that they called him 'Tailspin Tommy!' "

A few days after the attack, Kanaman joined his crew in the Navy Yard while his ship was made seaworthy again. In three weeks the *Tracy* was at sea once more. Just prior to the Battle of Midway, she was laying minefields in the vicinity of French Frigate Shoal; she went on to fight in the battle itself. For the next two years the ship and seven other minelayers worked throughout the South Pacific. Tulagi and Guadalcanal were on the *Tracy*'s schedule. In the middle of the war, Kanaman was reassigned to the invasion tanker *Camel* and participated in the landings at Guam, Saipan, the Philippines, and finally Okinawa.

Kanaman stayed in the Navy until June 1959, when he retired as a twenty-year man. He went to work for the Ford Motor Company for ten years, followed by fifteen years at the Western Electric Company. He retired in March 1985 and lives in Kleberg, Texas, where he raises and races horses. Of the attack he recently said: "I finished growing up on that day and learned that life was more than just a good-time roller coaster."

18
Gunner's Mate Third Class Frank Townsend
USS *Pennsylvania*

Many of Frank Townsend's shipmates called him "Tommy," but one outdid all the others by nicknaming him "Terrible Texas Tommy Townsend." That he had been born on May 13, 1920, in Morenci, Arizona, a company town founded by the Phelps-Dodge Corporation, made no difference. His family moved to El Paso when he was twelve, in 1932, and that made him a Texan forevermore. After high school graduation he joined the Navy, even though he had served in the Texas National Guard for several years. He chose the sea for romantic reasons, "drawn by posters and the prospect of foreign travel." He also was tired of lugging equipment for his National Guard machine-gun company around the Organ and Hueco mountains of southern New Mexico and western Texas. He thought that the Navy would be easier, with less heat and dust.

Following boot camp, which began in August 1939, he was assigned to the battleship *Pennsylvania* (BB38) because he planned to take the fleet examination for admission to the U.S. Naval Academy in Annapolis. He was among the first recruits to be sent to the *Pennsylvania* that year and, while waiting for the exam, served as a deckhand. Somewhere along the way, Townsend's aspirations to attend the academy disappeared, and he joined a gunner's gang in the ordnance storeroom. He rose to the rank of gunner's mate first class by 1943.

The *Pennsylvania* became the flagship of the Pacific Fleet. "After a while," Townsend said, "I became very attached to her and made a lot of friends on her." His job in ordnance required him to become familiar with all the materials related to the ship's guns and to make available everything from powder to wrenches. In the two years that he was aboard ship prior to the attack on Pearl Harbor, the crew spent time operationally between the mainland and Hawaii. They "were engaged in constant drill and were well trained." More training became necessary as the ship's company was increased during 1941 by new recruits, from the USN Reserves, or "feather merchants," as the old salts called them.

On December 7, 1941, the *Pennsylvania* was in dry dock number one, having arrived there the preceding day, as Townsend describes below.

"At noon we pulled into the dry dock. That's when they started pumping the water out of it. They got far enough along with it that they had removed one screw completely, and we had the deck division down there scraping barnacles and doing those other little chores that you do when they put you in dry dock. You scrape the bottom and get it ready for painting with red lead. In the meantime the shipyard workers do what they have to do—remove the screws, which are pretty big. All personnel on the *Pennsylvania* went off to use rest rooms and facilities that were on the dock. All this activity was going on on Saturday, so there wasn't too much liberty for anybody on that particular day."

Unable to go to town, the Terrible Texan went into "his usual routine": he played cards. "We had a coffeepot and something to eat, so we sat and played cards until about 9:00 or 10:00." The master-at-arms came around and told them it was time for bed. Townsend turned in about 10:30, looking forward to the next day, Sunday, which was a "day of leisure."

In the following passages he tells how he responded when the attack came early the next day. Like many of the seamen present, he saw little of it from his battle station belowdecks.

"I was asleep on one of these canvas cots. I remember that this gunner's mate first class, J.W. Fordemwalt, got up—I heard him—and he said, 'Do you want me to wake you for breakfast? I'm going to the dock.' I said: 'No, don't bother. I'm just going to have some coffee. I ate a lot of the baloney last night.' I went back to sleep.

"I don't know how long he was gone, but the next thing I knew was when he came tearing into the ordnance storeroom. I heard the hatch open, and he shook me. He said: 'Tommy! Tommy! Wake up! The Japs are bombing Pearl Harbor!' I said: 'Oh, come now!' He says: 'Yes, I'm not kidding you! By golly, they just bombed Ford Island across the way! And they're going to sound Air Defense at any moment!'

"While he was telling me this, I heard Air Defense go off, so I believed him. I got up, stowed my cot off to one side, and got out of there. This is what happens in Air Defense—get out of the ordnance storeroom and dog her down.

"By that time everybody was coming to their stations. The ammunition passageway was right in front of the ordnance storeroom, and my duty, Fordemwalt's, and another's was as the ordnance repair party on Air Defense. We were supposed to stay right there in front of the ordnance storeroom by the door, by the talker [a sailor with a telephone who passed information on to the other seamen] and just wait. Then, if anything was needed, we were supposed to find out what from the talker, and then we would open the ordnance storeroom, get it, and go about our business.

"So we stayed there, and, all the time that this was happening, we could hear the bombing. The hatch on the third deck was open, and people were streaming in from topside going to their stations. While we were standing there, the reports started coming in from the talkers. They said: 'My gosh, that thing's going down! The *Arizona* is on fire! The *Oklahoma* is capsizing!' It came through the communications system on the ship from the observers on the topside for the fire control, from the bridge, and everywhere else.

"I wondered: 'What's going on here? Where did these Japanese guys come from?' All of this was going through my mind. The *Arizona* had just blown up. Of course, the fire controlman stated from topside to this talker that they had dropped the bomb down the stack. It came to my mind: 'Well, we're here in dry dock, and, sure enough, they're going to put one through our stack!'

"We were waiting there when the ship just shuddered. It shuddered every time we fired our guns, but this was something different. We felt like the ship was just picked up and jarred down hard, from side to side. At the same time there was a flash of orange that just came overhead. About that time I looked over and hollered at the cooks and stewards who passed the ammunition: 'Close that hatch!' Two of them closed it and had just tightened the dogs real tight when I saw fire and sparks. The ammunition was down below. They closed this hatch, which the last guys hadn't, just in time.

"Immediately after they closed it, the word came down on the communications system: 'Ordnance repair party, lay up to the boat deck, gun number ten.' So we went up there. We tried to go up the ladder to it, but couldn't. There was oil, water, blood—so slippery you just couldn't get up. So we went down across the First Division deck, and we finally got a clear ladder and went up to the boat deck.

"We didn't know why all this stuff was coming down. We didn't know that we'd been hit until we came to the boat deck, and then, oh, was it ever a mess. I was in front, and the first thing that hit my eyes as I stepped out of the hatch was two dead seamen. One was a young fellow. He hadn't been dead too long. He was one of the recruits. I don't think he could have been more than eighteen years old. What stopped me in my tracks was the fact that he lost his hair, like somebody scalped him. He had just a hole where his head should have been. His head was hung down, and he was missing an arm and a leg, and he was hung up in an unnatural position—like somebody had picked him up and laid him over a boat davit. That was a gruesome sight. And another seaman was laying alongside him.

"While I was frozen there, the gunner's mate in charge of the air defense battery, a fellow by the name of Golding, came over. I had been standing watch on that particular gun, number ten, and so he said: 'Tommy, you know all about this gun, so why don't you go ahead and take over as gun captain?' The gun was still operational as far as training it or elevating it, but I doubt if you could fire it at all. But, anyhow, I told him I'd stay here.

"He had this man in the training seat—training is to move the gun in a horizontal position—and he was glued there. He was in shock. I could tell that. He had his hands tight on the wheel. Everybody seemed to be wide-eyed and in shock. I looked around. I could see the pall of smoke coming out of the *Arizona*. I couldn't see but just part of the *Oklahoma*. Everywhere I turned, I could see nothing but disaster—fires, smoke, and no airplanes. Over to my right, I could see a couple of seamen with dustpans, picking up bits of flesh and what-have-you and putting them in bags. I lost track of time.

"The firing had ceased when I got up to the boat deck. There were no more planes flying around. We were there for about ten minutes when all of a sudden a ship opened up, and, sure enough, they started hollering about planes coming up, and we saw three of them. They were coming across the island, and the guns started opening up. All right, we had our gun loaded, and they were trained up, but they couldn't elevate far enough up, so we just sat there and didn't fire. The planes were flying very high. You couldn't reach them anyhow. They were the only planes I saw. I remained on the boat deck at that gun until I was relieved around noon."

* * *

Townsend's interview continues with a valuable description of what happened the night after the attack. He explores the depths of emotion felt by the seamen who had suffered through the raid.

"The bad part came in late evening—4:00 or 5:00. After this letdown, everybody was talking, and rumors were flying: 'They're coming back tonight, and they're going to land troops, and they probably have troopships out there waiting until nightfall to come in for a landing,' and all sorts of things. Everybody was nervous. Everybody was still in shock. Nobody could believe what had happened.

"By that time, I had been called, along with some other people from the F Division, to identify a body in sick bay. This man was attached to the ordnance storeroom at the time to do some blueprint work, but he was really a gunner's mate first class from the Seventh Division. He was one of the fellows killed, a fellow by the name of Slifer. They weren't sure it was Slifer. He was badly burned, but we could tell. He was a tall man, about six foot three or four, and lanky, and he still had the skivvy shirt with three stripes. Most of the injured, by the way, were burned due to the scanty clothing.*

"About 4:00 or 5:00 we gathered in the ordnance storeroom again. The gunner decided that he had to sleep down there, too. He came down and we stayed there. We lost all track of time, but about 7:30 somebody passed the word that you could hear on the intercom: 'All hands, lay up to the armory and draw small arms. Repel boarders!' So we all ran up to the armory. I helped dish out ammunition and rifles. What a mess. Everybody was grabbing what they could. They weren't careful what they picked up—the wrong ammunition for the wrong rifle and everything else.

"We dispensed all the equipment, and then the word came back to secure from repelling boarders, so here comes all this stuff back. A little later we learned what had happened. Some Japanese fliers finally made it ashore; they were the Japs that were landing. But that night it was worse because of the uneas-

*Shorts and T-shirts were standard weekend dress on the ship while in Pearl Harbor.

iness. Guns opened up on the island, and we didn't know the reason. You heard the guns, you heard rumors, and we actually thought the Japanese were going to land, and we'd have to fight not as a naval unit, but as foot soldiers. We were in shock, all nervous, just awaiting word. Radios were not allowed to be turned on. That's the word that went down. Radios were shut off and turned in to the radio shack. They confiscated all radios, not because they didn't want us to hear the news, but because they felt the radios would tell the enemy where we were.

"We felt completely let down, like getting beat by a rival high school in your last game—just a complete letdown. When something like that happens, you can't ever get a chance to redeem it. You felt a lump in your throat when you saw all these ships the way they were, what had once been your pride—the Navy and all that—and then you thought: 'What will the folks think of us back home?' That's about the feeling that we had: 'Here they are depending on us, and look what we've done.' In other words, it was something that we felt. I felt responsible for it, though there wasn't anything I could do about it. I guess everybody felt the same way.

"As far as putting the blame on anybody, I don't believe anybody talked of that saying, 'That guy's responsible.' No, the media took that up later. But, knowing how the Navy works, and how any organization works, the man at the top has to take the responsibility. But at the time we didn't blame anybody. We knew that every man had done the best he could. I was very proud of those guys. Every guy stood by his gun. There wasn't anybody that I know of that shamed their ship in any way."

Townsend left the Navy at the war's end, having been on the *Pennsylvania* for the duration, through all of her Pacific theater battles. He returned to Texas and went to work as a manager for El Paso Gas Sales. Most of the remainder of his life, however, was spent managing Arrow Butane, which retailed bottled gas in the surrounding area. On January 5, 1980, at the age of sixty and on the verge of retirement, he died.

19
Fire Controlman Third Class Charles Horner
USS *Cassin*

As early as Thanksgiving 1941, Charles Horner believed that Japan was going to attack Pearl Harbor on November 30. His expectation was confirmed by the scuttlebutt aboard the USS *Cassin* (DD372) and the rest of Destroyer Division Five. In an interview in 1979 he said: "There was lots of Japanese girls in Honolulu, and the boys were going with them, and somehow or other lots of them would talk freely with you. I don't know, but that's the way I found out that they were supposed to hit us. The girls just lived there—lots of them at the time—and they were still loyal to Japan. They had gotten word somehow or other that there would be something like that going on. After it happened, why, I guess they disappeared." Whether what Horner described actually occurred or whether forty years of time confused his memory is unclear, but the increase in submarine patrols by the *Cassin* and other destroyers in the weeks before the air raid certainly was enough to cause a great deal of speculation in the fleet about a potential attack.

Horner, who was born on January 17, 1915, in Fayetteville, Arkansas, was not the type of seaman given to a great deal of gossip. He had been reared in Eram, Oklahoma, a village about twenty miles southwest of Muskogee in the eastern part of the state, and had joined the Navy on February 7, 1940, in Tulsa. With trouble in Europe he "saw war coming" to America and preferred the Navy to the Army. He wanted "a dry place to sleep when it started."

After nine weeks of boot camp in San Diego, he rode the cruiser *Memphis* to Pearl Harbor, where he was assigned to the *Cassin*, a one-and-one-half-stack destroyer of more recent vintage. At first he was a quartermaster striker, but, following a cruise to Australia in April 1941, he was sent to fire control school in San Diego. He left there a gunner's mate third class and returned to the *Cassin*, where as a pointer he helped lock the ship's 5-inch guns on target and then fire them.

At the time of the attack the *Cassin* and her sister ship, the *Downes*, were in the Navy Yard's large dry dock immediately in front of the battleship *Pennsylvania*. The *Cassin* had been there three days and was completely torn down in preparation for an annual overhaul, which included repainting, inspecting the engines, and refitting the guns. Her electrical power came from the shore, and she had been stripped of most of her ammunition.

That weekend the enlisted members of the crew were restricted to the ship in order to work on her. The officers were allowed to leave, but most did not. When interviewed, Horner guessed that on Saturday night, December 6, he was part of a "bull session" that often took place in the fire control tower. His narrative begins early the next day.

"I had the deck watch from 4:00 to 8:00 that morning. Everything was going fine. I was at the gangplank, and if anybody came aboard, I found out who they were. Of course, if you know the voice, why, then it's all right. If an officer came aboard, why, you have to greet him and everything.

"The crew was all aboard. Some of the officers had gone ashore that night. They had a big party in Honolulu somewhere, but I don't know anything about it. All I know is that there was a party for officers.

"Myself and another Okie, a young kid—I was about ten years older than he was at the time—stayed out on deck and talked. We talked to keep each other awake on that 4:00 to 8:00 watch. Then, when it was time to run up the colors, at ten minutes to eight, why, he went in and got the colors and came out and was holding them there.

"We were talking, and all of the sudden, why, we heard planes coming. I saw the red ball, and I said: 'That's the Japs!' He said: 'What do I do with the colors?' I said: 'Go back there and hang them up and then go to General Quarters!'

"I don't remember the direction they were coming; I forgot. Anyway, they were coming in so that they could hit the battleships in the side. There were one or two that came over us, straight over, and I recognized the red ball of fire, but most of them were out farther away from us. The ones I recognized weren't over, I'd say, two hundred feet high. They didn't bother us—the first wave—at all. They were coming in at a pretty good speed.

"I didn't try to recognize what kind of planes they were. After I saw the red ball, I knew it was the Japs. I hollered: 'The Japs are here!' About that time, I got an officer out on the deck. He sounded General Quarters then. We had a bell, and, whenever they hit it, it would go Ding-ding-ding-ding-ding-ding! Everybody went to General Quarters; about five minutes is all it ever took us—five to seven minutes at the most.

"I didn't leave the deck until the officer told me, because he was the officer of the deck. I was supposed to be relieved then, but nobody came to relieve me, because this attack hit. On destroyers you gave up everything at 8:00. My buddy ran up the colors, came back, and went to General Quarters, and I haven't seen him since.

"Well, we had either a .30- or .50-caliber machine gun up on the fire control tower, and we mounted it. What we could do with it, we did. One of the other fellows was on it. We looked around for a fellow name of Lovett, who was a first class; our chief had been transferred. We looked around, and Lovett was gone. Pretty soon he came back, and he was mad as an old wet hen. He went down to get firing pins for our guns. They were in the shop being repaired and checked.

"We had some ammunition down in the hold. Lovett came back, and he was mad. He said: 'They wouldn't give them to me! I could have killed them, and then I would have gotten the pins!'

"Well, all we could do was just stand and see the planes coming in and swooping down and hitting the battleships and Ford Island. We could see Battleship Row straight out behind us. It was a half to three quarters of a mile away. It was a clear, pretty day, and we had a fairly good view. There wasn't anything to obstruct the Japanese at all.

"I can remember I saw flashes and smoke go up. I saw them hit Ford Island, and they must have hit the planes, because black smoke came up from there. Really, they were making just any kind of swoops. At any ship that looked vulnerable, why, they would make a dive at it. I'd say I might have watched ten minutes. I felt angry because we knew we was up there like sitting ducks, and we could just watch and that was all.

"Then we came under attack from horizontal bombers. They

were trying to hit the *Pennsylvania*. The torpedo planes and the dive-bombers had come through, and then the horizontal bombers came through, and that was what hit us. We had one bomb that went right straight in between the powder magazine and the powder hoist in the stern. Then we had intervals in there where all of the bombs went all the way through the ship and didn't explode.

"We did catch one big one that exploded. One was big enough that you could have driven one of these big semitrailer trucks in there and had plenty of room in the hole that it made. Whenever it hit, why, we just felt a push-up when it exploded below. It just pushed the ship right up under me. It didn't knock me off my feet. If it did, I don't remember because right in there things were happening so fast that a person couldn't tell you exactly what did happen.

"It hit on the starboard side, right by the galley. It went through, but, if it had hit up above and exploded, why, then I wouldn't be here. But it didn't detonate until it got clear to the bottom of the ship. Then it just pushed everything up. The galley was, oh, ten feet back of us in the fire control tower—straight down.

"It didn't cause any fires. It just tore it all to hell, and there wasn't really anything left from that point up to the bow—half the ship was blown out. I would say it was probably twenty feet wide down at the base where it hit. Anyway, it took the biggest part of half of the bow right off.

"We weren't interested in the high-level bombers. We were watching all of the low stuff around, and we didn't know whether they were going to hit us or not. The high ones were too high for us to be looking at. All we were watching was the fighter planes that were protecting everything for them. The fighters didn't strafe us. I guess we were lucky.

"After the bomb the captain gave us orders to abandon ship. Most of our officers were aboard. The biggest percentage of them, even the captain, didn't go to the party that night. We only had one gangplank to go off on. Whenever they gave the word, why, then everybody ran to get off. We had some, I believe, that would have run overboard if there hadn't been an officer up there turning them. They were just going right straight toward the bow. I saw him hit a few to turn them. They had run past the gangplank to go ashore. I guess they had gotten scared and didn't know where they were. That's the only thing I could see.

"I hadn't left the ship yet. I saw this happen from up above. When they said: 'Let's go!' I left. When I came off the fire control deck, instead of going down the ladder, I just went ahead and jumped. It wasn't but about six feet. When I jumped, I landed right on Joseph Gagnor's shoulders. He hadn't been on the ship but a very short time. He didn't say a word. We both went and got off together.

"The first thing I did, I just ran over against one of the buildings and stood there a while. Then I kind of came to my senses after getting off of there. The crew was going just wherever they could go, and pretty soon I heard the word to go to the Marine Barracks, and you could get you a rifle and ammunition. So I struck out toward there. It was about a quarter of a mile away. I went up there and got me a rifle and came back. The attack was still going on. There was strafing then.

"I came back down to the ship, but I didn't monkey with the *Cassin* because she had already fallen over. The *Downes* was burning, so I went around over there. Some civilians came around, and they had a fire hose, and I started telling them to get the things going and get the fires out. So I stayed over there. There weren't any *Downes* men at all around, so I was the only one over there directing the fighting of the fire. I think there were three or four hoses. Well, they slowed the fire down, but it went ahead and destroyed both of the ships.

"I was letting others do the fighting. I was just standing there with my rifle kind of, I guess you would say, guarding. I don't know why. A plane came by, and the Jap pilot waved, and I raised my rifle up, and I let him have it. I don't know whether I got close or not. It looked to me like he wasn't over 50 or 60 feet high. He looked out over the plane and waved. So I returned it, but only with the rifle—I fired at him, yes, sir! That's the only round I fired.

"I was there at the *Downes*, I guess, maybe two or three hours. I don't know just how long. We had the fire pretty well down, and the captain of the *Downes* came and wanted to know what was going on, and I told him what we had been doing—

fighting the fire there for him. He wanted to know whether we thought he could get aboard. I said: 'I believe you can.' So he went aboard. I don't know what he got, but he asked my name and everything. I don't remember his name at all.

"Well, after that, they kind of got us together and sent us up to some barracks—I don't remember exactly where—for the night. We just bedded down, and then about 9:00, why, two planes came in. Of course, they were ours, but we didn't know it. They sounded General Quarters, and everybody ran out. They had been digging some waterline ditches or sewer ditches out there, and everybody fell into them. This one old boy had a submachine gun, and he didn't know how to operate it, and, whenever he fell down in there, why, he started shooting it. That really scared everybody. We didn't even see the planes.

"We stayed there that night. I don't imagine we slept too much. I don't remember if we ever got fed. We got a light breakfast the next morning. As for that evening, I don't remember. There was so much that happened that day that I don't remember whether we got to eat or not."

On December 8, Horner was assigned to the destroyer *Maury*. Three weeks later, because the *Maury* had a surplus of fire control petty officers, Horner was transferred to the *Gridley* and, soon after, to the *Clark*. He stayed with the latter for most of World War II. In late 1944 he returned to the United States to attend advanced fire control school and ended his military career teaching that rating to young seamen in Fort Lauderdale, Florida. He mustered out on February 7, 1946.

In civilian life, Horner went on to attend Northeastern Oklahoma State College, in Tahlequah. He married, had one child, took the railway clerk civil service examination, and, in August 1948, went to work for the Post Office Department. He retired in 1973 and now resides in Russellville, Arkansas. Much of his spare time was spent in attending John Brown University in Siloam Springs, where he earned 143 hours of college credit. At present he enjoys fishing, hunting, golfing, and traveling the United States. He is active also in various veteran organizations, including the Pearl Harbor Survivors Association.

20
Gunner's Mate Second Class Curtis Schulze
USS *Downes*

When Curtis Schulze graduated from high school in 1937, his
father told him: "Find something else to do because, if you go
to work in the mines, you'll be there for the rest of your life."
His father had worked in the deep-shaft clay mines around Vandalia, Missouri, most of his life. Vandalia, a small town about
thirty miles south-southwest of Hannibal, was where Curtis was
born on January 12, 1920. In those days the area was known for
its excellent firebrick made from local clay.

Curtis took his father's advice and enlisted. He chose the Navy
because his brother told him: "Join the Navy and see the world!"
Although he was accepted in June soon after graduation, he was
not inducted until February 8, 1938, and, when given a choice,
he considered the weather and picked San Diego rather than the
Great Lakes Naval Training Station for boot camp. After three
months of basic training, Schulze was sent to electric hydraulic
school for another four months and was then assigned to the
destroyer *Downes* (DD375). The ship's officers wanted him to
be a fire control or torpedoman striker, but, after a time on the
deck force and serving as coxswain on the captain's gig, he
managed to be assigned to a gun crew.

In 1940 the *Downes* was part of a fleet that sailed to Australia;
afterward, following repairs at Mare Island, she became part of
the destroyer force in the Hawaiian Detachment at Pearl Harbor.
Schulze liked the easy liberty policy, the food, the islands, the
recreation, and just about everything else the Navy offered. He
became a twenty-year man. His interview begins with the
Downes's entering dry dock number one in the Navy Yard, where
she was located when the Japanese attacked.

"The *Downes* had entered port, and she had some plates on
the bottom that had to be taken off and renewed. So we went
into the dry dock either Thursday or Friday, and they removed
the plates. They wanted to put an alteration on the breechblocks
for the guns, so they asked if they could take the breechblocks out of the guns and have them ready first thing Monday

morning. So we took them out and put them in the gun shelter and had them all ready to carry up there the first thing Monday morning. The gun shop was only about three or four blocks up in the Navy Yard. Then we took the .50-calibers down and stowed them away, put the ammunition down below, and, as I remember, we didn't have any 5-inch ammunition topside.

"In number one dry dock the *Pennsylvania* was behind us, and the *Cassin* was along our starboard side. She was about the same class destroyer. We were hooked up to the beach and drew all the power and got water and everything else from the beach—alongside the dry dock. We were at cold iron [no boilers were lit].

"On Saturday, December 6, I went ashore with a guy by the name of William White. We called him 'Willie.' He came from Ashland, Missouri. He was a good friend of mine. I saw him about two years ago [1986]. He's living up in Portland, Oregon, now. Willie and I went over and came back about 2:00 in the morning and got a good night's sleep. We had a few beers out on the beach—normal.

"On Sunday I got up at the regular time when the reveille went, and I went up to the galley and ate breakfast about 7:00. Then I went back to the number three gun shelter. I had to take the magazine readings in the storeroom. I had taken the duty for somebody, as I remember, so like every day I was going to take the magazine readings and turn them in to the skipper. I always kept a set of keys to the storeroom down in my locker. I wasn't supposed to, but I always did. I had the keys in my pocket, and I was going up to the number three gun shelter. When they blew the first Call to Colors, which was at five minutes until eight, like all good sailors, I stepped into the gun shelter so I wouldn't have to salute colors.

"I just happened to be looking over toward Ford Island, and I saw the first Jap plane roll out of the clouds, and I saw the second one, and I saw the third one. He had the meatball on him, and I think my exact words were: 'Well, those no good sons of bitches,' something to that effect.

"The first thing I did was run around and unlock all the magazines and the ready rooms and the ammunition lockers and the rifle lockers and the pistol lockers. Then I went down and opened up the after storeroom that belonged to the gunner's mates down in the compartment. That's where we had the .50-caliber machine guns—down there—so we broke them all open and put them in their cradles and brought some ammunition up and got some guys firing them. They were water-cooled, and some of the men worried about the water, and I said: 'To hell with the damned water! Don't worry about it! Just start firing the goddamned things!'

"At that particular time, I was the gun captain back on the number five gun. Walter Herzog, who was a third-class gunner's mate, went to work on number three. Even the snipes [crew assigned to the fire and engine rooms] were working and helping carry up ammunition, which is very, very hard to realize when the snipes are helping on anything topside. But they were carrying up ammunition and belting it and everything else. We were showing them how to do it. Then Walter got to working on number three, so I went up and helped him, and we got the number three gun in action.

"We got the number three gun into action. We sent some guys to the magazine, and they were running some ammunition up on the hoist. We fired a couple of rounds. Then I ran up forward to gun two because I knew Mike Odietus was up there trying to get gun two fixed. At that time, he was a first class gunner's mate, I think. I was second class, but he was first class. He had quite a bit more time in the Navy than I did. He was a hell of a good friend of mine and a pretty good gunner's mate.

"I was helping him, and I said to myself: 'When Mike goes, I'll follow him off,' because the number two gun was right up forward of the bridge. So he was working on that gun, and about that time the Japs dropped a string of bombs and hit just aft of the bridge and also a little in between the ships. Mike said: 'Let's get the hell out of here!' I said: 'Okay.'

"I watched Mike. When he left, the gangway was still up there. They had a crane sitting over on the dock. We went off on the gangway, and we had to crawl underneath that crane to get the hell out of there. About the time we got off, the ship did get hit some more then. We lost eleven guys that day. The yardbirds [shipyard workmen] were pretty nice about it. The twelve guys that stayed behind and helped salvage the ship—if they found a dead body the yardbirds wouldn't let us get around it. They'd get it out, take care of it, and keep us out of there. We stayed until the 20th, I think. We salvaged the ship.

"So we left the ship, and John Riley, who was the chief boat-swain's mate, went off with us. Some of the guys were crawling off the ship any way they could get off—jumping and everything else. They were starting to burn pretty bad. John was complaining about his back and his side hurting, so I took my handker-chief and gave it to him and started to daub his back and his side. I looked at him and I said: 'Mike, look here.' Poor old John had thirty-eight holes in him from shrapnel. Mike didn't have a wound, and I didn't have one either. So we went up and stopped a car and had them take John up to sick bay, which is where he stayed for a while. He got out two or three months later.

"I'd say it took us a half an hour to get all the 50s up and those two 5-inch guns. They had hit the *Pennsy* then with one bomb on a casemate. I think she lost three guys or something like that. They were dropping bombs at her, and they were hit-ting in between us and the *Cassin*. Bombs that hit behind the bridge and ones that hit between the ships keeled the *Downes* over. Just as soon as it started, why, the *Cassin* abandoned ship. They had a squadron commander aboard, but he hollered: 'Abandon ship,' and they left, and we stayed aboard. We were trying to get something done.*

"They were afraid the planes would hit the end of the dry dock and knock the caisson out and let the water come in, so they went down there and flooded it. They went down and had the guys sitting down there, yardbirds, I think, and they had them flood it. At first when they did that, all the oil and everything came to the top, and everything started burning, and it burnt pretty good for a while. They finally got it out, but the water was still in there. Then they took the water out and tried to get her sitting up on the keelblocks, but she didn't for quite a while.

"Eventually they salvaged the ship and took it back to the

---

*Charles Horner, who was on board the *Cassin*, gives a different picture in his interview (see pp. 136-41).

States and made another ship out of it. It never was very good. It wasn't true or anything else, but they did make a ship out of it. She fought in the war before the war was over. I think they did it more for looks than anything else.

"After we got off we went up to the head of the dry dock and stayed there until about noon, and then we went up to the receiving station and ate dinner. Then we came back to the ship, and then we went up to the receiving station and spent the night. Then the following day was when they told us to go and report back to the ship. They kept a couple of officers behind, and they made us clean up the ship. Oh, maybe there were about ten or something like that.

"While we were at the receiving station, we all had BARs [Browning automatic rifles] and guns and everything else. I think the rumor floating around was that Japs were landing some planes, and everybody and their brother was shooting up in the air at the planes. But they were our own planes. They weren't Japs; they were our own planes. It looked like the Fourth of July with everybody shooting up there. They had tracers. Mostly, it was small arms fire. The Marines were on the base over there and shooting up in the air, and there were a lot of guys up at the receiving station shooting up in the air. Finally, the word got out that they were our own planes, so they quit shooting. Then the rest of them came in. I think they did shoot down two of them, maybe.

"We heard rumors that the Japs were going to take over the yard. Guys that were on duty as watchmen would shoot at somebody if they'd see somebody. There were all kinds of rumors out. 'Don't drink the water because it is poisoned.' But it wasn't. It wasn't safe out that night.

"The next day, when we went to salvage, I think the *Helena* and *Oglala* were tied up down at ten-ten dock, which was right behind the dry dock where we were. They both had got hit. We helped them move ammunition around so they could get the *Helena* away. Battleship Row was just a big mess, but you couldn't see what the hell was burning, because of the oil. You took care of things in your own backyard. The *Oglala* was right behind us, and she capsized and got sunk.

"The *Shaw* got hit in the floating dry dock, and she lost half her bow. They made a temporary bow on her and made it watertight and then went back to the States. This Willie White went over there on her and came back with her. Then she got hit again after they fixed her up. She got hit again, but I think in the meantime Willie got on another ship.''

Schulze's interview ends with his comments on the Japanese. He expresses a sentiment not unanimous, but not uncommon, among Pearl Harbor survivors.

''I sure as hell didn't love the Japs, to tell you the truth. I believed then and also now that we ought to kick them out of the damned country and keep them out. I don't see giving them all that money and everything. Roosevelt put them in those camps, you know, to protect them because the Japs were bragging that they were going to do this and run everything on the West Coast, you know. And they didn't. They did actually hit the West Coast a couple of times, and Johnston Island was hit two or three times. So it wouldn't bother me a bit if they sent every one of them to the deep six!''

After working to help salvage the *Downes*, Schulze was assigned on December 20 to the USS *Mahan*. He stayed aboard her for most of the war, until June 1944, and took part in many of the amphibious landings made in the South Pacific. He was in the battles in the Marshall and Gilbert islands, and his ''tin can'' operated off Christmas Island, went to New Guinea, and landed at Milne Bay and Manus. He said that ''every Fourth of July or some damned holiday, we'd make a landing. That old [Douglas] MacArthur was a good general, but he left a lot to be desired. We were in MacArthur's Navy, the Seventh Fleet.'' He added that ''sometimes we were under air attack every damned day and every damned night.''

Schulze returned to the United States after June 1944 just in time, because the *Mahan* was sunk six months later in December. He became an underway ordnance specialist, riding various destroyers in coastal waters for several days at a time while repairing their guns. Before the war ended he was raised to lieutenant junior grade but afterward asked to revert to chief

petty officer, "the best rate or rank in the Navy." A twenty-year
man, he retired as a lieutenant in 1958. He now lives in Vandalia, Missouri, where he has served several terms on the city
council and is currently its municipal judge.

21
Yeoman First Class Leonard Webb
Fourteenth Naval District Headquarters

On Saturday evening, December 6, 1941, Leonard Webb was in
the kitchen of his Pearl Harbor apartment just outside the Navy
Yard gate reading the *Honolulu Star-Bulletin*. A story about Japanese reaction to the U.S.-encouraged embargo of petroleum
products led him to tell his wife: "We're going to have a war with
those people." Little did he realize, it would come the next day.

Webb, who was born in East Saint Louis, Illinois, on May 2,
1920, had been in the Navy since 1937. He had joined for "glory
and the romance of the sea." Money was not a factor, he already
had a job paying thirty-five dollars a week and traded it for
twenty-one dollars a month. After boot camp in San Diego, he
was assigned to the battleship *Mississippi*, where he wanted to
be an electrician's or machinist's mate. His high score on the
O'Rourke General Classification Test, which he took during boot
camp, and his ability to type resulted in his being assigned to
the ship captain's office, where he became a yeoman striker.

In time the *Mississippi* came under the command of Captain
Raymond A. Spruance, who as an admiral would be one of the
heroes of the Battle of Midway, in June 1942. Webb was the
captain's writer and provided the following description of Spruance.

"He was a cold and an aloof man. He was all business. He
was Navy 100 percent. He lived by the book. His manner let
you know that you would do exactly what the Navy expected of
you, and the whole crew did exactly that. He was the type of
person whose personality was demanding. There wasn't a man
on that ship that didn't know he would do his job to the best of
his ability because there was no doubt in his mind that Raymond
Spruance was going to require just that. He was a man who

could get the best out of you. His manner, his mode of operation, demanded this. He was a good commanding officer; he was a fine naval officer.''

Webb left the *Mississippi* in the spring of 1941 to avoid going to the Atlantic with the ship. ''I went to Pearl Harbor,'' he said, ''to get some easy duty. I outmaneuvered myself!'' He was assigned to the Fleet Hydrographic Office in Honolulu but later moved to Navy Operations, Overseas Transportation, at the Fourteenth Naval District Headquarters. He had married his boyhood sweetheart on September 30, 1939, and brought her and his young son to Hawaii. Life was easy—''lackadaisical,'' Webb said. But all that changed on December 7. In the next section of the interview, he describes the opening phase of the attack, as he and his family left home.

''I was laying in bed. I think about 7:30 I might have awakened, but I was in that never-never land in between—not awake, not asleep. My wife had gotten up to see about the baby; he was squawking as usual. She had gotten up to see about him, and I remember hearing a dull explosion.

''My wife came over to the bed and said: 'Hey, there's a big fire in the Navy Yard!' Well, I informed her that I wasn't a fireman, but I raised up on one elbow. Our bedroom was upstairs, and I looked out the window, and there was, indeed, a fire in the Navy Yard. About that time, three planes came over at about utility-pole height, and I saw red tails on them, and I questioned the parentage of these pilots. I assumed they were off the *Enterprise*, because Japanese planes and ours did look quite a bit alike, particularly the SBDs.* Like I say, I was questioning their parentage. Who would have the gall to buzz Navy housing before 8:00 on Sunday morning?

''At that time, right down the street from us was a multistory brick building they called the 'Receiving Ship,' a misnomer since it was not a ship. It was a building, but that was its title. It was multistory—four, five, six stories. The planes banked

---

*Webb undoubtedly means the SBD-3, the Dauntless, a carrier-based dive-bomber widely used during World War II.

sharply to the left, and, when they did, that's when I found out we were at war. I saw those red circles on the bottom of the wings. I heard that I broke all records in putting on trousers and shoes. At any rate, they were coming in behind this multistory Receiving Ship. When they got to the building, they banked to the right, and wouldn't you know that the whole battleship line was lined up out there! They couldn't miss. If they dropped a torpedo, it had to hit them, and that was their route of attack.

"At any rate, the wife and I grabbed the kid and ran downstairs, confused; I mean, this would be normal, particularly with 7.7s [shells] bouncing off your roof and coming through the wall. They were strafing all the way. There was a concrete stoop, a sort of concrete roof, over the front door. It was small, maybe 4 by 6 feet. Under the circumstances, with shrapnel, machine-gun fire, bomb fragments, and the whole bit, it was literally like falling rain. You could see the stuff bouncing on the ground. I kept my wife, the baby, and myself under this concrete porch, and we were trying to get our wits together.

"We're standing under this concrete stoop, and, in a house that was at a ninety-degree angle to ours, which was a duplex, there was a giant of a man who lived in there. He was a chief radioman. The first thing you know, this giant of a man came running out his front door and stood there. He eyed the Japanese planes, and he said: 'My word!' And he dashed back through his front door. There was something wrong, but it took me several seconds to figure out what it was. He had come through the screen door and gone back through the screen door without opening it.

"While we were standing there another fighter plane came directly down Center Drive, low, about utility-pole high. The pilot was looking over at me, and he couldn't have been seventy-five feet away and barely maintaining airspeed. The guy grinned. I'll always remember he had the biggest, shiniest, whitest set of choppers I've ever seen on a human being. The other guy—two men in the plane—was looking over there and laughing. They were making their approach, but the fleet wasn't yet in their range, but they were strafing everything in sight—Navy housing and what-have-you. Ethically, there was no excuse for that. There were women and kids out there.

"My wife was acquainted with a lady up the street several blocks away whose name was Fitzgerald. Her husband was an aviation machinist's mate stationed at Ford Island. His mother, good Catholic that she was, was going to Mass. She was in her fifties. They shot her through both legs with a .31-caliber machine gun. She was going to Mass, and she was laying out there! It was obvious she would never walk again; there was no excuse for that. Her legs were torn up. These are the kind of things you really don't want to remember, but that's the inhumanity of war. I don't know if they were actually shooting at her, but they certainly hit her.

"At any rate, in this same apartment area, we had a fellow named Jack Peavler, who was a boatswain's mate, and he skippered one of the tugs in the yard. So around the house comes the Peavler family Oldsmobile, all fenders rattling. It came to a screeching halt, and Jack's wife and their dog were in the car. He yelled at me to bring my wife and baby over there, that we had to get them the hell out of the place. He was right about that. It was a dangerous place. So I hustle my wife and kid over to their car. They had friends in Honolulu, which is where they were going. When we're almost to the car, my wife says: 'The baby doesn't have any diapers! Get some!' Here's the humor. Bear in mind that this is Armageddon, the end of the world, and my wife has me chasing diapers! And I went back for the diapers! But it struck me at the time: 'What am I doing, hustling diapers?' At any rate, the wife, the boy, and the diapers got in the car and went chugging off toward Honolulu. I breathed a sigh of relief and said: 'Come on, Jack, let's get to the Navy Yard!' This was during the height of the first strike."

In the second portion of the interview, Webb describes some of the activities in the Fourteenth Naval District Headquarters and the reactions of some Navy commanders to the attack.

"We got into the Navy Yard, and Jack and I said a hurried good-bye like: 'I'll see you.' I went to staff headquarters. Now I found out later that there was a watch officer, a lieutenant commander by the name of Kaminski, but my particular office was removed from the command duty office, and another yeoman, by the name of Allen, and I were the first two there.

"Kaminski got the word about the *Ward* sinking a Japanese sub. Now, I'm not blaming the man. You have to go back to that old Navy discipline, the idea that anybody with a half-stripe more than you had you under his thumb. He could squash you. Kaminski failed to report this to the commandant of the Fourteenth Naval District. Like I say, I'm not blaming the man. I may have done the very same thing. I'm not going to wake an admiral until I know something is for sure, and this must have been his reasoning.*

"At any rate, Allen and I are there, and these plane are strafing and bombing. I mean, it was a real turkey shoot, and there wasn't any doubt in my mind at least that they were going to land. So we decided maybe we better get some guns. Well, the armory was about two blocks away, and we beat it for the armory through all this shrapnel and what-have-you.

"We got over there, and there was a civilian armorer. I'm not knocking civilians, but what the hell was he doing in a Navy armory, running the show? We got in and explained to the man that we needed guns. He told us we'd have to have a chit. Now, this is Navy regulations—you've got to have a chit. Well, no amount of talking or explaining was going to change his mind. So we went outside and found a young, fuzzy-faced Navy ensign, and we actually physically assisted him in signing his name on this chit. We went back to the armory, and the man gave us an old World War I tin hat, Colt.45, holster, web belt, and three empty clips. 'Where's the ammunition?' 'I don't know!' The armorer didn't know where ammunition was!

"So we headed back toward staff headquarters, and I heard the Marines firing—the First Marine Defense Battalion. They never change. If we've ever had a fighting organization, it's been the Marine Corps. They don't know anything else. If they're not ready, they get ready—fast! They had small arms—machine guns, rifles (the old M-1s), Colt .45s. The Marines were out there. This was within twenty to thirty minutes from the time the attack

---

*The sinking, in fact, had been reported.

started. I'd bet that it wasn't five minutes until they had gotten out there and set up and were shooting.

"We headed for the Marine Barracks to get some ammunition and ran into a Marine gunnery sergeant I knew, and he had a sidecar on a motorcycle full of ammo. We motioned to the guns, and he threw us a couple of cartons of Colt .45 ammunition. We were under a big banyan tree. They are immense; they can cover half a block. We were under this tree, right on the Marine parade grounds, trying to load clips with seven thumbs on each hand. And here comes a Jap Zero in, just like in the movies—little puff of dust right across the parade ground and heading directly for us. We flattened out—me on one side of the tree, Allen on the other side. We didn't only flatten out; we went grass roots. I'm sure we got down to the roots. We were laying there, and the machine guns went on incessantly.

"Finally, even in my dazed state, I realized I didn't hear machine guns anymore, and I didn't see the plane. It was long gone, and the machine guns we were hearing were behind the latticework fence. The Marines had set up a .50-caliber back there. So I'm feeling real sheepish—scared or upset. Here I am, hugging the ground, and no plane. So I crawl on around this tree, and I didn't have to be sheepish anymore. I will still accuse Allen to this day of trying to dig a hole with the tin hat. He was really digging.

"We finally got our guns loaded, and I have to say that I didn't hit a single Jap plane with that Colt .45. The end of the barrel wouldn't stay still. It kept going in all directions.

"So we got back to staff headquarters, and by then Admiral [Claude C.] Bloch and his chief of staff, J[ohn] B. Earle, were there along with several other officers. J.B. looked at me and said: 'Webb, where did you get the guns?' 'Over at the armory, Sir.' 'Get some more.' So I went back to the armory, and things turned out a little better. The same armorer was at the counter, and he starts off on the old routine about you've got to have a chit. Well, I nervously showed him my .45. The clip was out, and I put it back in and said: 'This is the chit.' I got six guns with no further argument; I mean, he changed Navy regs almost immediately.

"So I went back over to staff headquarters, and it's still embarrassing, really. Those seven thumbs were still on each hand. Here was all the Navy high brass watching me trying to load clips, and I'm not doing a good job. At any rate, I finally got them loaded. I don't know why, but you do feel better when authority is armed—when the admiral and the chief of staff had on a .45.

"One thing that has stayed with me, that is almost heart-rending, was the agony on Bloch's and Earle's faces. I never saw any fear. They were old-timers. I would say, to me at that time, they were ancient, probably in their late fifties, but, hell, I was a twenty-one-year-old kid. They were pacing side by side on the second-floor concrete lanai, watching the destruction of their lifetime, watching the destruction of the American Fleet. It was their pride and joy, and I will remember the frustration and agony on those two men's faces as long as I live. There wasn't anything they could do. Their whole life was going down the tubes out there, and they were helpless—nothing they could do. I believe I can still see it. I've never seen two more frustrated humans in my life. They were agonizing over their fate. Their life's work was going down the tubes, and they were helpless. To me it was one of the saddest things I ever saw.

"At the time, as I understand it, once the fleet was in port, the commandant of the Fourteenth Naval District and General [Walter C.] Short were the two who had responsibility for the defense of the fleet. Now that doesn't mean that the fleet could only fire back on order of Admiral Bloch. He really had problems, but he had no difficulty explaining later during the investigations as to why this Japanese fleet wasn't discovered. He had maybe 10 percent of the number of Navy PBYs and PBMs that he should have had to patrol the area.

"Maybe I've overstated it, but he couldn't possibly have had over a third of the aircraft he needed to do the job. We're talking about thousands upon thousands of square miles to patrol. Naturally, Bloch had the planes patrol the most obvious areas. The route from the north Pacific was not even remotely a possible area for patrol. Smaller ships at sea needed to be refueled in two or three days maximum, and you don't trust the north Pacific that time of year. I've been there in the wintertime. It's cold; it's rough; it's stormy. It is no place to refuel. So Bloch's idea of patrolling the obvious areas of attack was all right as military strategy. The Japs just put a shuck job on us, a real good con job. They did the unexpected.

"Also, everything else military was going to the East Coast at the time. The country was oriented to the war in Europe. We lost carrier after carrier, ship after ship, to the Atlantic Fleet. Pearl Harbor was the last place we felt Japan would strike— Alaska, or some place like that, but not Pearl Harbor. They did a job on us, and they did a good job."

In the concluding passages, Webb discusses his activities in the period after the attack, once more providing insight into operations at naval headquarters.

"Later on in the day—it seemed like an eternity before the air strikes stopped—why, Navy efficiency came to the forefront again, and an organization was immediately started, trying to get communications not only between the naval headquarters and the ships, but with the Army, Army Air Corps, and what-have-you. We really didn't have the equipment for it. We had telephones. I went on duty about 8:00 A.M., and I was relieved either seventy-four or seventy-six hours later. I don't think that I was much good the last half of that period, because by then you're almost dead.

"I was worried to death about my wife and child because, in my mind, the Japanese were going to invade. I didn't see her for, I guess, the better part of a week. There wasn't any way we could get together. Telephone calls were restricted. They allowed no civilians back into the naval defense area, and, of course, they allowed no sailors out of there either.

"At headquarters there was complete astonishment, disbelief over the attack: 'This can't be!' In other words, the Japs had taken on one of the strongest military installations in the world, and they literally crippled us. They did a job, but they could have done an even better job. I will never understand why they did not bomb, particularly with incendiaries, all these multihundred-, thousand-, even million-gallon fuel tanks surrounding the harbor. They would have wiped out everything in Pearl Harbor. I think those people were probably the kind who do exactly as planned, no variance. They could have literally wiped us out with another three or four strikes, but they did what the battle plan was, and then they retired.

"Another little humorous situation happened late in the morning or in the early afternoon. I was manning the phones in the chief of staff's office and got a call from this Major So-and-so at Bellows Field. I knew it wasn't a sailor by the language. 'We have a submarine tied to a tree,' he said. *Tied* is the word, the operative word. Not *secured*, *moored*, or *lined*, but 'tied to a tree.' And he was excited. 'You goddamned sailors, get somebody over here to disarm these torpedoes!' 'What torpedoes, Sir?' 'It's got torpedoes sticking out of the front end of it.' I thought: 'Oh, man, this guy is way out!'

"I kept trying to bleed more information out of him, and the chief of staff said: 'What do you have there, Webb?' I said (with my hand over the mouthpiece): 'I have an Army Air Corps major here, Sir, that I think must have been shot in the head earlier this morning.' 'Why?' I said: 'He's got a Japanese submarine tied to a tree!' The Old Man, with all these terrific problems he had, said: 'He does sound like he's been hurt.'

"At any rate, I gave the major a three-digit number to call at the submarine base. Actually, I was brushing the guy off. I'm thinking: 'Submarine; this can't be.' You don't tie submarines to palm trees. I gave him the number and assured him he'd get help if he called there, which he said he would and added some more unkind remarks about the Navy.

"I was embarrassed sometime later, several days later. I was close to the main gate, and here comes a big tractor-trailer, flatbed trailer, and guess what—it had a two-man submarine on it that they had picked up over at Bellows Field. The man wasn't out of his head. He had had a submarine tied to a tree.

"During the first week, I had a chance to survey the damage. Is there such a thing as a king-size junkyard? Here are these mighty battleships. The *Oklahoma* has rolled completely over. I saw the *Arizona* blow sky-high—broke her back when she went in the air. The *Maryland*, *Tennessee*, and *California* were down in the water. They were sitting on the bottom.* Having spent

---

*Neither the *Maryland* nor the *Tennessee* sank to the bottom.

years on these things, it was incredible to me that you could inflict this kind of damage. Yet, when you stop and think, the conditions under which the punishment was inflicted, yes, it could happen. They were sitting ducks.

"I really thought that we'd had it, because I was still battleship oriented. You win a war or lose a war with battleships, and we didn't have any. I mean, the *Nevada* is aground, and the *Pennsylvania*, as I recall, was in dry dock, and she was shot to smithereens. I didn't pay much attention to the smaller vessels. I didn't know how we'd ever survive it, and I'm not real sure the high-ranking officers, who knew all about naval tactics and warfare, knew. Thank God that the carriers were at sea and weren't there, since the war turned into naval air warfare, really.

"You got over the anxiety, the amazement, the astonishment, and by then you were cold mad. We would fight until the last man. I didn't have any idea if I'd ever get back to the United States. We'd fight Japan until the last man died, and I hoped I was going to be the last one."

After the attack, Webb stayed on at the Fourteenth Naval District Headquarters but shifted to combat intelligence under Commander Joseph J. Rochefort. He was separated from the Navy on June 19, 1944. In civilian life he worked as an aircraft machinist, retail sales manager, real estate agent, and personnel manager with an independent oil company. Having retired, he still lives in East Saint Louis.

22
Private Leslie Le Fan
Marine Barracks, U.S. Naval Station

Leslie Le Fan joined the Marine Corps on July 23, 1941, in his hometown of Temple, Texas, where he had been born on September 7, 1921, and graduated from high school. He chose the Marines because he "had a great admiration for marines; they had always fascinated" him. He explained it to his parents this way: "Look, my time is coming up sooner or later, anyway. Why not give me a choice of what I want to do? If I want to go, I want to be first class—a marine."

Sometimes in boot camp at San Diego he told himself that "I had made a drastic mistake." Boot camp was serious business. But, as he later recalled, after nine weeks of training he was assigned to the aircraft carrier *Saratoga*. The *Sara*, as many called her, patrolled the West Coast from Bremerton, on Puget Sound, to San Diego. In November 1941, Le Fan was sent to join the Pacific Fleet at Pearl Harbor.

Arriving in the Hawaiian Islands on December 1, Le Fan and fourteen other marines were detached to the Marine Barracks at the U.S. Naval Station where they were to train men for sea duty or as embassy guards. In the week he spent there before the war broke out, he had three night liberties and pulled security guard at the main gate once. The day before the attack he had his last liberty in Honolulu. His friend Jack Thorpe, from Kansas City, and he left the post at noon, December 6, and went to Waikiki Beach, where they swam and surfed until 5:00. They then joined two sailors, with whom they shared barracks, in the only luau in Le Fan's life. It cost $1.00, or 5 percent of his monthly pay. He ate poi, getting more on his uniform than in his mouth, and had a few drinks. The men were home by 11:00 and soon went to bed. In the interview, Le Fan demonstrates an amazingly detailed memory of his experiences during and immediately after the attack.

"On the morning of December 7, I awoke at approximately 7:00. I made up my bunk, put on my trousers, and went to the head along with thirty or forty other sailors and marines. I took a shower and was chatting with my friends. Jack Thorpe said: 'Are we going to church this morning?' I said: 'Yes, I think we'd better. I promised the chaplain that we'd be there.' He said: 'Fine. I'll go along, too, and then we'll have a bite of breakfast after.' This particular Sunday morning we didn't want the normal breakfast—beans, corn bread, and coffee—so we were going to go outside the post to get coffee and a doughnut or roll.

"I was shaving at approximately five minutes until 8:00. We heard planes, and we heard explosions. The first thing that went through my mind was that the stupid Navy was holding maneuvers on Sunday morning. They couldn't do it another time; they had to do it on Sunday morning. We could feel the concussion.

We were that close. I thought: 'Well, they're sure playing rough.' The sailor down from me says: 'That can't be the Navy. That's got to be those stupid jar heads [Marines]. They're holding maneuvers. They don't have any better sense anyway.' We were all friends, and it was pretty much a joke.

"I finished shaving. In fact, I was almost through when it started, and I had on khaki trousers, a T-shirt, and my shoes. All I had to do was put on my shirt and field scarf and go to church. Then General Quarters sounded. We started running down the corridor in the barracks. As I passed the gun rack, I grabbed my rifle. Jack was with me, and he grabbed his rifle, too. The sailors didn't have rifles.

"We were running down this corridor as a Zero strafed the barracks. The sailor approximately six feet in front of me fell. He was hit in the back of the head with what I think was a .50-caliber because his face completely exploded, and he fell. I thought: 'Well, if they're playing war games, they're sure playing rough.' I stepped over him, and I remember thinking to myself: 'That's the first dead man I have ever seen,' and I was scared. I didn't know what to think. We saw the holes in the overhead, and we heard planes. We ran outside, and the first thing I saw was a low-flying torpedo plane.

"I would say the plane was less than one hundred feet off the ground, because they were making the run at Battleship Row. From where I was, I could see the superstructures of all the battleships. I could also see the red circles under the wings, the meatballs. I said: 'There's the meatball!' The lieutenant standing by me said: 'We're under attack by the Japanese! Get your rifles!' Well, I already had my rifle.

"I had no ammunition at all. So the sergeant in charge told us to fall in. Then he said: 'Disregard that order! Don't fall in! You'll make too big of a target! Scatter!' So we scattered. There were some planes coming over us, but they were firing over our heads.

"This sergeant put us behind a retaining wall approximately four feet high, facing the harbor. Somehow he got hold of about six bandoliers of '03 ammunition that was in '03 clips.* We

---

*This was ammunition for the bolt-action Springfield rifle, model 1903.

were all armed, ten of us with M-1 rifles—M-1 Garand, semi-automatic, .30-caliber. They would fire the '03 ammo, but we had to have a special eight-round clip to go into the M-1, and we were given bandoliers of '03 ammunition for the Springfield, with five-round clips. I opened the receiver of my Garand and put one round into the chamber and closed it. The number of that rifle is 351735. I've wondered many times where it is. I carried it until 1944. It made some good Japs out of some bad ones.

"We were given orders that when the planes came over us to follow the sergeant's instructions: 'Ready, aim, fire,' and that we would get some shots off, which we did. I recall one Jap pilot coming over, and he waved at us as he did. He was very low—less than a hundred feet high—because he was going to Battleship Row. They would wave at us, and we were throwing .30-caliber rounds at them as fast as we could, firing single shots because we could not fire semiautomatic. I fired sixty rounds, because I recall this particular bandolier that I got had sixty rounds in it.

"There was a Marine officer and a naval officer who walked out of the barracks. They were undoubtedly going skeet shooting that morning. They both had automatic twelve-gauge shotguns, and I'm going to say that each one was carrying a satchel filled with four boxes of ammo. They stopped right in the middle of the parade grounds in front of the barracks, loaded their shotguns, and began to fire. The thought went through my head: 'What do they expect to do to an airplane with a shotgun?' But a man had to do something.

"There were other people shooting .45 pistols. One man got hold of a BAR and began to fire it. We were firing our M-1s. Anyway, everybody was shooting, and I've often wondered what the Japs thought when they got back aboard the aircraft carriers, looked at their planes, and saw all of those number nine shots that probably didn't even penetrate. I wonder if they thought: 'Well, what are they doing to us? Are they sending bees or kids or throwing rocks?'

"On one occasion when we were back of the wall, a machine gun had gotten into operation on our left. A BAR was in operation to our right, and this one plane came over real low. We were given the order: 'Ready, aim, fire,' and we all fired at the same time. The machine gun opened up, and the BAR opened up. The plane exploded. Of course, we all hollered: 'We got him! We got him!' Until this day, God only knows who hit the plane—we may have—and set off a bomb. It burst into flame and fell right into the harbor.

"I saw several planes go down. I saw a Zero crash into the ground. I saw a torpedo bomber go over a ship and burst into flames, and a couple or three dive-bombers did the same. I believe they were dive-bombers with the fixed landing gear. During the attack there was a lot of confusion. After I had fired all of my ammo, I was watching everybody else fire. We were trying to stay as organized as possible, but there was a terrible lot of confusion. Scared? Yes. Excited? Yes.

"I went back into the barracks and grabbed a shirt and put it on. I went outside and was given a steel helmet. It was the first time I had ever had a steel helmet on in my life—what we called the 'Steel Kelly,' the old British helmet. I was given a gas mask that I slung over my shoulder. I filled up my cartridge belt with a hundred rounds, but, here again, I had only the '03 clips.

"We were waiting outside when the attack ended abruptly. Our lieutenant came up and said: 'Let's get to the water's edge and see if we can help those people in the water.' We ran as fast as we could—I'm going to guess, say two hundred yards—to the dock area. The oil on the water, much of it was burning. Some of the sailors and marines in the water were trying to get out. They were covered with oil. Some of them were obviously dead. They had been blown off the ships or had jumped off. Some of them were badly burned. Some had limbs missing. For the first time in my life, I thought I was going to get sick.

"We proceeded to try to pull as many men out of the water as we could. Some of our men got into some boats that were tied up alongside and rowed or paddled out to pick up people. They were covered in oil. Many were burned beyond recognition. Some were wounded. It was an awe-inspiring sight in a sense, but it was devastating.

"Then, as we took these people out, we were laying them on the dock and making them as comfortable as possible. Now, some few that we pulled out were in shipshape condition. They were swimming like mad, and they began to wipe the oil off. I remember one sailor that I pulled out of the water, and I took my handkerchief and wiped the oil from his face. I couldn't tell if he was a black man or a white man or a Chinaman. But I did wipe it off, and he said: 'Thanks,' and then he jumped up. I always wondered what happened to him. I've never seen him since. There was another one that we pulled out that had a leg missing. Obviously, the man was dead. I think he bled to death. I guess we had twenty-five or thirty laid out on the dock, and ambulances were coming up, and corpsmen were trying to get these people to an aid station as soon as possible. Now, how many were alive and healthy and just scared and full of oil, I don't know.

"Now, the ten of us were under this lieutenant, and he said: 'Get those people out of the water! Get them out of the water! Lay them up here!' And I said: 'What's going to happen to them?' He said: 'That's up to the corpsmen and the doctors! Let's get them out of the water before they drown!' We knew that they were badly burned, mutilated, hurt, and that some were even dead. We knew that.

"In the confusion, time passed very fast, and the second attack started. This time the high-level bombers came in—what we referred to as the 'Betty bombers.'* They were at high altitudes, dropping bombs, and they dropped them in our area. We could feel the concussion from them and could hear the shrapnel hitting our barracks, either burying itself into it or bouncing off. There were bullets flying everywhere—some ours and some theirs—because in the second attack we were also being dive-bombed and strafed. We were ordered back to the retaining wall. We hesitated leaving the wounded on the beach, but we had no alternative. We were ordered back. This time we fired some more. We were even firing at the high-level bombers.

"I did see the *Oklahoma* when she turned turtle. When it flopped over, I saw it roll. I had a horrible feeling! I thought to myself: 'If she's going to roll over, that's the end! There's people in there! What are we going to do?' I could feature these sailors

*Bettys were twin-engine land-based bombers that were not used in the air raid.

and marines in that hull when she rolled, and I thought: 'Well, I've seen the top of a lot of battlewagons, but this is the first time I've ever seen the bottom of one.'

"I saw the last torpedo that slammed into the side of the *Arizona*. She just buckled right in the middle. It just quivered, buckled, and then settled. You could see the sailors running around. Many of them were in their whites, some were in their skivvy drawers and T-shirts, and some of them were stark naked. They were given the order to abandon ship. Some dove off the side; some tried to go down Jacob's ladders. But the flames were getting to most of them. I personally believe there were as many people killed by flames as by shrapnel or bullets or anything else.

"The dive-bombers were coming down pretty thick and heavy in the second attack. The high-level bombers were laying their eggs right down Battleship Row and then hitting the sub base, which was out of my sight. I didn't know what was going on at Hickam Field or Schofield Barracks. At the time I was trying to keep my composure. I heard of the devastation there later on, but not that day.

"Then we went back to the rescue operations, down to the water's edge. We laid our rifles down, but we were told this operation was being taken care of, and we were ordered to an ammo dump. It took us about an hour and a half to go to the dump, the magazine, get the ammo, and get back to the harbor. Our men had already set up three machine guns. The Navy was getting their guns into operation. There was no attack going on, but they were loading up, and they were ready in case the Japs came back, because we definitely expected another attack. By this time they did get some M-1 clips. We formed our ammo so that we could fire semiautomatic and were sticking around this wall.

"It was approximately 10:00. Now, this is a guess. A watch was the last thing on my mind. Time was irrelevant at this point. Being a marine and being a rifleman, I was given three sailors to go with me if we had to evacuate to the hills. I was given one boot [a trainee fresh from boot camp], one sailor that had been in approximately five years, and one sailor that had been in twenty years. This last one came over to me, and he said: 'Will

you show me how to load one of these things?' He had a Springfield rifle. He said: 'I fired one of these twenty years ago in boot
camp. I haven't fired one since. I'm a cook. Now what do I do?'
So I showed him how to load it. He said: 'Well, I've got orders
to stick with you. If anything happens, we're supposed to go
into the hills where there's ammo, clothing, medical supplies,
and we're going to fight guerrilla warfare.'

  "The sailors that were in whites were dipping their whites in
coffee in order to camouflage them. That's all they had. They
didn't have time to get any khakis. They dipped their whites in
black coffee, put them on; some of them were still wet. If the
Japs couldn't see them, they could sure smell them.

  "After a while our officer came back and said: 'Well, obviously the invasion was scuttlebutt. You sailors go this way, and
you marines come with me.' We were sent to the main gate to
keep everyone out. Civilians were trying to get in; civilians were
trying to get out. There was an awful lot of confusion. There
was still some spasmodic shooting. I didn't fire a shot after the
attacks.

  "We were reformed that afternoon and were sent to Oahu
Cemetery. Oahu Cemetery is located near Honolulu. At this
time, we were fully armed. We got on a truck, and we went to
Oahu Cemetery. They were beginning then to bring in the bodies
of the dead. We were gotten together. There were ten of us, and
a corporal was in charge. The corporal said: 'We have our orders. We are here to keep everybody out. Now we're going to
spend the night here in this morgue.' There were bulldozers
digging trenches at this time. They dug them all afternoon. And
he said: 'We have orders to keep everyone out unless they have
a special ID.'

  "Trucks were bringing in these crude, makeshift wooden
boxes approximately 7 feet long, 2½ by 2½ feet. There were
dead soldiers, sailors, and marines killed during the attack in
them. We were given orders that the Japanese were going to try
to count the casualties and to shoot anything that moved. That
was our orders. 'Don't ask any questions. Shoot anything that
moves.' We walked post in pairs.

  "They brought bodies in all afternoon. The bulldozers were
digging two long trenches. I'm going to guess and say they were

The repair ship *Vestal* ran aground on the Aiea Shoal after pulling away from the USS *Arizona*. Joseph George graphically recounts his experiences aboard the USS *Vestal* that won him a Navy Commendation Ribbon. *Courtesy National Archives*

Martin Matthews and Archie Wilkerson describe the damage done at Ford Island Naval Air Station, including hangar number six, shown here in flames. Planes parked on the ramp were totally destroyed early in the assault. *Courtesy National Archives*

Taken two months prior to the attack, this photograph shows the tank farm, the submarine base, and CINCPAC (commander in chief, Pacific Fleet) headquarters located on the Southeast Loch at Pearl Harbor. During the raid these installations were untouched, and, as several survivors point out, the Japanese failure to destroy the facilities proved to be a fatal mistake. *Courtesy National Archives*

Leslie Le Fan describes a scene similar to this burial of men killed during the attack. He said in 1976: "Today I can smell fresh pinewood, and the memory comes back to the day at Oahu Cemetery when I saw blood and oil seeping out of these boxes and knew that only yesterday these men were live human beings." *Courtesy National Archives*

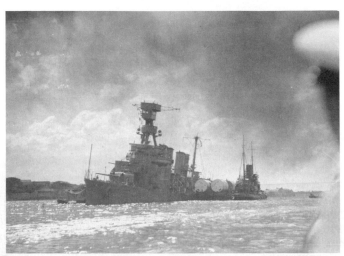

Despite being heavily damaged, the USS *Raleigh,* moored just north of the target vessel *Utah,* continued to fire back at her attackers. Seamen from the *Raleigh* used acetylene torches to cut through the *Utah*'s hull and rescue John Vaessen after the converted battleship turned over. *Courtesy National Archives*

Men set up guns in a bomb crater near hangar number 15-17 at Hickam Field. *Courtesy National Archives*

Wheeler Field on fire. Several survivors describe the action there. *Courtesy National Archives*

The Wheeler Field barracks were heavily damaged by the attack. *Courtesy National Archives*

Destruction and death were the fate of American pilots, their fighters, and hangar number three at Wheeler Field. *Courtesy National Archives*

Seamen at Kaneohe Naval Air Station work between attacks to save a burning PBY seaplane. Twenty-seven of these planes were destroyed at the base by Japanese airmen. *Courtesy National Archives*

Kaneohe Naval Air Station lies in ruins after Japanese planes have departed for their carrier task force *Kido Butai. Courtesy National Archives*

A damaged P-40 at Bellows Field. Phillip Willis describes the unsuccessful efforts of American fighter pilots to get airborne during the attack. *Courtesy National Archives*

150 feet long each and 5 to 6 feet deep. They were laying the boxes side by side. They were beginning to smell pretty strong. Blood was running out of the boxes.

"One flatbed truck came up, stopped abruptly, and a box fell off. It hit the concrete and burst. There was a trunk of a man, three arms, and one leg in this particular box. The Navy man, who had on a face mask, put the remains back in the box, sealed it up, and laid it into the ground. They were laying them in as fast as they possibly could, side by side, with identification marks as best as they could make them. We walked post that night out of this morgue area. We had no food and no coffee; we had nothing. We couldn't burn a light.

"Actually, eating was the last thing on my mind. I wasn't hungry. I didn't think about food. I kept thinking about what my mother must be thinking, knowing I was at Pearl Harbor, because the week before, when I first got there, I sent some mail home that I was at Pearl, and we were having a big time on liberty. I sent some canned candy home—some Hawaiian candy for Christmas. That just about depleted my supply of money. That's one reason I was broke then.

"That night in the morgue, I watched my first cremation of the civilians who were killed in the attack in Honolulu. I later learned that many were killed by our own shells that didn't go off and landed in Honolulu. Of the people with me that day, I can remember Raymond Langlois from New Orleans, Raymond Jones from Arkansas, and Jim Harvey from Kansas City. We weren't supposed to keep diaries. That was a no-no, although I did keep a small one—just a notebook with a few notes in it. But I remember Jones, Langlois, and Harvey because we walked post that night together.

"It rained that evening, and, while walking around, we each had our rifles and pistols loaded, and we were given orders to shoot at anything that moved. On one occasion there was a car that came by, and we were at the main gate of the cemetery. They had their lights on. Raymond Jones and I were together at this particular time. Raymond said: 'Turn off your lights!' And they told him in no uncertain terms to go to hell. He walked in front of the car, and, with his rifle butt, he knocked out both lights, and they proceeded on their way, cussing us.

"The next morning there was another occasion when a carload of youngsters, teenagers, drove by applauding and waving Japanese flags. I never wanted to fire a shot so bad in all my life, but I couldn't pull down on kids. Anyway, they were of Japanese origin and were probably trying to change sides real quick. They just drove by and were applauding and waving Jap flags. The more meatballs I saw, the madder I got.

"There was a couple who lived at a florist shop across the street from the cemetery. They came over. Well, we stopped them immediately, and they asked us if we wanted breakfast. Well, this was a real delight. We had no coffee. So we went over two and three at a time and ate breakfast and came back to stand at our post. I'm going to say that about 8:00, six of us were selected as an honor guard. We had our rifles, and we were given three rounds of blank ammo, which we loaded into our rifles, and the chaplain, who was a captain in the Navy, gave a prayer. His words came, at the end, with tears in his eyes. Believe me, there were grown sailors and marines standing there, big men, who were crying, unashamedly crying. They had lost buddies; they had lost friends; they had lost their ships; they had lost everything they had, more or less. The scuttlebutt was still so thick that we didn't know exactly what was happening. You could hear anything you wanted to hear.

"The chaplain said, when he wound up, that 'we are beaten to our knees, but we shoot pretty good from that position.' He said: 'With God's help we will win this war. It's going to be a long war. It's going to be a short war. Your guess is as good as mine, but we will win eventually because God is on our side!' It was an inspiring speech. I was privileged to be on the six-man honor guard that fired as they covered up the graves.

"I learned later on that at Red Hill Cemetery the same thing was going on. I don't know how many were buried there that day. There were several hundred of these boxes laying side by side. Today I can smell fresh pinewood, and the memory comes back to the day at Oahu Cemetery when I saw blood and oil seeping out of these boxes and knew that only yesterday these men were live human beings. Foremost in my mind, right then, was: 'These Japs aren't going to get away with this!'

"Monday night we were ordered back to Pearl, and I went to

Ford Island to guard and take care of the oil depot and the ammunition depot, because we just knew that we were going to be invaded and that this material was essential. I stayed there approximately three days and then went to a place near Aiea, Richardson Recreation Center. There was a swimming pool. I finally did get one message off to my mother, a cablegram. All I could forward was two words: 'Am Safe!' She cherishes them today—'Am Safe,' two words.''

On December 15, Private Le Fan boarded the USS *Tangier* as part of a force assembled to relieve Wake Island, which was besieged by the Japanese. The task force was ninety miles from Wake when a last message was received and piped through the ship's public-address system: "The enemy has landed, and the situation is in doubt." The sending radio went dead; the ships turned around. The *Tangier* ran slower on the way back to protect the force's hospital ship, the *Solace*. Both vessels arrived at Pearl Harbor on January 1, 1942.

Le Fan left the Hawaiian Islands in March, going first to the New Hebrides and then to Espíritu Santo. He made the landing at Guadalcanal on August 7, 1942, and was later part of the invasion forces that leapfrogged their way toward Japan, establishing beachheads at Tarawa, the Marianas, and Okinawa. As soon as the fighting ended, he left the Marines and returned home, where he worked for the next twenty-seven years in the circulation department of the local newspaper, the *Temple Telegram*. Leslie Le Fan died on October 4, 1986.

Chapter IV

North Northwest of Ford Island

Some American defenders of Pearl Harbor believed that the Japanese attacked the northwest side of Ford Island—the side opposite Battleship Row—because they expected to find the Pacific Fleet's aircraft carriers docked there. This was their normal berthing (F-9, F-10, and F-11), but they were at sea when the assault began.

A popular notion, which is probably wrong, was that some of the Japanese fliers thought that the battleship *Utah* was a carrier, since she had been converted to a target vessel and had wood planking laid across her main deck. On the weekend of the attack, she also had two cranes on board to shift some of the vessel's timber ashore, which added to her appearance as a carrier. But a Japanese pilot would have required a vivid imagination and bad eyesight to mistake the *Utah* for the USS *Lexington* or USS *Enterprise*.

Such an error was not the case when Lieutenant Heita Matsumura led the fourth group of torpedo planes in phase one of the attack to the opposite side of Ford Island at 8:00 A.M. He was upset that two of his planes attacked the *Utah*, because he knew from earlier study that she was a target vessel. Nevertheless, the *Utah* was struck, and by 8:05 "abandon ship" was ordered. Seven minutes later, at 8:12, the *Utah* had capsized.

The USS *Raleigh*, a light cruiser moored just north of the *Utah*, was missed at 8:00 by a torpedo that went between the *Raleigh* and another light cruiser, the USS *Detroit*. Around 8:05, however, the *Raleigh* was not so lucky, for a torpedo hit just outside the number two fireroom causing it and the forward engine room to flood. Immediate counterflooding kept the ship from rolling over. Her crew fought back and claimed several kills before being bombed around 9:08, when one missile dropped nearby and a second penetrated her decks and detonated on the harbor floor. The resulting explosion caused her to list further, but nothing more disastrous happened. At 9:20 another bomb dropped close by, but no damage resulted.

The *Detroit*, slightly farther north along the island, was unaffected by the torpedo launched between her and the *Raleigh* at 8:00. Two bombs exploded within 20 to 30 yards at 9:05, but they, too, failed to cause damage. The only other ship along the northwest side of Ford Island was the seaplane tender *Tangier*. She was moored just south of the *Utah* and unscathed by the early part of the attack. At 8:40 her return fire inflicted heavy damage on the Japanese, as her gunners shot down three enemy aircraft. She also fired on a midget submarine operating in the vicinity. Around 9:13 bombs hit near her, and fragments shattered a small boat and windows in her pilothouse. A third bomb fell close enough to splinter a wardroom and wound several seamen.

From around 8:50, Japanese dive-bombers concentrated on the west side of Ford Island, and a few minutes later, about 9:00, the USS *Medusa*, a repair ship in the entrance to the Middle Loch, had a bomb drop near her. Earlier she had fired on the same midget submarine that the *Tangier* attacked. The craft was finally sunk by the destroyer *Monaghan*, which rammed it and dropped depth charges at 8:43.

North of Ford Island, in the East Loch and elsewhere, were several destroyer nests. Most of these vessels got under way early in the battle and began firing at the incoming planes; the USS *Aylwin* made such a foray. However, the USS *Dobbin*, a destroyer tender, came under dive-bomber attack at 9:15 and 9:45. In the first assault, three planes launched bombs that missed, but fragments killed one man and wounded four others, two critically.

As in all phases of the raid, uncoordinated strafing occurred repeatedly. In fact, in the area north-northwest of Ford Island the onslaught seemed even less planned, less prearranged. Although damage here was not so severe as that along Battleship Row, it was bad enough for the survivors, and, on some of the ships not represented in these interviews, men died in agony. Aboard the USS *Curtiss*, a seaplane tender anchored near the *Medusa*, twenty men lost their lives and fifty-eight were wounded when a disabled Japanese plane crashed into her at 9:05.

23
Seaman Second Class John Vaessen
USS *Utah*

John Vaessen was born at Saint Francis Hospital, San Francisco, on July 10, 1916. At his mother's insistence, he graduated from high school; then, after a few years during which he took various jobs, he entered the U.S. Navy on May 27, 1941. The offspring of a seafaring family, he was naturally pulled toward that branch of the service. He spent two years in the naval reserve before his unit was activated, and, having once worked for an electrical contractor, he was first assigned for further training to the signal and radio school in Chavez Ravine, Los Angeles.

Vaessen's only ship assignment prior to the attack on Pearl Harbor was aboard the USS *Utah* (AG16), a battleship that had been converted to a mobile target vessel. It was used by airmen from the various services for bombing practice and by the Navy for torpedo drill. He boarded her at San Pedro, California, in September on the day before she sailed for Hawaii, and he was assigned the duty of electrician's mate striker. Because the *Utah* was a target ship, Vaessen did not have a battle station but pulled watch on a frequent schedule.

Unlike the many men who relished duty in Hawaii, Vaessen found it less than exciting. "When you go downtown and see nothing but everybody in white and white hats bobbing all over the street, and you line up for everything you do," he said, "it's not really encouraging.'' Despite his complaints, he and a friend, John Wallis, went to Honolulu on December 6 on liberty. The former wanted to buy Hawaiian Christmas cards, and the latter planned to get a tattoo. After Vaessen made his purchases and mailed a few cards to friends on the mainland, the two men ''had a few drinks'' so that Wallis could fortify himself for the ordeal ahead. He was tattooed on Hotel Street, in the town's red-light district, and they returned to the ship on the 11:00 P.M. liberty launch.

Since the *Utah* did not have a regular berthing place but had to occupy other ships' spaces, it was docked in the area normally used by aircraft carriers, which were at sea and not expected to return until December 7 or 8. The target vessel was covered by large, thick planks of wood designed to protect it during bombing practice. On the weekend of the raid, having just finished an assignment, the crew was preparing to shift the lumber to the Navy Yard. Two huge cranes placed on ship for the task, along with the expanse of boards, gave her the appearance of a carrier, and, although it is doubtful, some confused Japanese pilots may have believed that they were attacking such a craft when they torpedoed the *Utah*.

On December 7, Vaessen had watch beginning at 8:00 A.M. in the switchboard room, which controlled the ship's electrical system. According to custom, he arrived on the fourth deck at 7:45, and he relieved a seaman named Joe Barta. As he left, Barta said that he was going to pick up a newspaper. Vaessen never saw him again; he would be numbered among the missing that day at Pearl Harbor.

The *Utah* took two torpedoes, which, at the time, Vaessen thought were generator explosions caused by the ship's being rammed. She rolled over, trapping Vaessen below decks. His one advantage was a thorough knowledge of all parts of the vessel, information he had gained during the previous two months while stringing wires and lights for crews working below. After the ship capsized, he made his way to the bilge area by crawling toward the lower decks.

''I always heard the attack was 7:55, but it could be that our watch was wrong, because I had it a little ahead of that. I'm putting batteries in the flashlight, and all of a sudden there's this Thunk in the blister, and water is coming in. Well, just before I had gone down the hatch, I noticed a ship go by. I believe it was the *Arizona*, but I couldn't swear to it. So I said: 'Gee, they must have rammed us.'

"We had a telephone switchboard down in the room next to me, but it didn't go into operation until 8:00. This was a patch-cord telephone system. So I knew it wasn't operating. Then pretty soon I felt another thud, and more water started coming in. It really started pouring in. We had emergency-lighting acid batteries, and the water started closing on them and shorting everything out. The power started dimming. I knew to keep the lights on on the ship, so I pulled the vent. I figured I needed to keep the lights on so people could find their way to where they wanted to go.

"I thought we were rammed. The ship turned pretty fast, so I grabbed this flashlight which I was repairing, and I headed to the hatch. The one going up where I was was all dogged down because it was just painted. I went past the radio room and said: 'Well, I'll go across and go to the other side, cross the ampli-dyne room and go up.' But by the time I got to the door, the ship rolled over.

"I was hanging onto everything, the door and anything I could grab. The deck plates came flying by me, fire extinguishers, everything loose. I was hit in many places but not by sharp edges. I was just lucky that God was with me, that's for sure! Anyhow, the ship rolled over, and I crawl over the amplidynes and go up to the bottom.

"The amplidyne motor room was for the guns, the control to keep them in phase. So I go up to the dynamo flat. I thought the guy in the dynamo room would be there, but he had gone up the hatch already. I looked around. I didn't see anyone. So I went up to the bottom, and there was a wrench that opened the bilge. There's a little clip that holds the wrench, and many times the wrench is not there, but this time it was. I picked it up, and there are four great, big brass bolts that are well lubricated and a brass cover over the bilge. I open it up, and the door swings open. It's where they kept the spare asbestos. So I got showered with that, like a snow shower. I could look down below, and I could see the water bubbling up pretty fast, and every once in a while something on the superstructure, which was holding us up, would snap.

"So I said: 'Pull yourself together. I'm gonna go up to the bilge.' My light—it would be one of those with the switch that's not the greatest—would go on and off at times. I crawled along, and, every time I looked down at the water, I got more scared because it was bubbling up. But then it slowed.

"With the wrench I'd kept with me, I hit the bottom of the ship. I said: 'It sounds to me like it's out of water,' but I wasn't sure. So I hit it again and again and again, and I guess I kept it up for quite a while. I hit as hard as I could. I had a blister on my hand that you wouldn't believe. I just banged and banged, and nothing happened for quite a while. Then all of a sudden I heard a rapping on the outside and voices, but I couldn't understand what they said.

"I had control of myself. I said: 'As long as it's out of water I could close the hatch and stay there a while.' When I first looked, there was 8 or 9 feet of space, but gradually the water came up. I guess the weight inside of the ship would make it heavier, and you could hear a snap. We had cage masts,* so maybe the superstructure was collapsing. I don't know what was holding it up. So I crawled along and pounded away. I heard a tap back and voices and then nothing.

"I had the light. I could look around, though I didn't know how long it would last. It was a three-cell light. I still have it. I had the end wrench, maybe 10, 12 inches long. It's an end wrench, just for a hatch, nothing else, absolutely nothing. It weighs about a pound and a half, two pounds. I got a big blister, but that didn't stop me from pounding. I just kept pounding."

Although he did not know it at the time, the sounds Vaessen next describes were caused by a second attack. The Japanese pilots were trying to strafe seamen who had climbed on top of the ship's hull after it rolled over and were trying to rescue

---

*The *Utah* had one cage mast at the time of the attack.

Vaessen. At the same time, Japanese planes were firing at gunners on the USS *Tangier* who were providing covering fire for the rescue crew. Some of the enemy shells inadvertently hit the *Utah*.

"Like I said, I heard voices and then silence. I strained my ears to hear, and then there was all this silence. Then all of a sudden I heard RAT-TAT-RAT-TAT-RAT-TAT-RAT-TAT! I said: 'Well, they are using these pneumatic chisels, that's what they're doing. They're getting hoses, and they're going to cut a hole in here.' I heard this RAT-TAT-RAT-TAT a couple of times. I'd hear it by me, and then it would be in the other end. I said: 'That's somebody in the other compartment. I'll just have to wait my turn.'

"I learned later that the RAT-TAT was the planes coming in strafing. The *Tangier* was tied forward or aft—I forget which—and they were firing with their antiaircraft guns to keep the planes away from the rescue party, because the *Raleigh*'s guns were all out of shape.

"Pretty soon, some voices came back, with more people, but I still couldn't understand them. I'd hear a rap. They tried to signal with code or something, but I didn't understand. Then after a while I saw a little red spot—somebody with a cutting torch. They got a little hole burned, and the torch went out. Then I panicked. I had 3 or 4 feet of space. I had to crouch down to stay in there. I'd see the glowing metal caused by the torch again, and it would go out. Finally, Hill* held it a different way, so it wouldn't go out. Anyway, they burned a circle maybe 16 or 18 inches. I don't quite know the size. I'd always heard the stories of how thin the hull of the ship was, but that was an inch, maybe more, of thick steel.

"I had shorts on at that time—the last time in my life I ever

---

*William Hill was a shipfitter assigned to the cruiser *Raleigh*. After his ship was put out of action by Japanese bombs and a torpedo, Hill operated the acetylene torch that freed Vaessen. Years later, he saw Vaessen's name mentioned in Walter Lord's *Day of Infamy* (New York: Holt, Rinehart, 1957). He located the seaman through the Bureau of Navy Personnel, and the two have become good friends.

wore shorts—and a T-shirt. The sparks were coming down on me, but I didn't care. I stayed right under there. The best shower I've ever had! They were trying to holler in, but it was just 'Stay back,' and that kind of stuff. I see all the red flame go out, but the slag was holding the piece in. Then pretty soon a guy goes Bang! Bang! Then I backed away. The thing came down, and I was out and gone. They had a fellow there with a bucket of water to cool off this because the metal was pretty hot, but I was already gone. He didn't even get the bucket turned over. When the plate came in, I was out!

"Our crew had a boat over on Ford Island and an engineer to run it. They took me to the shore. Hill says that I said: 'A generator blew up,' but then I looked at the *Raleigh*, and it was down in the water, and I said: 'What happened?' They said: 'We're at war!' I said: 'Who with?' They said: 'The Japs!' "

After leaving the *Utah*, Vaessen went to Ford Island, where he had his burns and bruises tended. He next went to the "lucky bag," a collection of various articles of clothing left unclaimed by a ship's crew, for clothing. "I got ill-fitted," he said, "but that was the best they could do." According to rumor, his tribulations prompted the Navy to search for other survivors in airtight places on ships that had been sunk. As a result of further searches, a small number of sailors who might otherwise have perished were saved. For having kept the lighting system working on the *Utah* as she sank so that others might escape, John Vaessen was awarded the Navy Cross.

Soon after the attack, he managed to send his mother a message by the Pan American *China Clipper*, which flew a regular route through Honolulu at this time. At first, Vaessen lacked an assignment and toured the naval base. He said: "We walked over by the *Arizona*, and the bodies were stacked up. There were blankets that covered them. We were cold, so we each borrowed one. It was not a nice thing to do, but. . . ." Later he was assigned to assist a civilian company, Merritt, Chapman, and Scott, which performed salvage operations at Pearl Harbor.

After working with the various groups clearing the port,

Vaessen was sent in June 1942 to the shipyard at Alameda, California. He helped put the USS *Starling*, a minelayer, in commission and served aboard her for much of the war. He left the Navy on September 3, 1945; worked for many years as a civilian electrician, a skill that he had perfected in the Navy; and finally retired in San Mateo, California, where he currently resides.

24
Seaman First Class Nick L. Kouretas
USS *Raleigh*

In 1940 country and western stars sang a popular melody entitled "I'll Be Back in Just a Year, Little Darlin'." It had been inspired by the Selective Service Act, which provided for the drafting of men between the ages of twenty-one and thirty-five for one year. The first lottery drawing was held on October 29. In Nick Kouretas's words, when Washington officials drew birth dates, "my number came up." Faced with the certain prospect of being drafted into the Army, he joined the Navy.

His decision to enlist was made almost on the spur of the moment. Kouretas had accompanied his younger brother, Jimmy, to the local naval recruiting station in Sacramento so that the latter could enlist. While there, Nick, gregarious by nature, told the officer in charge that his "number had been drawn out of the fishbowl" and he soon would be following his brother into the military. The recruiter said: "Why don't you join the Navy with your brother? We'll keep you two together; we'll put you through training; you'll go aboard the same ship." After realizing that, as a one-year draftee, he in fact would be committed for the duration of the impending war, Nick said: "Why not?" Thus he volunteered with his brother on February 11, 1941.

Kouretas was born on June 27, 1919, in Sacramento to Greek immigrants. He grew up in the section called Alkali Flats, graduated from the city high school, and got his first job with Fredrikson and Westbrook, a local highway-building firm. As an assistant timekeeper, he had a well-paid steady job in the waning years of the Great Depression. Life looked "pretty rosy" for him until his "number came up."

His situation did not seem bad even after he finished boot camp in San Diego. He and his brother were assigned to the light cruiser *Raleigh* (CL7) in Pearl Harbor, and Nick felt that there would be no fighting "until Hitler got things going." Since Nick was joining the Pacific Fleet, he and the war would still be an ocean apart. "What a surprise," he later mused; "you know, the *Raleigh* was the first ship to get torpedoed at Pearl Harbor."

Duty on the *Raleigh* was not easy. A light cruiser with four stacks, she was the flagship for Admiral Robert A. ("Fuzzy") Theobald, commander of Destroyer Flotilla One. She was a dilapidated, unforgiving vessel built in 1920, without bunks and infested with "rats the size of dogs!" Of his first days aboard, Kouretas, who quickly became a yeoman striker, said: "It just scared me to death, trying to sleep in a hammock, the ship rolling, and the rats running alongside on the pipes. I just couldn't believe it. I said: 'Jeez, say this isn't so!' "

All things considered, however, his few months of peacetime duty were mostly enjoyable. He had the money and pull to rent a one-room apartment, with a kitchenette, just opposite Waikiki Beach near the Royal Hawaiian Hotel. He spent a lot of liberty on the beach, eyeing women. "You know," he said, "I felt I was a young, debonair playboy, living the free life. I loved being with girls. They all knew Nick, Nick off the *Raleigh*."

Kouretas was possibly the only seaman first class in the Pacific Fleet to have an apartment in Honolulu. He could afford it through his "ill-gotten gains." A shipmate, Jack Moser, said: "You know, that Greek racketeer had everything going aboard ship. He was in the four-for-five racket, ran a couple of crap games, and made lots of money." Nick learned the "four-for-five" racket, or loan-sharking, by watching old chiefs lend young seamen four dollars at mid-month and collect five dollars in return on payday.

The interview opens with Kouretas's activities on Friday, December 5, when he began a weekend that started out like many others he had spent in the months before the attack. It ends on the Wednesday after the battle.

* * *

"Those days [just before the attack] were every-days in my life. It was routine. When we pulled in, I made a liberty that Friday. I went to my apartment. Of course, being a peacetime Navy, we could wear civilian clothes. I changed clothes. I got into a sports outfit, and I went carousing and barring. I don't know, I might have got lucky that night. I used to fairly often. But I know, Saturday morning, I came back to the ship.

"One thing I'm very proud of is the fact that, during my entire naval career, I had a 4.0 conduct rating. I was never put on report. I never got in trouble. I had a 3.89 proficiency rating in leadership of men. So I learned discipline. It was inbred through my family, and I tried to play the game by the rules. I wasn't going to fuck up like a lot of guys. I was proud, so I made it a point that, when my liberties were up, I would get back aboard ship.

"I remember that I came back aboard ship Saturday morning. I knew it was my turn to catch the duty. So everybody made liberty, and I just went about my daily routine—work in the office, had dinner—and that evening it was a regular routine aboard ship. I went down and chitchatted with the sailmaker and one of the boatswain's mates, played some dominoes, and then retired for the night. I knew I was on call, but as a yeoman nothing ever came up. That Sunday morning I knew that as of 8:00 I was off duty, and I was eligible for liberty. Liberty started at 10:00 for regular people, but, being a gamer, I said: 'I'll take the 8:00 church boat.' Now, I wasn't going to go to church. But that gave me two hours to get ashore, get to my apartment, clean up, and go downtown to see what's happening. So, at any rate, I went down to breakfast, and we had sunny-side eggs. I'll never forget it—bacon and sunny-sides and hash browns—because, boy, they were spread out. Those yellow yolks were looking up at you. Everybody was running down those decks. So I ate my breakfast, and I headed up to put on my uniform. I had already shaved and showered.

"I felt that I had a bowel movement coming on, and I thought: 'Well, I'll go down to the head and take care of business.' I went to the head, sat there, and I noticed a funny book. There were a lot of eighteen- and nineteen-year-old sailors aboard ship who bought these comic books. At the time, Superman and

Captain Marvel were very popular. So I picked this comic book up, and I was kind of looking at it. All of a sudden I heard this BAA-WOOOOM, and, Jeez, it blew me out of my underwear and over the top of the bulkhead. You see, there were two rows of crappers and then maybe a five-foot bulkhead separating them from stainless steel urinals. You'd urinate on one side and do number two on the other. So the blast blew me over the top of the bulkhead, headfirst into a urinal.

"I got up, and I thought: 'Holy Christ! The ship blew up.' I said: 'How in the hell can the ship blow up? We're tied up, and the engines are secure.' And I thought: 'What in the hell has happened?'

"Then I thought that another ship had rammed us, so I ran to the portholes, because, at that time, we had portholes open when we were tied up. I looked out the porthole, and I saw this plane that dropped a torpedo pulling up out of its dive. I saw this big rising sun, and by then I said: 'Holy Christ! The Japs!' Everybody started hollering and screaming: 'The Japs are here! The Japs are here!' So, with just a T-shirt on and nothing else, I started running to get topside. I had nothing on below, and I was barefoot. I fought the war in the nude! I didn't look for my skivvies; I was just trying to get out of there.

"My battle station was on the 3-inch gun on the well deck, so I started running back to get to it. The head was just aft of midships, and the well deck was three hatches up, so I went up the after hatch, the midship hatch, and the forward hatch. I went up the after hatch, climbed up on the main deck, and then climbed up and went up on the well deck because that is off the fantail. The other 3-inch guns were lined up on the port and starboard sides and on the forecastle.

"When I got there, the gun crew was almost there. You know, the funny thing about it was that everything was secured. When we docked, some of the gunner's mates went on liberty with the keys to the ready boxes. We had the awnings up, with the tie-ties lashed to the grommets, to shade the ship. So we broke into the butcher's room, where they carved the meat, and got cleavers and knives and cut the tie-ties and then cut the awnings down. With big sledges we broke off the locks and got into the ready boxes where we didn't have the keys. Some of the gunner's mates were there, and they opened their ready boxes. So we started firing.

"Our ship was credited with knocking out six planes that morning—six Japanese Zeros.* I can't say that my particular gun got any credit for them. A lot of times planes were coming at us from all angles. I'd try to concentrate on one target. They'd say: 'Get this guy!' you know, and I'd lead him, hoping I could get him. I know I was scared as hell.

"During the attack, the entire United States fleet at Pearl Harbor got only six planes in the air, and Lieutenant Don Korn, a young guy that we called 'Popcorn,' got one of those planes up, one of our scout planes. They sent him to search for the Jap fleet in the north. I had a lot of admiration for Lieutenant Korn.

"It took me six or seven minutes to get from the head to my battle station. I think all the torpedo planes had dropped their torpedoes by then. In fact, this torpedo plane that dropped the torpedo that hit us—the pilot and his radioman—they circled our ship at least two times. I recall the Japanese radioman looking out there with his shiny teeth, and he was giving us this handshake gesture. His palms were together right above his head, and he was waving them back and forth as they rounded the ship. They weren't more than 75 to 90 feet in the air—telephone-pole height.

"Well, the torpedo hit between the number one and number two fireroom and the forward engine crew. It was a foot and a half off dead center of the total length of the cruiser. Fortunately, we were tied up. We had no engine crew down below decks, or they'd have gotten killed. It made a hole big enough to drive an Army dump truck into. When I saw the *Raleigh* in dry dock, I couldn't believe my eyes.

"Immediately the ship started to list to port. We were tied up at [pier] Fox 12 off Ford Island. In front of us was the USS *Detroit* at Fox 11, the same class cruiser as us. Behind us was the battleship *Utah*. You know, it was a target ship by then. When the Jap pilot saw the *Utah*, he thought it was Battleship Row. He peeled off and dropped the torpedo.

---

*It is unlikely that the *Raleigh* shot down six Zeros, since the Japanese strike force lost a total of nine.

"We didn't have any power and had no way to start it. So immediately, when the *Raleigh* started to turn over and stretch her ties off Fox 12 where we were tied, the first lieutenant in charge of damage control ordered us to flood the starboard compartments. She filled up on the starboard side and came down in the water; she just leveled down in the water. In the meantime, they had gotten two tugs to bring over two big buoy tanks. Divers went down and tied cables around her, and they put two buoy tanks alongside of her and kept her afloat.

"I think Captain Simons was aboard when the attack started, but I'm not positive. I remember him being up on top of the bridge with his helmet and screaming orders. I know that between the first attack and the second, when the high-altitude bombers came over, he gave orders from the bridge about the listing. You know: 'Stand by! Prepare to abandon ship!' And we passed the orders along. There were vocal orders coming down from the bridge, down to the deck off the forecastle, and, by the time it got to midships and then on back to the fantail, it was: 'Abandon ship!' People were diving off into the water and swimming to the island.

"When the second wave, the high-altitude bombers, came over, we got hit again with a five-hundred-pound, delayed-action bomb. It went completely through the ship, came out the bottom, and then blew up. I saw this plane coming in—and I was firing at them—and I thought: 'Holy Toledo!' I saw it drop that bomb, and I thought: 'It's coming right for me!' Now, it wouldn't have done a damned bit of good, but I stopped firing, and I ducked my head—you know, tried to cover my head with my arms. It's just a natural reaction. The bomb hit right on the edge of our ready box, about seven feet away; went through the well deck, down through the main deck, down through three or four two-inch steel-plate decks, down through the fuel tank; and then blew back and made a hole in the fuel tank. Fortunately, it was a delayed-action bomb; if it weren't, I wouldn't be here talking today.

"Well, this shook me up. I don't know when I got myself back together. I remember there was a lot of commotion, and I left my battle station because they told me that the first lieutenant wanted me up on the bridge. The planes had sort of slowed down; a lot of them had left; there were very few in the air. The antiaircraft fire had slowed down, too.

"So I ran from the well deck back toward the main deck, along the side of the ship, and yet there was a plane strafing. I thought: 'Oh, Jeez!' I could hear those slugs chipping paint, you know. At times I dove for shelter, and then finally I got to the bridge. I remember the first lieutenant telling me: 'Kouretas, the .50-calibers have stopped firing up on the tripod.' We had a tripod mast with a deck and three .50-caliber machine guns up there. So he says: 'Climb the tripod and see what's happened.' So I started going hand over hand up the ladder, up the tripod, and the machine guns were swinging around toward me, and I felt: 'Oh, God, they're going to get me! They're going to get me!'

"I finally got up there, and the degree of disorganization was unusual. There were all young seamen up there, and they didn't know how to operate the .50-calibers; they had them all jammed. None of them were hurt, but the machine guns were all jammed. They were trying to read the manual on how to unjam the machine guns. Then I helped them, and we got the guns unjammed, and I came down. Then finally I started to get oriented again.

"I would say that the *Raleigh*'s crew acted almost totally in accordance with its training, but, after the attack was over, then there was shock. That's the way I reacted. I knew from my training what I had to do. I wasn't scared during the initial attack, but after it was over I started coming apart. I recall that, when the attack ceased, and the planes were gone, and there was no more firing, orders came that we were to abandon ship and get over to the main island.

"Then Captain Simons got on the bridge and said the Japanese were landing troops on the other side of the island. He ordered the first lieutenant to break open the armory, pass out rifles and ammunition as far as they would go, and for everybody to get on the island and shift for themselves, give them hell, and go down fighting. I recall that plainly.

"I remember that I got all shook up. It was at that point that I realized that I didn't know where my brother was. But, in the meantime, I had gone down and was one of the first ones to get my share of rifle bullets, a rifle, and a .45. I went by Paduca, a Filipino messboy who was the captain's cook, and he gave me a big butcher knife and a cleaver. At that time, black people and Filipinos were mess stewards; they weren't rated or anything in the Navy. I thought: 'Well, now where am I going to go?'

"Well, I left. I went to Ford Island, and it was just total confusion. They were trying to muster different ships' crews, trying to find out who people were, where they belonged. Late Sunday afternoon they started mustering our crew, and then my brother's name came up as 'missing in action.' I remember there was an ensign who was in charge of my brother's division who came over and asked me when was the last time I had seen Jimmy. I said: 'Well, I didn't see him this morning because he got up early and took Captain Simons over for some errand to a fort and then brought him back.' I thought: 'Jeez, where is he?' Then I realized how many people had been killed, how many were dead. 'Where do I look?' I thought: 'Where do I go?'

"This is where I started to go into shock. Up until then I handled the war. But now shock set in. I began to think of my parents, my sister, my family, and I thought: 'What am I going to say to them? What am I going to do? How can I explain this?'

"Then I was assigned to this boat crew to pick up bodies. We would take them over to Aiea Landing, and the hospital corpsmen would jump in the water with sheets, tied, and scoop the bodies up. We didn't bring them aboard the launch; we would lasso a leg, an arm, a head, and slowly tow four, five, or six bodies behind the launch over to the landing.

"Every time we brought a load over to the landing, I would jump off and run up the landing, because they were laying them like cordwood, a body here and a body there, with a walkway down the center where they would try to identify them by their dog tags, with the heads pointing into the walkway. I would run along the aisle and, knowing my brother's characteristics, look for him. He chewed his nails. I knew where he had a wart; I knew every little mark on his body. I would get so far, and I'd say: 'Well, this guy looks like him,' but I couldn't see a face. I'd pick up a hand, and I'd say: 'No, that's not him,' and then go on. By the time our launch took off, I'd be ready to go, and then the next crew would bring bodies in. I knew where I'd left off. I did this for a couple of days—Monday and Tuesday.

"That Wednesday, about 10:30, I was at Ford Island at the mess hall, getting something to eat. I was just about ready to enter the mess hall when I seen this fellow walking across the runway, and I recognized his walk. It was that of my brother. But he had a sailor's cap and a lieutenant's blue coat with gold stripes and a pair of shorts on—a mixed uniform, you know, anything he could get hold of.

"So I broke the line, and I ran out there, and I hollered: 'Jim! Jim!' He said: 'Nick! Nick!' And I said: 'You son of a bitch!' and I hit him. That was my first reaction. I now look back on it, and it was stupid. He didn't raise his hand to me. I said: 'Where in the hell have you been?' He told me: 'I was on the *Blue*, the USS *Blue*!' He said: 'You think they're going to break radio silence to tell you where the hell I am at? We've been out chasing carriers!'

"When he was coming back from somewhere in the launch to get back to the *Raleigh*, as I said, the last planes had dropped their bombs, and they were strafing. There were maybe forty-five men in the launch, and they all jumped overboard. He looked up, and he saw the *Blue*, and he swam over to it. She was a destroyer that took off because she wasn't hit, and she went out in the Pacific chasing the carriers. She didn't come back in until Wednesday. So finally we got back together."

After the *Raleigh* was refloated and put to sea, Nick Kouretas and his brother served together once more. But in 1943, after the five Sullivan brothers died on board the USS *Juneau*, the Navy issued orders that brothers, if they were the only sons of a family, could not serve together. Nick, feeling he could adjust to changed circumstances more quickly than Jim, volunteered for duty aboard an oil tanker and spent time in waters around Alaska. He then transferred to shore duty with the Twelfth Naval District's discipline office in San Francisco.

After the war he opened a bar and then worked as a dealer, maître d', and bartender in Reno, Lake Tahoe, and San Francisco. Finally, he entered law enforcement, becoming first a narcotics officer and later a consultant to various police organizations, including the U.S. Bureau of Prisons. For the remainder of his life, he remembered the horror of pulling bodies from the waters of Pearl Harbor. He died of cancer on December 27, 1979.

25
Radioman Third Class Clifton Bellew
USS *Detroit*

The location of the elevator in the downtown Federal Building in Oklahoma City determined that Clifton Bellew would fight in the Second World War as a sailor. "I think," he said, "the reason I joined the Navy was because the first military recruiting office after you got off the elevator was the Navy's." He had come to the city to enter the service because, after leaving Seminole High School, he could only get low-paying odd jobs and was determined to find something better.

Bellew was born on February 12, 1921, in Achille, a small town in the Ouachita Mountains near the Red River in southeastern Oklahoma. After joining the Navy on October 12, 1940, he was sent to three weeks of boot camp in San Diego and then transferred to the training center's radio school, where he spent the next sixteen weeks learning to be a radioman.

After a two-week leave, he was assigned to Commander, Destroyers, Battle Force, Pacific Fleet, Pearl Harbor, whose flagship was the USS *Detroit* (CL8). The vessel, an old four-stack light cruiser, was a sister ship of the USS *Raleigh* and, like the *Raleigh*, had two 6-inch guns mounted forward of the tripod mast, one 3-inch antiaircraft battery forward and two midships, and two seaplanes with catapults about two thirds back from the bow. The radio shack, Bellew's duty and battle station, was on the port side of the tripod mast.

On the weekend of the attack, Bellew stayed aboard ship, in part because radiomen pulled split duty and in part because, although he was paid on December 5, he still could not afford liberty. On Saturday he worked from breakfast to lunch, lounged around in the afternoon, and then returned to the radio shack for the shift from supper to 1:00 A.M. On Sunday he planned to eat breakfast—fried eggs were served on that day only each week—read the newspaper, wash clothes, and sunbathe.

The *Detroit* was moored in its usual place opposite Battleship Row and near Ford Island on the Pearl City side. It was toward the north end of the harbor, a point from which Bellew could see the Ford Island airstrip and some of its buildings; the destroyer tenders *Dobbin*, *Whitney*, and *Dixie*; and some of their charges. The interview begins as he finished his meal.

"After breakfast I went up to the quarterdeck, which is where the officer of the day spent his time. I bought a Sunday paper, and I started aft to read it and enjoy the rest of the day. As I got back to the area of the ship where the catapults were, which is more or less an open area—that's where they showed movies—there was a sound of diving airplanes. I didn't know what to think at first. I looked to my left and saw the dive-bombers diving on Ford Island. I watched about four of them drop their bombs on the hangars on Ford Island.

"There was a sound from the other side, to my right. I turned and looked, and it was torpedo planes that had come in over Pearl City. There was just enough water for torpedo planes to drop their fish. I saw one—he must not have been more than fifteen feet off the water of the bay—drop his torpedo. I had seen pictures in movies of these planes, but I had never seen one in actual fact. He continued straight at us, firing his machine gun. I was frozen at that moment. He veered off toward the bow of the ship. Then I saw a second plane drop its torpedo. About that time, somebody yelled: 'The Japs are attacking!' because, as the first plane had winged up, you could see the big rising-sun emblems.

"They dropped torpedoes aimed at the *Detroit*, *Raleigh*, and the *Utah*. The torpedo aimed at the *Detroit* missed and stuck in the mud along the Ford Island shoreline. The torpedo aimed at the *Raleigh* penetrated the hull and went into the engine room. The engine room was flooded, but the torpedo had apparently not traveled far enough to arm itself and therefore did not explode. The *Raleigh* was tied up to this big concrete pier or block. Her bow was probably 75 to 100 feet from our stern.

"As I say, the torpedo missed the *Detroit*. There were, I

think, two machine-gun bullet holes in the stack, and, as far as I was able to find out, there were only two people on the ship that got a scratch. One was one of our radiomen, who, on his way up to the radio shack, apparently got grazed by a bullet right under his arm. And one of the gunner's mates got a graze on his leg. They were the only two guys on the ship that got a Purple Heart that day. We were very fortunate.

"Well, about the time somebody hollered 'the Japs are attacking,' I headed for the radio shack. It was about the time the second plane dropped its torpedo when this fellow hollered. Some of the crew had painted half the deck, between the quarterdeck and the superstructure forward, where the radio shack was located. No one paid any attention to that paint. I went right on across it and up the ladder. They had the ladder tied off, but I went over the ropes and into the shack. I don't know how so many people got there before I did. Only a couple of minutes had passed when I went into the radio shack. Of course, the reason there were so many people there was because the oncoming shift had arrived, and many of the offgoing shift were still there. There didn't seem to be any room for me.

"Anyway, I got run out. They said: 'Go outside!' So I went outside, and that's when the planes—I'm not sure if it was the torpedo planes—had come back around for another pass with their machine guns. By that time, some of our guns were firing. I don't know how these people got into action so fast. The only answer I have is that training, that practice, that they had caused it.

"Nearly all the ammunition was down below at the time in the magazine, but someway or somehow they got some of it up there pretty fast. The planes made only a couple of passes with their machine guns, and they left because they had dropped their torpedoes, and they were on their way back. The dive-bombers did the same thing.

"After my dash for the radio shack, I remember looking back past the *Raleigh* to see the *Utah* roll over. She apparently got two torpedoes. And, being in port on a weekend, everything was open; all the compartments were open. Watertight integrity was at a minimum. She took two torpedoes and flooded right

away, especially on the port side, and then that thing just rolled
right over.

"I saw people scrambling out in their underwear. Fortunately, the ship didn't roll fast. More people would have been
trapped. But as it rolled over, I saw people scrambling up on
the bottom. A few of them had their trousers on. Of course, we
did wear shorts out there. We cut off our white pants and made
shorts out of them. Some of them were in that, and some were
just in their underwear. Immediately, I thought: 'How many
guys are trapped in there?'

"At the time, I didn't know what was happening on Battleship
Row. The only thing I knew was that there was an awful lot of
black smoke going up over there in that direction. Later, when
we left the harbor, as we rounded what I'll say is the channel
side of Ford Island, we saw that the *Nevada* had its stern beached
after it had taken a bomb. We were told that a quartermaster had
given the engine room a stern command—to move the stern—
and had backed the *Nevada* up on the bank so it would not sink
in the channel.

"The planes and hangars on Ford Island—seaplanes in their
hangars and what few land planes, mostly trainer planes that
were on Ford Island—were just a shambles and a mess. There
were still fires, and smoke was billowing from that. As we got
a little farther there, we could look back and see Battleship Row.
In all the commotion the *Oklahoma* had turned over, and, at the
time, we weren't sure just what she was. Oil was all over the
harbor. There was some activity in small boats. Mostly,
they were ferrying people from their ships that were destroyed
to the beach, where they could go to the hospital or something
in that order. We couldn't see the naval shipyard, but they had
been bombed over there.

"I was still outside the radio shack. Every once in a while I
would stick my head in to see if I could do anything or see what
was going on—if there was any information. When I first went
out, during the attack, I was in an area of the deck outside the
radio shack about 6 feet wide and 12 or 15 feet long. That's
where we held our training sessions, our verbal training sessions. I was out there, and some people started bringing up
ammunition boxes for our .50-caliber machine guns in what we

called the 'crow's nest,' up above the bridge. The only way that you could get ammunition up there was to hoist it up on a line. So I proceeded to help them in this chore. I spent my time out there until we didn't have anything else to shoot at.

"To me the attack was just one continuous battle. I don't recall a lull in it. There may have been one, but, as I recall, I don't remember any. I remember this flight of bombers of ours that tried to land over on Hickam. Naturally, they were large planes. I was out on the deck there, and I could see them. They were trying to land, and I could see shells exploding around them. I can imagine what the men on those planes thought.

"During the time that we were passing the ammunition up to the crow's nest for our .50-caliber machine guns, there was a two-man sub that got into the harbor, and one of our little four-stack destroyers, that used to nest over at the Pearl City area, got under way and got a bead on this submarine and rammed him.* I saw that. He hit him, and the bow went out of the water and came down on the submarine. I saw the sub later on after they raised it, about a month or two later, when they took it over to the submarine base. It was kind of smashed up.

"One incident I would like to mention was that heretofore, when we got under way, we always had a small tug—we called them 'donkeys'—come out and pull us away from these piers that we were tied up to. That morning around 9:30 we left our pier, and we went out into the channel of the harbor, turned around, came back into the pier, and tied up without any assistance from one of these donkeys. The only assistance we had may have been from one of our ship's boats, and that was just handling the lines. I think this spoke well for our officers, who are supposed to be proficient in ship handling.

"Our intention when we first left was to leave the harbor. But, for some reason, after we got out away from the pier, something changed their minds. They probably got a message from CINC-PAC, commander in chief, Pacific Fleet, to wait for the admiral. The admiral was not on board. I believe that the chief of staff was aboard and some of the staff. The captain was back aboard

*The midget submarine was rammed by the destroyer *Monaghan*, which did not have four stacks.

by that time. We went back, tied up, and it was close to noon when we left the harbor.

"We left with a group of destroyers—I don't recall how many or which ones—and proceeded, I think, about northwest. I think we were looking for submarines and possibly a landing force. I do know that, on the second day out, during lunchtime, we did a hard turn, and everybody left their food where it was, and it didn't stay where it was. It scattered all over the place. We had a narrow miss on a torpedo. The destroyers, we were told, did sink a submarine.

"We stayed out five days. One reason that we didn't stay out very long was that we were fairly low on fuel. I think it was five days we were out. I know that we didn't waste any time getting out with the destroyer escorts. I'm not sure whether we had three or four. As I say, I don't recall who they were, but I know that we headed out looking for submarines in particular and surface ships, also.

"We were at General Quarters, naturally. We stayed at General Quarters for about three days. All the compartments were closed up, and I think no one went down to our compartment to sleep that first night. I slept in a space that I wouldn't believe that I could get into. It was underneath our radio room equipment. Being out in the tropics, some of the crew slept out on deck.

"I know that, the second night out, I was so tired that I said: 'I don't care what happens. I'm going to go down and get in my bunk and go to sleep.' I think I had duty up until midnight, and I could hardly keep my eyes open the last couple of hours, so I went down and got in my sack. I think that there was another guy down there. We were just dead to the world."

After the *Detroit* returned to Pearl Harbor the USS *Whitney* became the admiral's flagship, and Bellew transferred as part of the flag personnel allowance of the admiral. Later, Bellew served on the USS *Dobbin* and the USS *Dixie*. He was in Alaska for two years, returned to the United States for another year, and went to China with the Sino-American Cooperative Organization (SACO) to set up weather and radio operations in 1945.

Bellew spent twenty years in the Navy, retiring on June 30,

1961. He went to work in the computer industry in Dallas as a repair and maintenance man, first for Collins Radio Company and then for Rockwell International. He retired a second time in 1983 and lives in the Dallas metropolitan area in the town of Richardson.

26
Storekeeper Third Class Robert N. Isacksen
USS *Tangier*

The seaplane tender *Tangier* (AV8) had an unhappy crew, in Robert N. Isacksen's opinion. The men were primarily naval retirees, who resented being called back to duty in mid-1941, and Navy reserves, who would have preferred to be almost anywhere other than aboard the *Tangier* in Pearl Harbor. To make matters worse, nearly all of her officers except the captain were "ninety-day wonders," or graduates of Officers Candidate School, which took about that long to complete. According to Isacksen, "During the attack, the commander ordered all the officers below—out of the way—and let the chiefs run the vessel."

Isacksen was a volunteer and a most unusual sailor. Born in Des Moines, Iowa, on December 14, 1918, he had moved with his family to Oakland, California, in 1924, where he finished high school, got a job, and for two years attended college nightly at the University of California, Berkeley. He joined the Navy in June 1941 to keep from being drafted into the Army. Like many of his contemporaries, he wanted to escape marching; he also wanted to avoid basic training and beginning as a lowly buck private.

The Navy let him bypass boot camp and made him a storekeeper third class. The recently commissioned *Tangier* needed someone to run her storeroom, and Isacksen, trained at college as an accountant, was the man. Two days after getting his uniform, he boarded the ship at Mare Island and stayed with her for the next five years. In charge of the storekeeper's office, he requisitioned food, handled the ship's pay, ordered all seaplane repair parts and other supplies, and kept books for the gedunk, or exchange store. He was perhaps the busiest member of the crew, which numbered between 1,600 and 2,000 men.

Soon after Isacksen joined the *Tangier*, she sailed for Bremerton, Washington, to pick up a load of torpedoes. The ship then cruised the West Coast to San Diego, went back to Long Beach, and from there sailed for Hawaii in late August or early September 1941. At Pearl Harbor the crew had very little to do except practice, since the naval air stations in the Hawaiian Islands took care of planes that the tenders normally serviced at sea. Once the war began, however, the *Tangier* became the floating base for a squadron of PBYs and briefly for Marine Corps bombers. Under wartime conditions she rearmed, refueled, and repaired her charges, which engaged in observation, dropping bombs and torpedoes, and laying mines.

In the interview, Isacksen describes the attack in a way that undoubtedly reflects the experiences of many that day. He was too busy at his battle station to observe much of what was occurring around him, and the excitement of the moment kept him from remembering many specifics.

"We were out on Saturday practicing. The reason I remember is because we came in, and we had not gotten our ammunition stored below. That's a strict rule, and the captain was an Annapolis man, and he was very, very strict on rules. He lived by the book. But we still had some ammunition on topside by the guns.

"Nobody had liberty that night because we always had to be back by 5:00 P.M. We could get off as early as 8:00 in the morning and spend the whole day, but we had to be back by 5:00. I may have watched a movie that Saturday night, because we had a movie on topside every night.

"When we came in, we took the *Lexington*'s berth on the side of Ford Island opposite Battleship Row. She was there the day before but left that night. We were to pick up supplies and then go to Guam or some other island; I don't remember which. We were scheduled to leave Monday. I knew that because I had been told I could have liberty on Sunday.

"I know that Sunday I got up and ate breakfast and then put on my dress whites. I was on deck waiting for the liberty boat to take me to church. I belonged to the Christian Church at that time, and I had friends who were working in Honolulu; they belonged to the Christian Church, and I went to their church with them quite a bit.

"I don't remember what time it was—around 8:00, I guess—but I happened to look up, and I said something to an officer. I said: 'Boy, they're sure getting these war games very real,' because we had been playing war games. I remember saying that to him, and he looked up, and he said: 'War games, hell!' He hit the General Quarters alarm, because that was a Japanese plane up there. Then I remember running for my battle station. It was a .50-caliber machine gun on the starboard side near where the captain stood.

"The first group of Jap planes I saw came over a little high, and then they dive-bombed the *Utah*. We were about fifty yards from the *Utah*. They were diving down on it, and everybody was running. I would guess that they wouldn't be much more than 20 or 30 feet above your head when they were diving. I guess the thing that impressed me was the fact that the one I noticed came over, tilted his plane a little bit, and he just had a big old grin on his face looking down at us. I guess that rubbed me wrong.

"Well, I got to my position, and the two men who ran the gun had it going. I grabbed for the ammunition. Of course, we didn't have enough belts, and I started belting right away. We didn't have electric belts, so we did it by hand. During the Pearl Harbor attack, all I did was belt ammunition. I did it as fast as I could, trying to keep the right number of shells, since every third shell is supposed to be a tracer-type shell. I did that for pretty close to thirty-six hours without stopping. The minute we would get a bunch of ammunition belted, somebody would come over from another ship and pick it up and take it, and we would go on again.

"I don't know if the men on the gun were firing before I got there, but they were firing at about the same time. Everything went so fast that it would be hard to say when they started. I really felt numb. You really don't think. It's more or less instinctive. I don't recall anybody panicking.

"One time we ran out of ammunition, and I went below, and

I don't remember whether it was two or three decks down. They had ammunition in wooden boxes, and they had wire across them, zigzagged across. I remember that I went down there and grabbed one of the boxes, put it on my shoulders, ran up the ladders with it, and didn't think anything about it. The fact is, I didn't even wait for anybody to clip them with the pliers. I tried to break them with my hands. I know that, a couple days later, I couldn't even pick one of those boxes up with two hands, let alone put one on my shoulder. I don't know what the source was, but you just did things you normally couldn't do.

"Our ship was not one of the Japs' primary targets. We had some strays that, when they realized they might have been too late, tried for us. They missed. We did have some shrapnel from bombs that hit close, burst, and came across us. But I do not remember any strafing. The best I can recall, I think one or two torpedoes went completely under us, and that's because they were aiming for someone else. I don't believe they ever tried to hit us. We were not important to them. In fact, I think the whole war was that way with us, and I'm very glad.

"Now, when the *Utah* turned over, they yelled, and I looked over. I did not actually see it turn over myself because I was busy. When I looked over there, I also saw the *Raleigh*, which was on the other side of the *Utah*. It was sunk down, and they were standing in water and still shooting. It went straight down and didn't turn. That was quite an experience. Later, I understood that one of our sheet-metal men went over and cut into the hull of the *Utah*. The chief did that. I knew him very well. He was a big man. He was very quiet and wouldn't talk much about it. He used a blowtorch [cutting torch?]. I didn't see him doing that either, but I heard about it.

"Now this may not sound true, but my reaction during the attack was that I worried how my mother and father were taking it in the States, not about my own personal safety at the time. I think I was numb. Anybody that says they were not scared—I just can't believe him. It's a different-type thing. Things were happening so fast you didn't have time to think. We were working automatically.

"Like our captain, he was trying to get ammunition passed and in place, and some of the officers were just out of college and were getting in the way, so he ordered them below except for the exec [executive officer] and himself. Of course, the chaplain refused to go below. He said his place was up there with the men. The fact is, he sat in the line where they passed the ammunition, and he was right in the middle when they were passing it.

"I couldn't detect a lull between a first and second attack. I was too busy. I don't think I ever remember stopping. I stayed right there and belted. I didn't move. The best I can remember, I stayed about two days. The fact is, they even brought sandwiches to you. You didn't go down to eat.

"It may sound funny, but we had about three of us lined up there with these hand belts, and we just kept belting ammunition. The guns were firing right beside us, and they'd grab a belt as fast as we did it. When they'd quit firing, we'd just keep belting; and when we'd get up a load, somebody would come and take them, and we'd keep going on.

"I think our ship did a professional and automatic job during the battle. I think we did it very well. I still say that, if I had to go back through it again, I'd rather be on my ship because of the fact that they did perform as well as they did.

"When I think about Pearl Harbor and the attack, the only thing I can say is that it was a horrible thing. The attack itself was not as bad as some of the other battles we had later. We lost more men, but we went into them prepared. What made Pearl so bad was it was such a surprise. Some of the things you saw when they picked up men that had been in the water—burned, holes in their cheeks and trying to smoke, and things like that—it just sets an image that is everlasting on you."

On December 9 the *Tangier* took a company of marines to sea. Joining one of the aircraft carriers and its escort vessels, the tender sailed toward Guam, which fell to the Japanese before they arrived. The *Tangier* then went to Midway Island, unloaded the marines, and in early January 1942 returned to Pearl Harbor. Isacksen said that this was the first time he realized the extent of the damage done on December 7. "There was lots of oil," he recalled, "and the ships were in bad shape. I even think the *Arizona* was still smoking. I can still see it smoking now."

Before he left the service on September 15, 1945, Isacksen rose to the rank of chief storekeeper. He and the *Tangier* were involved in several Pacific campaigns, including the liberation of the Philippine Islands. Upon his return to civilian life, he attended a business college briefly and then went to work for Traders and General Insurance Company. He spent most of his career, however, in Dallas, Texas, as chief accountant for the Lone Star Wholesale Liquor Company. He retired on the last day of 1980 and resides in Dallas. "To this day," he has written, "I am proud to have been in Pearl Harbor and survived, but I still feel that Washington could have warned us of an impending attack. Since then I have not trusted our government totally."

27
Water Tender Second Class Emil T. Beran
USS *Allen*

Emil Beran quit the Hadley Vocational School in Saint Louis, Missouri, during his second year because he became more interested in girls than mechanics and because, in his words, "I don't think I done too good at school." Moreover, his family was poor and could ill afford to keep him at Hadley when he could have been working to help them make it through the Great Depression.

Born on August 22, 1916, in Saint Louis, Beran joined one of the four local naval reserve divisions, the Thirty-fifth, in 1937. The division was an engineering group, and, when it was activated in January 1941, Beran entered the service as a fireman on the USS *Allen* (DD66). His skill and fearlessness in managing the ship's boiler got him promoted to water tender second class by the time of the attack. Part of Task Force Four, which was responsible for the security of the Hawaiian Sea Frontier, the *Allen* had the duty of antisubmarine patrol in the waters around the islands.

The ship was a World War I two-stack, split-deck destroyer. Beran said: "It was fairly seaworthy, but we had a lot of work to do to keep it in shape. It looked like an old Model-T Ford." Despite considerable tension between the ship's 135 Navy regulars and 50 naval reservists, morale was fairly high. When resentment flared, Beran noted, "you'd say to them: 'You god-damned regulars couldn't get a job, and you came in here to eat and sleep.' Sometimes it would get quite serious, and other times you'd just shake it off and forget it and shake hands."

On liberty following the usual weekly patrol tour, Beran, who was known by his first and middle initials, was quite a "rounder." As he said, "Being a young man and a week away from a woman and some drink, why, the first thing we'd look for was a drink and then for the girlies at houses of prostitution, or stables, as we called them." He added that each group or ship had its favorite stable and that the sailors he "bummed with always headed for the New Senator Hotel." However, nearly all seamen, when first ashore, gathered at the Black Cat, a bar near the Honolulu YMCA. The latter was an economical place to stay for those given overnight liberty.

During the week before the attack, the *Allen*, which was having trouble with its sonar, returned to port on Wednesday, the 3d. Beran believed that they stayed on full alert for several days after docking, because a U.S. submarine had reported sighting the Japanese fleet near Hawaii. The craft, he stated, "lost sight of the fleet in heavy weather. They ran into storms, and, when they finally up-periscoped, they couldn't see a thing in clear weather."

Despite what Beran thought had been an advanced warning, on Saturday, the *Allen*'s skipper canceled the alert and granted his ship full liberty while the vessel was fumigated. Since two thirds of the crew went ashore, only sixty to seventy men remained on board. Beran was one of these. He kept an auxiliary watch to maintain enough steam for power to the galley and bathrooms.

At the time of the attack, the *Allen* was moored next to the USS *Chew*, a short distance west of the *Nevada* and just north of Ford Island. The interview illustrates the degree to which many sailors at first believed that the attack was just another drill.

"I had the 0400 to 0800 watch. My relief came down at twenty minutes until 8:00, and breakfast was already served in the compartment, so I had to take my plate and go up to the galley. I got two eggs and some bacon and bread and coffee, and I went down to the compartment to eat.

"All of a sudden, I heard gunfire, not too much gunfire, but bombs bursting. Well, they were constantly training, towing targets and firing their guns at flying targets. Then I heard the damnedest bang under the hull of the ship. I'm eating, and this machinist's mate first class from Minnesota, named Gross, came running down and went to his footlocker to get his money; he was lucky at craps, and he had quite a bit in there. He said: 'The Japs are here, and they're sinking the fleet!' I said: 'Oh, boy!' I tramped my feet and said: 'Here I go!' I thought he was kidding.

"I looked at the man's face, and I could see fear on him. He was pale, and his eyes were wide, and his lips were sort of trembling as he ran by.

"About that time the General Quarters bell went off, which means man your battle stations. I took an extra bite and jumped up, and I ran up the ladder and stepped out on the deck, and I saw this Jap plane flying by. He must have been about one hundred yards away. I could see his teeth, and he was grinning, and he had his flight glasses on. I thought: 'Well, this is it,' and I stepped out.

"Three weeks before the attack my GQ station was changed. Then I had been on a gun. I was number one shellman, which means I was the one that pushed the antiaircraft shell into the barrel. I was transferred to the fireroom due to the chief water tender's recommendation that I was not afraid of boilers.

"So I went down, and the man I was to relieve, Rominick, he had a pair of boobs on him like about a twenty-one-year-old woman. We called him 'Tits.' He was sitting down there, and he was writing a letter, and he would look up sometime at the steam gauge and the water gauge on the boiler. He said: 'What is it? A drill?' Naturally, he believed that.

"To back up a little bit, when I stepped out of the hatch, the *Arizona* was already burning, and the *Oklahoma* had a ninety-degree list and was turning very slowly and burning fiercely. That's the one that capsized completely, rolled over.

"Getting back to Tits Rominick—he says: 'Is it a drill?' I said: 'Get off your ass! The Japs are sinking the fleet! Make up some burners! Let's get up some steam!' The burners put the oil through an atomizer, under pressure, that forms the gas that burns.

"Between him and me, we had a full head of steam up in nine minutes, which was against regulations. Normally, you should build up steam in a period of twenty minutes to half an hour, but it was an emergency. The entire fireroom was under pressure, and we had to go through an air chamber, or an air lock, which meant you would open a hatch topside, step on this ladder, pull the hatch closed, dog it down, go down, and then you had to undog this other hatch before you went into the fireroom, and then you went down the ladder to the floor plates.

"I remember, as I closed the first hatch on myself, I said something like: 'God save us! This is the last time that I'm ever going to see the sunshine!' I gave myself up then and there. I was thinking, as just a small potato in the military: 'Well, if they're here now, they're really here in force!' I pictured an invasion with such terrific bombardment that there wouldn't be a ship afloat.

"One guy became so frightened that he tried to crawl under a locker on deck that only had about a six-inch space—the locker where they stored their movie machines and projectors. He was so scared—frightened—that he actually tried to get under there, and he couldn't get his ass under. Another guy, a yeoman, Johnson, who was regular Navy, a con man and a sharpie, he put on a tin hat, as they termed a helmet, the old World War I style, and he was actually shaking in that thing, and he looked comical. The thing was just flopping around on his head, almost making a complete circle because he was shaking.

"Then the officer came down and he stood there with a .45. He was pale, and he had a life preserver on and a big .45. I think he was more scared than we were. I don't know whether he mistrusted us or what, but there was no telling what he was going to do. He probably had orders to shoot us or try to stop us if we panicked and tried to run out, but that was the farthest thing from my mind. I was trained to do what I was doing, exactly, under emergency.

"So we had 66 men aboard. All of sudden, we got word: 'Prepare for sea! Get under way!' Our regular complement, I

would say, was 175 to 200 men.* We had approximately one
third of the men assigned to the ship, because two thirds had
liberty. They were prepared to fumigate the ship, to delouse it.
They took these canisters of gas that were supposed to kill the
bugs and threw them over the side. Everything that was topside
went over the side, including the mess tables where we were
supposed to eat. With axes they cut the hawsers that had us tied
up, we backed out, and we went to sea.

"I was down below, but I believe the raid was over by then.
In fact, it was, because it must have been close to 10:00 in the
morning when we pulled out. The raid had been under way since
five minutes until 8:00. When I went below, they were still
concentrating on the battleships and cruisers. They wanted bigger game, thinking that the carriers were in there, which was
their primary target. Like I said, being just a small spud in the
Navy, with ammunition ships and tankers all around the *Allen*,
I pictured that the island was going to be blown to pieces. I
expected the Japs to do their damage and neutralize as much as
they could and then have their landing barges out there so they
would land troops, which would have been very easy for them
to do.

"Anyway, we pulled out to sea, and I think everybody in the
back of their heads thought: 'We're hauling ass! We're going
home to the States!' We were thinking that. Yet, two thirds of
your mind was thinking: 'That's not it! We're out looking for
these bastards,' which we were.

"To get back to the duty aboard ship—I would spend two
hours in the fireroom, which was my duty station, two hours
topside manning guns, passing ammunition, lookout, or whatever was necessary. No sleep at all. We were fed on the run—
coffee and sandwiches. Whenever they'd think they missed you,
they'd bring you a couple of sandwiches. Nobody was interested
too much in food.

"We got out that night, and we ran into the *New Orleans*, a
cruiser. In the meantime, I guess, militarily being way down
the line, the Hawaiian Sea Frontier, we were not given our recognition—wartime signals and code name. The *New Orleans*

---

*The *Allen*'s crew consisted of 100 to 115 men.

already had theirs. So they're blinking lights at each other. Their skipper's telling the signalman what to blink to us, and our skipper was telling ours what to do. Our skipper knows that's the *New Orleans*, but their skipper didn't recognize us. Finally, they got on what is termed a ship's phone, and they talked to each other. Our skipper told them: 'Goddamn it, I had six tubes on you!' The skipper of the *New Orleans* said: 'Well, goddamn it, I had 8-inchers on you!' So there would have been two ships blown out of the water, just like that.

"I don't recall if it was two or three days that we stayed out, actually looking for the Japanese. They went one way, and we were cruising around and looking the other way. I'm not positive on the time.

"Anyway, while we were at sea, that evening, December 7— it was dark—we saw firing over the island, which we took to be another attack. It was antiaircraft guns and tracers. By tracers, they shoot up the red ones, and then they follow that pattern. That was when we heard that [Admiral William F.] Halsey and his carrier were coming in. Usually, they land the airplanes first, because there is always that danger of the ship being sabotaged or running into a mine. Being at war already, a submarine could have been at the entrance. As these planes were coming in, some happy trigger-fingered guy on the island just hollered: 'Enemy planes! Air raid!' He fired one shot, and all of a sudden the whole island opened up. We couldn't see the planes, but we could see the shell fire.

"We pictured it as another attack, thinking: 'I'm damned glad we're here at sea! What good would we be there as a stationary target tied up to another ship?' We talked a lot. It was just: 'Well, what did you do?' 'Were you scared?' 'Did you shit in your pants?' We said stuff like that, as we passed. There wasn't too much of that. I think we were all, deep in our hearts, scared about what had actually happened, knowing that they came close to five thousand miles and practically snuck in on us, right through the open door. We didn't know at that time about the foul-up of communications and things like that. When you see it now, you almost think it was a damned sellout by some politician to get us in the damned thing. Being a good Republican, I always blamed Roosevelt.

"I was topside, off duty, when we came back, and I could see the damage that was done. The ships were still smoking and burning. We would get word on how many battleships were hit. We knew that the *Oklahoma* and the *Arizona* were totally disabled, sunk. The *Nevada* beached itself. The *Utah* was turned over. You could see the damage on others that had holes in their decks. The *Cassin* and *Downes*, they were in the floating dry dock with the *Pennsylvania*.* The *Shaw* was in the floating dry dock, and her bow was shot off and exploded. In fact, one of the reserves from Saint Louis was killed fighting fires on the *Cassin* and *Downes* when some of the ammunition exploded. In fact, there were two of them killed.

"Every Sunday closest to December 7, another fellow and I go and put a little Pearl Harbor marker and a flower on their graves at our National Cemetery in Saint Louis. They don't normally allow flags. Only once a year do they allow flags, and that is Memorial Day. Usually, the Boy Scouts or different organizations put a flag on each grave. There is a constant big flag always flying over National Cemetery.

"Oh! Oil and debris were floating all over the place when we came back. Our crew was scattered all over on different ships. Some of them helped fight fires, like the two I said, and some of them worked at the hospitals bringing in the wounded. Others were just jerked aboard different ships. We had some that were on the cruisers *Phoenix* and *Detroit*. Whenever a ship was pulling out, they'd jump into a whaleboat, and, if they couldn't get to ours, they just went aboard another and performed regular duties like they would on our own ship.

"When we came in and saw the damage, it was heartbreaking because a lot of men died. I think in every enlisted man's mind they more or less thought somebody sold us down the river. To this day, I don't believe that I've seen all the facts and read them. There was a foul-up in Washington. I believe it was just the stupidity of our politicians and State Department. We had it in Korea, and we had it in Vietnam. Our politicians are damned fools. They just don't realize what is going on. When a military

---

*The *Cassin*, *Downes*, and *Pennsylvania* were in a graving dock, a type of dry dock used especially for cleaning the underwater surfaces of a ship.

man is smart and tries to tell them, they say: 'Listen, you are in the service, Buddy. You'd better keep your mouth shut.' And like good school boys, military men just go ahead with what they're told to do.''

After the attack, Beran was with the *Allen* in the Pacific as she supported aircraft carriers and landing forces. He served at Truk, Palau, the Marianas, and the Philippines and on the cruiser *Biloxi* at the Bonin Islands. He was discharged on September 28, 1945. Back in Saint Louis he went to work for the Anheuser-Busch Brewing Company. Thirty-six years later, in 1981, he retired, and he currently lives in his hometown.

28
Yeoman Second Class Kenneth Isaacs and Eliza Isaacs
USS *Dobbin*

The mysterious and unexplained disappearance of an officer from the destroyer tender *Dobbin* (AD3), five months before the Pearl Harbor raid, set Kenneth Isaacs to thinking after the attack. According to Isaacs, in July 1941 the ship's captain went ashore to hike in the Aiea hills and never returned.

"We had a Commander [Thomas C.] Latimore come aboard in about April 1941. He was from Navy Intelligence. He was captain of the ship—a commander in the Navy but captain of our ship. They had transferred him from Washington, D.C. He was a very quiet, solitary, and elderly man, and he would take hikes up into the Aiea hills, which were surrounded by sugarcane and pineapple fields. The area was not built up with fortifications as at the present time. It was a real wilderness. In some of the areas the only way you could get in was just cut your way through the brush.

"Captain Latimore came back to the ship one time, and he had an arm wound which he said that he had hurt in a fall. For a while he had his arm in a cast. It healed, and then in July he left the ship again, wearing a khaki uniform and an old hat and carrying a walking stick which, evidently, was a souvenir to him from somewhere else. And he didn't come back to the ship.

"After we realized that he was absent, well, we sent searching parties of about three hundred men from the area and from the ships in the harbor. The Honolulu police and the Army were notified. They had tremendous searching parties out, and they searched for approximately a month trying to locate him, but they never did find him. They took their trackers from Schofield, who were familiar with the area, with dogs, and they didn't find anything.

"There was no evidence of his remains anywhere. At first we figured it was a result of foul play. Later on, some of the talk was that he went up into the hills and ran into Japanese spotters who were plotting the fleet, and they killed him and did away with him, or we had a feeling that what he might have discovered had caused him to leave the area because of his intelligence background and take the information with him to Washington."

Exactly what happened to Latimore has never been explained; he was declared officially dead on July 19, 1942. The incident has been forgotten by almost everyone except Isaacs. He and his wife, Eliza, had been in the Hawaiian Islands a little more than one year before the disappearance. Married on July 13, 1939, in San Diego, Isaacs was sent to Pearl Harbor aboard the *Dobbin* soon after his wedding. Eliza did not follow until June 1940. At first they shared an apartment briefly with another sailor and his wife on Beretania Street. They next moved to their own apartment near downtown Honolulu, where they were living when the attack occurred.

For two people born in southern Illinois, the islands were a pleasure. Eliza called living there "real wonderful." Social life involved picnicking on Waikiki Beach, sunbathing, swimming, visiting with other naval personnel and their wives, and attending free sporting events—for midwesterners this meant especially basketball—and free shows. They were particularly impressed by the islands' bands, including that of Harry Owens, the composer of "Sweet Leilani." Mrs. Isaacs also worked at a large department store, the Liberty House.

Isaacs was born on July 13, 1915, in the section of West Frankfort, Illinois, called Little Egypt. His father was killed in a coal-mining accident when Ken was three years old, and his mother raised the family. In 1935, unable to find work, Ken joined the Civilian Conservation Corps and served two years. It was during this time that he met his future wife in Lawrenceville, Illinois, where she had been born on September 19, 1909. Isaacs joined the Navy in 1937 and extended his tour for two years in September 1941.

On the weekend of the Pearl Harbor attack, he began liberty at noon on Saturday, left the *Dobbin*, and arrived home about 2:00 P.M. After a nap, he and Eliza visited Bland McConnell and his wife, a Navy family they had known since their time in San Diego. They came home early that evening, listened to the radio, and went to bed at 10:00 P.M. Ken Isaacs's interview begins about one hour before the attack.

"We slept real sound. Mrs. Isaacs got up first. Normally, she would click the radio on, but she didn't. We feel that she was up around 7:00. She went ahead and fixed breakfast, and then she called me, and then she turned the radio on. The announcement came over the radio: 'All military personnel, report to your ships or stations!'

"The radio did not announce an attack. We were approximately ten miles from Pearl Harbor. It was only about a five-minute walk from downtown Honolulu, where I would normally catch the bus or a jitney to the ship landing. We did not hear explosions or anything of that nature.

"I said: 'Honey, it's just a drill. It's just a drill.' And I think I started to go out the door, and she said: 'Well, I already have breakfast. Why don't you sit down and eat breakfast?' So I sat down and ate breakfast. I still felt that it was a drill.

"I left the apartment probably at a quarter after eight. Then, as I walked out of the house, and I had gone maybe two blocks, I realized all of a sudden it wasn't a drill. I realized that there was just no tomorrow, that we were faced with a war, and we were going to have that problem, and I started running. I'd run a while and I'd walk a while the five minutes that it took to get down to the bus or jitney station. There was a jitney there. There were four or five sailors around. We all piled into it, and we headed toward Pearl Harbor and the landing where the ship would pick us up. Even at that time, there were planes overhead, and you could hear strafing. Even in Honolulu there was noise going on, so I knew this was for real. It wasn't a play thing.

"So, after we got in the jitney, it was sort of a hectic ride. He was moving as fast as he could, and everybody was excited. We all wanted to get back to our ship or station. We tried to pay the driver, and he wouldn't take any money. We had to go through the gate there with the marines. There was no problem. They let us go right in. We could have been Japanese agents, and we would have gone right on in because everything was thoroughly mass confusion.

"Then we came down to the landing dock where normally our liberty boats would come in and pick us up. I lucked out. There was a fifty-foot motor launch that came along from our ship. They picked me up, and we started back toward the ship.

"As we went back, we turned facing Battleship Row—the area that the torpedo planes came down on. As we turned facing it, I saw this big hulk that looked like a barge or something that had been turned over. There were a couple of other men in the liberty boat with me, and we were discussing it, and coxswain said: 'Well, that's the battleship *Oklahoma*.' It was upside down, and it had capsized. The *Arizona* was on fire at that time, and there were still airplanes overhead.

"To see a battleship capsize like that is a horrible thing because you realize how much of a battleship is underwater. It's enormous. You can imagine what the biggest whale would look like. Well, that's what that turned-up *Oklahoma* with the keel sticking up looked like. In the background was the *Arizona* smoking. My thought then was that I didn't know if we were ever going to get out of there alive or not. I had the feeling that it was just the end of the line. The man upstairs had called your number, and you were going to get it before the day was over.

"Going down Battleship Row, facing it, we then veered off to the right, and we went partly around the island, which would be about half a mile, and we were tied up in that area there. The *Dobbin* was tied up to a buoy at the northeast end of Ford Island with its destroyers. There were five destroyers alongside. They called us Destroyer Division Number One, plus the USS *Phelps*.

The destroyers that were alongside were the *Blue, Helm,* Hull, Dewey, Worden, MacDonough,* and *Phelps.* They were tied alongside. We could nest as many as wanted to nest on one side of us. There were several other nests of ships that were tied up to other buoys thereabouts, too.

"The motor launch I was on was not strafed. The harbor was full of oil, lots of oil. It was afire around the *Arizona* and where the battleships were located. It was burning—the water was burning. The *Oklahoma* was leaking oil, and, of course, it was on fire. The torpedo planes had done their damage, but there were still Japanese planes overhead. In fact, the *Dobbin* was not attacked by the enemy planes until, oh, 9:10, because their primary targets were the battleships and the dry docks. After they had attacked them, then they were looking for other targets. Of course, one of the reasons they would move to us was because we had an admiral aboard ship, and with an admiral aboard ship, he has his flag. They knew that they were hitting a command ship of the Navy, which they actually preferred to do.

"I would say that I arrived at the *Dobbin* at 9:30. Coming aboard, the thing that they handed you first was a life jacket. The next thing they handed you was a helmet, and the next thing was a gun. They were well organized for a destroyer tender, which normally is not a fighting ship.

"We had a very good commander who was a repair officer. I remember he was at the gangplank when we came aboard. His name was Skinner. He was a lieutenant commander, a naval academy graduate, and the crew respected him a lot. The fact that he was there when you came aboard, it gave you that sense of security. All our motor launches—I imagine we had eight— were in the water picking up survivors, taking them back to their ships, and doing what could be done. We had no small boats aboard our ship at that time. They were in the water doing what they could do.

"The main attack was over when I came aboard. It had occurred twenty minutes earlier. There were still miscellaneous Japanese aircraft overhead. They were still bombing, and our antiaircraft guns were still shooting. At the same time that all

---

*The *Blue* and the *Helm* were not tied alongside the *Dobbin*.

this was going on, we were passing provisions and, more important, ammunition to the destroyers that were still alongside so that they could get under way. All of the destroyers that were alongside of us left with a full complement of provisions and ammunition.

"They headed for sea, and also some of the destroyers were partly dismantled. So all during the attack, and all during the day, we were repairing and getting them ready to go to sea. It took some time, and it was the middle of the afternoon before our ship was completely cleared of the destroyers.

"I went immediately to General Quarters. I was in the deciphering organization. My only job was to carry messages from the deciphering room to the captain. I went to that area, but there was no activity, and, after the man in charge secured me, I was free to report to the navigator, my particular section. I was the only one in the section; I was there as a navigator's yeoman. I had a lieutenant in the reserves who was the navigator.

"We had three naval reserve officers. A dentist came aboard, and it later turned out that naval life wasn't for him. He had been at Coronado, California, servicing the teeth of the wealthy, and the Navy wasn't his dish. We had two merchant marine officers who were in the reserves come aboard, and the one who was my boss was a J. F. Acker, Jr. He was a fine, young navigator and a fine, young officer. He was a lieutenant junior grade. We had an ensign aboard who never adapted to the Navy life. He was an old-time merchant marine officer, and they are really something to behold.

"Most of the officers had been ashore, but most had returned. Our two doctors were aboard in the sick bay. The commanding officer lived aboard ship. Our executive officer lived ashore, but he was back aboard ship. I would say that by the time I was back that most of all of the officers were aboard ship.

"The *Dobbin* sustained only shrapnel damage. As far as a direct hit, we didn't receive any. The material damage was minor. We lost a motorboat hull that we were repairing. We had a number of small holes through the decks, bulkhead, beams, and we had damage to three radio transmitters. We were set up for tremendous communications as a flagship. Of course, we were able to repair all of that damage except for the motorboat hull, which was declared a total loss.

"Action on the *Dobbin* never stopped from the time I got aboard all through the night. We had a continual influx of survivors from other ships. We took on two hundred Navy men from the USS *Raleigh*, which was a cruiser. We had other survivors who, when the destroyers got under way, were men still ashore, and we took them aboard and logged them in and fed them and berthed them until we could get them back to their own ships."

While Ken Isaacs made his way to his ship, his wife learned about the attack. She describes her activities on December 7.

"I went about cleaning up and wasn't aware we were being attacked. I went out to the trash can, and the landlady's daughter said: 'Isn't it awful about the Japanese attacking us!' That was my first knowledge, so I went back in, I listened to the radio, and they said: 'The rising suns have been sighted on the planes' wings! Stay in the house! Get off the streets! Don't look up!' So what do we all do? All the Navy wives in the house go out and look up to see what's happening.

"Then we just more or less got together and talked. The landlady's husband was a Navy Yard worker, and they had to go back, too. He left with his house shoes on because he thought he'd be gone about thirty minutes or so. Late that afternoon, Mrs. Keyes decided to go over to her mother's, and she told all of her tenants that they could stay in her apartment because there was a telephone there. We kept thinking we might get word.

"So we stayed there. We just talked and kept wondering what was going to happen. That night was the longest I ever put in. A woman from across the street came over there, and she was very excitable. She stayed with us for the night, and she got real upset at every little movement. Anyway, during the night it was real moonlight, as clear as could be, and she'd look out the window and see a shadow of a tree, and she'd want to call the police. She finally did call them. Then we insisted that she not call them anymore because we might need them, and they wouldn't come. But they told us on the radio to go about our business the next day. We were to go to our job, and, if we didn't, we were to go about normally.

"Along about 3:00 in the morning, there was an elderly Japanese couple that went down around Circle Lane, and this lady from across the street got so excited she wanted to call the police again, and she was 'Blank, blank, blanking' us because we wouldn't let her.

"One other girl worked at Liberty House, so we decided we'd try to get some rest. About that time Mr. Keyes managed to get home, and we told him where his wife was. He left, and I guess he arrived over there all right. About 4:00 A.M. some activity happened over around the waterworks, which was not too far from us, and they fired their machine guns. Man! You should have heard this woman! She was trying to put us all down on the floor, and finally she said: 'Well, if you want to get your heads blown off, go ahead and do it!' It was a real experience. It really was.

"We were worrying, of course, about our husbands. We were wondering. We kept thinking: 'Well, we'll get some word. We'll get some word.' But I didn't get any word from him until a week later. He had written a letter and mailed it that night. It took a week to get there. When it came it was cut right in two. I don't know why. Half of it was about four lines by four lines.

"I went to work the next day. The Liberty House was turned into sort of a guard station. The upstairs could be blacked out, and they had patrols for the city, you know, night patrols. Anyway, they could feed those people. The Liberty House, then, became sort of a kitchen for the change of the guards—the civilian guards.''

Shortly after the attack, Mrs. Isaacs, like most naval dependents, was ordered back to the United States. In the concluding portions of the interview, first Eliza and then Ken explain their feelings about the Japanese in light of what happened.

Eliza Isaacs: "One of the cashiers in the department store where I was working was a little Japanese-American woman, and when they were outlining the areas that we could go to in case of an attack, Jane said to me: 'You can come to my house,' because it was in that area. They kidded me quite a bit about that—that a Japanese offered me a place to come to in case of an attack. But she was a Japanese-American.

"My attitude toward Japanese didn't change. There was one maid in the Liberty House that I didn't like very well to begin with. When the convoys left there after the attack, or when they began to move the families out, you could see from the top of the Liberty House where the ships were pulling in to tie up. She and one of the other janitors would get together and talk. They'd be hanging around and trying to listen, it seemed to me, and I feel that she was maybe spying. She probably wasn't, but that was my feeling."

Ken Isaacs: "I really hated the Japanese, and I think the one thing that really sparked that hate was something there that afternoon when I went back to the fantail of the ship, and we had two canvas covers with bodies. They were fellows that I had known and who had been killed during the attack. We lost three men off the ship. They were on a three-inch antiaircraft gun. The moment of truth probably more than anything else, and the hatred that one would feel, really came out because these were fellows that I had known from the time they'd come aboard ship, being in the personnel office. One of the men I had worked with on deck when I was a deckhand. You felt at that point that anything Japanese or anything pertaining to them was bad. If I'd had fifty Japanese standing in front of me, and they'd given me a gun to mow them down, I would have mowed them down!"

Following Mrs. Isaacs's return to the United States, Yeoman Second Class Isaacs served in the Battle of the Coral Sea, where he aided in transporting bombs to the fleet's aircraft carriers. In 1943 he transferred to an attack passenger ship that carried assault troops in the battles at Ulithi and Suva Bay. He returned to Portland, Oregon, to help commission the USS *Arneb* and later the USS *Barnstable*. He left the military on September 13, 1945.

In civilian life, Isaacs worked first for the Bureau of Internal Revenue in San Francisco; then, for two years beginning in 1948, he and his wife served with the special services branch of the Army in Japan, Ken as an accountant, Eliza as a secretary. Ken eventually began a career with Trail Mobile, Inc., and transferred to San Antonio, Texas. He died on October 30, 1976. Eliza, who still lives in San Antonio, said of her experience: "Because of Pearl Harbor I understand the feelings and emotions of war, and I can understand the feelings of all people who must suffer it."

29
Machinist's Mate First Class Rudolph P. Zalman
USS *Medusa*

Not every young couple in Honolulu enjoyed its resort atmosphere in late 1941. Rudolph Zalman and his wife found it hard to make ends meet on his Navy pay and the small salary she earned. Married in October 1941, they lived in a modest cottage in the Punch Bowl area, and much of their free time was spent at home. They were saving to buy a car so that Rudy would not have to ride the bus back and forth to the pier where he caught a boat almost daily to his station on the USS *Medusa* (AR1).

Zalman, who was born in Mart, Texas, near Waco on January 9, 1911, joined the Navy in 1931, about one year after finishing high school. His decision was an easy one. The family farm was too small to employ him gainfully, and he did not want to work for one dollar per day as a farm laborer. He chose the Navy because he had a relative who had served in it and because he thought that it offered the best chance to learn a skill. He was right. After boot camp in San Diego, he spent nine months learning to be a machinist's mate at the Navy's technical trade school in Norfolk, Virginia.

He first served aboard gunboats and destroyers in the Asiatic Fleet off Shanghai, but in 1939 he was assigned to the USS *Medusa*, a battleship repair vessel with a complement of welders, shipfitters, machinists, foundry workers, and other men derisively called shallow-bottom sailors. Zalman resented the epithet, which was given to sailors on ships that rarely left port. The *Medusa* joined the Hawaiian Detachment at Pearl Harbor in early 1941.

Although Zalman usually received liberty three out of every

four days, during the two weeks before December 5 he was continuously aboard ship since his vessel was under Condition Two, or ready for attack. That Friday, however, he was given leave at 6:00 P.M. and went home. The next day a neighboring couple and the Zalmans attended a football game between the University of Hawaii and Willamette College of Salem, Oregon. After the game the couples went to the Zalmans' home, ate, and had a few drinks before their friends left. Rudy read for a while and then joined his wife in bed at about 11:00 P.M.

The events that Machinist's Mate Zalman relates in the following pages are possibly typical of what happened to quite a few seamen caught in Honolulu on the day of the attack. He made his way from his home to his ship, saw a great deal of history in the making, but affected it very little, if at all. The battle was over when he boarded the *Medusa*.

"The first thing I heard just before 8:00 was BOOM! BOOM! BOOM! Then I heard sirens going—fire engines. I said to myself: 'That must be some fire they are going to.' My wife said: 'Go out there and stop that boy who's throwing that ball up against the gable of the roof, because it's irritating me.'

"So I got out of bed, put on a robe, walked out the back, and looked around. Nobody was there. No kid was out there throwing a ball. But I heard the guns sounding off up at Fort Armstrong. Then I stepped out and looked toward Pearl Harbor, and there was a haze, smoke, and so forth. I saw the puffs of antiaircraft firings, and that BOOM! BOOM! was the antiaircraft shells going off. So I said: 'What in the world is going on?'

"Then, while I was taking another look, I saw three planes swoop down. They came over the Punch Bowl hill. I immediately recognized them; they were Japanese. They were flying at about one thousand feet, but they were low enough that you could read the insignia and know immediately. There were three, and they veered off toward Pearl Harbor.

"Meanwhile, a neighbor across the street came running up and said that the Japanese were attacking Pearl Harbor. I liked to dropped dead. I said: 'No way!' He said: 'Yes, they are!'

"We had what they called a second level underneath our house because it was built on the slope of a hill. Our basement was quite large, and that's where I kept my whites. I had my uniform there. So the first thing I did was rush down there and start putting them on. I tried to get one leg in but managed to get two in one leg, and so it went back and forth. Meanwhile, my wife was screaming: 'You're not going out there!' I said: 'Yes, I am!' and I did!

"I finally got dressed, got my white hat on, but had my neckerchief in my hand. So I rushed out down to Beretania Street and turned right. What I had in mind was to catch a bus down at the Black Cat Cafe, where all the buses left from to go to Pearl Harbor. It was a little bit farther than a mile to the Black Cat. I got to Beretania, and I thought I'd run into some sailors. But I didn't see sailor one. I said: 'What the heck is happening? I wonder if they called everyone to battle stations last night, and they missed me.'

"So I started running, and I was running down the street when WHAM! right behind me. I don't know to this day whether it was a bomb or one of our antiaircraft shells, maybe from a three-inch gun. I was passing this Chevrolet agency, the only one in Honolulu at the time, and the shrapnel hit above me and knocked a hole in the agency. The last time I passed through Honolulu was in 1954, and that hole was still in the same building. I wanted to go in and tell the guy: 'You ought to save that hole for a souvenir. That's my souvenir.' You can laugh about it now, but at that time things got serious because I saw a man go down. I believe he was a Chinese national. He was in the middle of the street, about 50 or 60 feet behind me. I just kept on going.

"My mind was to get back to the ship. A little bit farther along, here came a chief and a couple of other sailors in a Ford or Chevrolet. He said: 'You want a ride?' I said: 'Yeah.' So I hopped in, and we're going down the street just about where the fire station was, and there was another explosion. I don't know what it was, but the car's engine caught fire. So we bailed out. Two of us went one way, and I don't know what happened to the chief.

"We headed up the street toward the hills, a short cut to Pearl Harbor. A young fellow came along with a station wagon, and we got in and were rolling along pretty well. We got a glimpse of the fires and everything. I said to myself: 'Well, all the oil tanks must be burning.' I was surprised later that the oil tanks, the oil supply, were untouched.

"We came out in the housing area and tried to get to the main gate at Pearl Harbor. They had us blocked off. I think the Army had the road blocked off. They were firing, so we took an intermediate road over to the main road from Honolulu to Pearl Harbor.

"It was a little bit rough going until we got to the gate. Of course, the Marines were already at the gate with their machine guns. Somewhere near there a 3-inch antiaircraft gun was firing. With the noise and the dust and the marines waving us on, we went in as if we were going to catch a liberty boat back to the ship. The second attack was under way when we got there.

"Another fellow and I headed out toward the receiving station, a block away from the main gate. We went around the building, looked up, and a plane came in firing. We looked over to the right, and three planes came in from that direction. They were firing. We noticed a dump truck that had been turned over, and it had a steel bed and access to get underneath it. Somehow or another, and I forget to this day how, we managed to get underneath that dump truck bed. It was right there on the landing where our boats came in.

"We remained under the truck about four or five minutes, until all the shooting was over with. Our next goal was to catch a boat back to the ship. So we managed to get a motor launch, a fifty-footer, and we got out in the channel and headed back. There were people from different ships on board, and they hollered out to the coxswain which ship they were going to go to. So we went out, and it took an hour to get to the *Medusa*. We had to stop, turn around, do this and that.

"Meanwhile, I noticed the hull of a ship was sticking up. I said to myself: 'Well, that's the USS *Indianapolis*,* the cruiser, that was always anchored at a fjord in the channel on our starboard side. It never dawned on me that we were south of Ford Island. Not then, but later on, as we went alongside the *Arizona*,

---

*The USS *Indianapolis* was not at Pearl Harbor on December 7 but was part of Task Force Three, which was reconnoitering in the area around Johnston Island at the time.

I noticed that it was the *Oklahoma* that was turned over; it was not the *Indianapolis*. The *Indianapolis* managed to get out.

"Meanwhile, while we were coming down this channel, we looked over toward the entrance, and there was the *Nevada*. She was just about ready to block the channel. Then we noticed that a couple of tugboats hurried over there, and they did just manage to turn it. They were fighting fires everywhere. I think the *Oklahoma* had the *Maryland* penned in. The *Maryland* had no way to get out. So we went on and went past where the *Arizona* was burning. The *Vestal* was over there, a bomb had dropped through the holds, and it was halfway sunk on the starboard side.

"Through a clearing I saw a bomber above. I didn't know that it was one of our bombers coming from the States. I said: 'Uh-oh, we've had it!' Talk about someone being scared—we were. We'd seen all these battleships and cruisers burning. The *California* was settling down, the *Oklahoma* turned over, the *Arizona* burning, the *Maryland* penned in.

"Then, going around Ford Island, I saw the *Raleigh*, which was a four-stacker cruiser, and it was down at the stern, but it seemed to be in action. Further on was the *Utah*. The Navy used that as its target ship. The deck had heavy timbers on it, and it looked, coming over the horizon at a distance, like an aircraft carrier. I found out later that that's what the Japanese mistook the *Utah* for. They sent a lot of torpedoes into her, and she overturned. She laid with her deck out to the midstream. I said: 'Next thing, the Japanese Navy will be firing on us.'

"Well, we went around the island and kept on going until we got back to our ship.* We passed the *Curtiss*, which had a fire on the topside, and they were fighting it. We found out later that a Japanese dive-bomber crashed on them when they shot it down. When I got back to the ship, I told the fellows about all of this, but they didn't believe it at all. They couldn't believe that the battleships were sunk or anything like that.

"I was anxious to know if the Japanese fleet was coming. That puzzled me. Of course, all that day there were rumors that they landed paratroopers and captured the water system,

---

*The *Medusa* was anchored off Pearl City near the Middle Loch, slightly behind the *Curtiss*.

and they had landed at Kaneohe Bay on the other end of the island, and that there was sabotaging going on. I mean this wasn't hard to believe.''

Once aboard ship, Zalman took up his battle station, which was in damage control on a lower deck. That night he listened to the wild firing that occurred, which he likened to the sound of an air gun or chip hammer, a pneumatic tool for removing paint, being used on the side of the ship. Following the attack, he worked a seven-day week, running lathes and milling machines and making smaller parts for the battleships that were under repair prior to being refloated.

For the remainder of World War II, Zalman served in the Pacific theater, most of the time on the *Medusa*. He stayed in the Navy until July 1, 1954, when he retired after twenty-three years of service. As a civilian, he worked for Phillips Petroleum Company and later the Hercules Powder Company. He eventually returned to the region where he had been raised and, on September 1, 1987, died at his home in Waco.

Chapter V

Hickam Field, Fort Kamehameha, and Tripler Army Hospital

Hickam Field and Fort Kamehameha were located adjacent to each other on the east side of the channel that led into Pearl Harbor. To enter the fort, one had to pass through the main gate at Hickam and drive south along the length of the airfield to where "Fort Kam" began. It and Fort Weaver, located on the west side of the channel, were the main coastal installations protecting the harbor from attack by sea. Established in 1913, Fort Kamehameha was named for the first monarch of Hawaii, King Kamehameha the Great, who reigned over the islands from 1810 to 1819. The fort was considered a smart installation, something of a showplace. The well-trained artillerymen who manned its coastal guns were useless, however, on December 7. The post had some antiaircraft batteries as well, but these were not manned and were likewise of little value on that day.

Japanese airmen understandably showed minor interest in Fort Kamehameha, for they were not coming by sea to mount a landing or bombardment of a traditional sort. One incendiary bomb burst near some coastal batteries, a mess hall and barracks were damaged, and a Japanese plane crashed into other buildings. Yet the greatest danger came from the machine-gun fire as Japanese planes briefly strafed the area about 8:13 A.M. It was then that soldiers at the camp returned gunfire and shot down at least one enemy plane and perhaps several more.

Hickam Field was of much greater concern to the Japanese, and it received more attention and sustained more damage during the attack than any other installation. Founded as a bomber base, the airfield was built beginning in 1934 and was completed in 1938. It was named for Lieutenant Colonel Horace M. Hickam, who had died in an aircraft accident in Texas in 1934. When the Hawaiian Air Force was organized in late 1940, it took control of all Army Air Corps installations on Oahu, including Hickam.

At the time of the attack, as a precaution against sabotage, planes at Hickam Field were ranged across the warming-up aprons three or four abreast, with 130 feet between the rows and 10 feet from wingtip to wingtip. Hostilities may have started when one Japanese group leader, Lieutenant Commander Kakuchi Takahashi, misjudged the signal for dive-bombers to attack and commenced operations against Hickam and Ford Island at 7:55 A.M. At the time, the air base's strength was in B-17s (Flying Fortresses, four-engine long-range bombers), A-20s (Havocs, twin-engine bombers), obsolete B-18s ("Bols," Douglas twin-engine bombers), and at least one B-24 (Liberator, four-engine long-range bomber) undergoing repairs.

Different descriptions of the attack on Hickam Field exist, but it appears that this first encounter lasted about ten minutes, until 8:05. It began with nine dive-bombers attacking the Hawaiian Air Depot. These were joined by three additional planes, which hit the target from the northwest. A few minutes later, nine more aircraft, approaching from the southeast, bombed the hangar line and were joined by seven more from the east.

The second attack began at 8:25, when nine planes bombed and strafed parked bombers, the technical service building, a large consolidated barracks, a beer hall, a guardhouse, a firehouse, and the number one aqua system, which supplied water for the base. High-altitude bombers appeared a bit later, hitting, among other targets, the baseball diamond, which the Japanese may have believed to be a gasoline storage area. This attack lasted fifteen minutes or more.

Around 9:00 a third attack followed in which Zeros and

dive-bombers strafed planes, repair areas and buildings, the Hawaiian Air Defense Building, the parade ground, and the post exchange. The onslaught ended about 9:10 A.M. A great deal of material, including most of the B-17 and B-18 bombers, was destroyed, and 129 lives were lost in this high-intensity raid.

Tripler Army Hospital, like several other military installations on Oahu, was spared by Japanese pilots intent on more important targets. The hospital, located several miles northeast of Hickam Field and north of but nearer to Honolulu, was undergoing expansion at the time of the attack. As with other hospitals in the area, its work began after the air raid, when the wounded were brought in.

30
Private First Class C. R. ("Jim") Gross
Hickam Field

C. R. ("Jim") Gross entered the service in late 1939 in order to find himself. "I didn't know what I really wanted to do," he said; "I had two and a half years of National Guard, some ROTC in college, and thought I would like military life with the opportunity to go overseas. So I just went in."

Gross was born in Owen County, Indiana, on July 1, 1920; finished high school in Bloomington; and spent one year at Indiana University before joining the Army Air Corps. He trained for two and one-half months at Mitchell Field, on Long Island, New York, before shipping out for Hawaii on the Army transport *Republic*. He sailed down the East Coast, through the Panama Canal, to San Francisco, and then on to the islands. He arrived at Hickam Field on March 20, 1940, and was assigned to the Fifth Bomber Group.

Early in his career he had attended clerk-typist school at Wheeler Field and, after finishing, managed to be transferred from the Air Corps to the Finance Office, an independent branch of the Army in those days. When World War II began he was a private first class in the Finance Department at Hickam, working on payrolls.

On December 6, Gross and a married couple who had befriended him, Bill and Mildred Goodwin, rode the post bus to

Honolulu. As they were leaving Hickam, Jim noticed an anti-aircraft unit arriving from Fort Shafter and remarked that the general alert at his post was reaching a higher level of preparedness. In town the trio shopped for phonograph records and material for a divan cover. The Goodwins also bought a parakeet, birdcage, and stand. They returned by bus at 10:00 P.M. While Mildred worked on the cover the men "had a few drinks and talked." At 2:00 A.M. they went to bed. Gross spent the night at the couple's home, which was located a few blocks from his barracks.

In the following interview, Gross relates the reaction of a noncombatant, a payroll clerk, to the Pearl Harbor attack, and his statements mirror some of the confusion on the part of the Army commanders. He emphasizes the much-discussed bombing and strafing of the Hickam Field Post Exchange (PX), where he took shelter and where he was slightly wounded.

"At 7:55 we were awakened. The first thing that came to my mind was the antiaircraft outfit that they had put on the base the day before. I heard a lot of antiaircraft fire. I couldn't imagine what in the world was going on! I knew the island was under a general state of alert, but I thought this was a very unreasonable time to start anything like that. I tried to hide my head under the pillow and drown out some of the noise. I just stayed there.

"Shortly, I heard Mildred getting up. I thought: 'I hope she goes back to bed, because she's going to get Bill up pretty soon, and when he gets up, then I get up.' She was talking in a very excited manner. The next thing I knew, Bill came bursting through my bedroom door and said: 'Gross, what's the insignia on a Japanese plane?' He had a look of shock on his face that I had never seen before. I said: 'Well, they have the rising sun on their wings and fuselage where we have the star. Why?' And he said: 'Get up, dammit! They're here!'

"I thought he was crazy, but I got up in my BVDs and ran out in the front yard just as the initial attack was pulling off. They were flying in beautiful formation. I'd say they must have been 8,000 to 10,000 feet high. They were directly over Pearl. There was a tremendous antiaircraft barrage that was 2,000 to 3,000 feet below them and not doing a bit of good. Smoke was pouring up from a lot of the facilities on Hickam as well as over Pearl. You could stand in Bill's front yard and throw a rock over the fence into Pearl Harbor. We were about as close to the action as you could have gotten.

"I knew what was taking place, but I really didn't know what to do about it. It was like: 'Holy mackerel! What do I do now?' The one thing that stuck in my mind was: 'I've got to get in uniform.' I'd been in civilian clothes the night before, and I was concerned about getting in uniform. So Mildred had a little bicycle, and I rode that thing back up to our barracks and went in and got dressed.

"None of our people had left the barracks. They were quite excited about what was going on. We had no combat mission. We really didn't know what to do or where to go or what-have-you. The only place we had to go, in fact, was the finance office, and you don't fight a war from the post headquarters building.

"So we started to the headquarters building. We could see the runway from our barracks. You could see a black wall of smoke that you knew was a gasoline and oil fire. I could see, down at the end of the base, the old Hawaiian Air Depot area. I noticed the damage, but I didn't take time to see what the nature of the damage was. We started toward headquarters, and about midway between our barracks and headquarters was the post exchange. I got that far when the second attack came in. I wasn't exactly where I wanted to be. Some of our guys stopped in the exchange to get a cup of coffee.

"We heard later—I don't know if this is true or not—that the original plans for Hickam Field called for the headquarters building to be where the post exchange was eventually located. There had been changes along the way. In any case, the Japanese worked over the PX pretty well. Several of us were in there.

"The PX was sort of a U-shaped building. The main store was on one side, and the cafeteria and snack bar on the other side, opposite it, and the rest rooms and so forth were on the base, or bottom, side. I don't recall where I was when they came back, but I remember trying to find any place to hide. I know that at one point I was curled up under the wash basin in the ladies' rest room. I don't know how long I was there.

"The PX had one of these big walk-in coolers, refrigerated

areas. I know that some of the guys went in there, and they were killed by concussion. Several were wounded. One of the men in our outfit, Marvin Wingrove, from Tucumcari, New Mexico, was in the snack bar drinking coffee, and he got a piece of shrapnel in the calf of his leg and couldn't walk. I got a piece of shrapnel through my left shoulder, two holes about an inch apart, but they didn't hit the bone or anything. I didn't even know I'd been hit. I think it was while I was outside lying up against the building.

"I remember this one plane that looked like he was coming right at me, and I remember that, as he started strafing, I saw the shells going right across the ground. And I thought: 'Holy mackerel! This is it!' I was behind some hedges, shrubbery. I don't know what happened, whether he quit firing or whether one hit in front of me and one hit up on the wall behind me. I was still lying at the side of the building. I never felt that my time was as short as I did when I saw the shells coming.

"I really don't know how long this took. I know that it seemed like a long time, but, as far as putting any specific parameters on it, I really don't know. You sure are glad when something like that is over. It let up enough for us to run over to headquarters. The attack was still going on. They just diverted their attention somewhere else.

"As I was going over there, I remember seeing this guy whom I had known for a long time, who was a professional wrestler, standing out in the middle of the parade ground holding a .30-caliber machine gun in his arms, firing at the aircraft. He lived through the attack, and I think he got credit for knocking one down. I was amazed at this guy. He was always somewhat of a character around the base. Everybody knew him, a great, big fellow. I think he weighed 225, 230 pounds. This was one of the most amazing things I ever saw. It sticks in my mind.

"We got over to the office and were issued old World War I–type helmets, a .45-caliber pistol, and a gas mask. I had a big red spot on my shirt from where the shrapnel had entered down through my pocket. It didn't soak through my pocket, but I had this bloody left shoulder.

"It was decided by somebody that we should get some of the women and children off the base. So Goodwin and I went down and picked up these families, those of Master Sergeant Rutherford, the chief clerk, and Captain Charles H. Miles, the unit's commander, as well as Mildred Goodwin. We picked up a couple of other women; the names I don't remember. We saw one woman running down the street, hysterical. One of the women in the car said she knew her, so we picked her up. We went to the foothills behind Honolulu, where friends of the Goodwins lived. They had a small one-room house, and we barged in with eight or ten people. They had no children, so everything was fine with them.

"As soon as we had done this, we came back to the base. There were still fires along the hangar line, and aircraft were still burning. I recall no fires as far as the barracks area was concerned or the married-couples area. There was damage. There had been a lot of strafing, particularly in the barracks area. This large barracks, which was pretty much the center of Hickam, had many machine-gun holes through it and some shrapnel and the whole bit. There were no windowpanes left in the building. I guess there had been some bombs there, too.

"So when we got back, the captain told me: 'You go to the hospital, because there's a reaction to things like your wound, and I'm not going to have you running around like this.' So I went over, and they put me in bed for the afternoon. I think I got a package of cigarettes and a Baby Ruth candy bar out of it. Later that afternoon, the doctor came around and asked how I was doing. I said: 'Fine.' He took a look at my shoulder, put a new bandage on it, and said: 'Okay, come in in a couple of days and get the bandage changed.' That was the extent of it."

In the concluding paragraphs, Gross comments on the period following December 7 and reflects on the nature of America's surprise by the attack.

"We spent the first night in the headquarters building. Of course, the first few days following the attack were worse than December 7 because of uncertainties and all the rumors we were hearing, that paratroopers had landed, that there were transports on the windward side of the island unloading. We felt the island was going to be in Jap hands in a matter of hours.

"There was a great deal of fear about the possibility of fifth columnist activity. I suppose it was a typical case of American overreaction. It was something we saw in the papers or heard on the radio or this type of thing. It was all secondhand. I saw nothing.

"There were a lot of trigger-happy soldiers and marines that night. There were a lot of fires along the Pearl Harbor area. We got an eerie feeling from the reflections of these flames. I guess we lost about as many aircraft to our own men that night as we had during the day, that is, among those that did get in the air. There were Navy and Army planes lost. There was a safe avenue to come in, but they didn't get around to telling all those gunners about it, I guess.

"We didn't go back to our office for a few days. We were out filling sandbags, working with the ordnance people. I don't remember how long it was, less than a week, but I know that we did go back. We got around to putting out payrolls again in four or five days. Life had to go on; each had to play his own role. We wound up working a lot harder than ever before, on a seven-day basis. When you were working under blackout conditions, and there was no air-conditioning, that could get pretty uncomfortable.

"You hear so much about Pearl Harbor being the epitome of unpreparedness. I don't think that's the case. We had enough over there that we could have defended against this carrier force and knocked them off or suffered very little damage. There's a lot of difference between being alert and being prepared. We were simply not alert. This was the problem. We were not alert.

"It's hard to blame some lieutenant who was on special duty at 8:00 in the morning, when he gets a call from a guy fiddling around with the radar unit. Most of us couldn't even spell radar at that time. You really can't fault that guy.

"Joe Lockard, who supposedly identified the Japanese group coming in, was a pretty good friend of some of the guys in our office. They had come over on the same boat. But radar was one of those newfangled things that nobody knew about. I don't know whether I would have put any faith in it or not.

"I have felt very strongly about this through the years, and I hope that this point is brought out. It was not a matter of being unprepared so much as it was of not being on the alert.''

Jim Gross left the Hawaiian Islands on September 3, 1942, when his enlistment expired. He reentered the service immediately to attend officers candidate school and was commissioned as a second lieutenant on December 9, 1942. In 1945 he was released again and attended the University of Iowa in Iowa City to complete a bachelor of arts degree in economics. He rejoined the Air Force in 1948 and spent another fourteen years before retiring in 1962.

He next worked for several firms, including Republic Aviation and Xerox, before taking a position with the U.S. Civil Service. At the time of this interview, he was employed in the Office of Economic Opportunity in Dallas, Texas. He retired in 1982 but continues his mania for big band music and is currently an officer of the Dallas–Fort Worth Metroplex Big Band Society. He has said that experiencing the attack at Pearl Harbor has had little effect, if any, on his life since. "It is," he adds, "an icebreaker in conversations sometimes, depending upon the circumstances.''

31
Staff Sergeant Frank Luciano
Fort Kamehameha

Frank Luciano was born of immigrant parents in Everett, Massachusetts, a Boston suburb, on June 10, 1921. In 1939 he graduated from high school and, facing bleak economic prospects, joined the U.S. Army. He saw the service as a chance for education, training, and, more important, a job.

Luciano had initially tried to enlist in the Coast Guard but was one-quarter inch too short to meet its standards. He next volunteered for the Marine Corps, but once more was rejected because of physical problems. He had two bad teeth, injured in a boyhood accident. Then the Army checked him over and decided: "You're all right!" Trained at Fort Plattsburg, New York, and Fort Hancock, New Jersey, he was first an infantryman but soon decided that the branch best suited for his purposes was the Coast Artillery.

Reassigned to the Coast Artillery, Luciano requested duty in Hawaii. Although he had seen pictures of the islands and of hula girls, romantic reasons had nothing to do with his choice. "I just wanted to get somewhere," he said, "and to settle down and see if I could learn something. Hawaii was just a good spot." In late April 1940 he began a nineteen-day voyage aboard the World War I transport *Chateau-Thierry* from Brooklyn to Pearl Harbor, passing through the Panama Canal.

Arriving on May 4, Luciano was immediately assigned to the headquarters at Fort Kamehameha. At the time, the fort was the Army's largest Coast Artillery outpost, with a contingent of about twenty-five hundred men, most serving in the Fifteenth, Forty-first, and Fifty-fifth Coast Artillery Battalions. During the next nineteen months, Luciano became a master gunner, involved in many of the functions of a headquarters outfit. He surveyed, gathered data, and made maps for placing the various-sized weapons controlled by Fort Kamehameha, whose soldiers manned all the coastal guns on Oahu. He was also responsible for locating the sixty searchlights used by the Coast Artillery. The units had 12-inch coastal guns, 155-millimeter howitzers, mortars, railway batteries, 16-inch barbette guns, and several rapid-fire antiaircraft weapons. The coastal guns were given personal names, for example, Battery Selfridge or Battery Closson, which were located on opposite ends of Hauula Point.

During maneuvers, Luciano was sometimes aboard ship with a splash camera, taking photographs so that ultimately the gunners could know the patterns being made by the long-range artillery shells they fired at imaginary attacking vessels. At other times, he was in the battery's OP (observation post) plotting incoming ships as information was relayed from forward observers on land, at sea, or in the air. In case of a real assault, Luciano was required to help prepare a 14-inch mortar for firing and then to take his position in the OP.

In the first passage of his interview he discusses what might have happened if the Japanese had tried to land on Oahu on December 7. In this respect, his view differs radically from most Navy personnel interviewed. However, his attitude toward Japanese and Japanese-Americans on Hawaii was fairly typical of most American military men.

"As a master gunner I knew what we could do. A lot of people didn't know. Don't misunderstand me, now. A lot of people said: 'Well, they could have taken us.' I don't think so in a mass invasion, as some people thought, for the simple reason that we had guns all around that island. We could've moved other guns around; we did move some guns around. We had searchlights set up. Inside of two hours, every searchlight could have been lit up. So if the Japanese didn't hit us within three or four hours, no way, and, if they had come at the same time as the attack or just an hour later, I think they might have had one beachhead, but I don't think they could have gotten any further because of the guns we had.

"We never thought they would hit us, because we thought we were too strong. We were strong on that one island, Oahu. Any other Hawaiian island, I would say, No, we couldn't; they would be able to take any one of them.

"We thought that if they were coming in full force, their supply lines would be stretched out so long that I think they would have been vulnerable, and I'm certain that sooner or later we would have annihilated them one way or the other. I think they used common sense in their own judgment. We would have lost quite a few men. Don't misunderstand me. I think we would have lost quite a few men. They may have had a beachhead quite a while before we could get them off of there, but we were closer to our mainland than they were to their mainland.

"I don't think the Japanese in Hawaii would have caused much of a problem. There were a few diehards. We caught a few of them. We knew that. We caught a few at Hickam Field. I went over there to investigate. I was sent on the morning of December 7 by Lieutenant Twining. He sent me over there because he heard of saboteurs. I took a squad to the lumberyard. When we got there, we were pushed into the service of helping the wounded. The biggest problem was finding saboteurs; there weren't any. In fact, half the kitchen personnel that were supposed to be working were Japanese, and they were not there.

"There was a potential among the Japanese, but I don't think any of them would do anything. They loved Hawaii as much as we did, and I don't think that they would turn on us in that respect. I knew them very well. I had a lot of friends of Japanese ancestry over there, and a lot of people who came from Japan to live there.''

In the concluding portion of Luciano's interview, he discusses his activities from Saturday the 6th until the morning of December 8. He had been on maneuvers for six days prior to the 6th, but for some reason the Army canceled the practices then. Luciano provides some of the flavor of garrison duty for noncommissioned officers in the cluster of forts and camps around Pearl Harbor.

''Well, on December 6, we were still out on maneuvers, and they called it off—the maneuvers—around noon. This other staff sergeant and I were both working plotting boats at the command post, and we were told to close it down. So we did and came home.

''We were living in this shelter—what we called T-34, which was a bachelor quarters. Only sergeants and above could live in those quarters. Everybody else had to live in the barracks. I couldn't live in the barracks. I made staff sergeant, and they kicked me out. 'You're a staff sergeant now,' they said, 'you've got to go.'

''We went home after maneuvers were called off, and then we figured: 'Heck, let's go to town.' We had a little money left because we were on maneuvers, and we never spent anything while on maneuvers. I said: 'I'll tell you what. Let's go to confession first.' My buddy was Catholic and so was I. I said: 'We'll go to confession first, then we'll go downtown, have a nice meal, come home, and tomorrow get up and go to church.' He said: 'That's a good idea.' So that's what we did. The rest of the day we went downtown, went to Waikiki, went swimming, and had a nice time. We ate and came back about 8:00 or 9:00 that night.

''We were asleep next morning when all hell broke loose. We were going to go to 9:30 Mass, and, of course, we weren't going to eat anything before. Both Weisnger and I were living in this place. Frank Weisnger, he was the sergeant I went to town with.

We had another sergeant there, too—he was the telephone communications sergeant—in another room. We each had a place there.

"All of a sudden we heard this bombing, and we heard the machine guns. 'What the heck's going on? We just went on maneuvers. What's going on?' Weisnger said: 'I don't know.' I said: 'For crying out loud! There must be something out there!' So I went and opened the door to my house, and right in front of my home—right in the center—came a burst. I said: 'Those guys must be nuts!'

"But Weisnger was a flying nut. He used to love planes. In fact, he could fly his own plane. He had his license—pilot license. He wanted to get in the Air Corps. That's why he took the Coast Artillery—so he could later get in the Air Corps. He looked up and said: 'Frank, those are not our planes. Look!'

"I looked again and saw the red ball on there. 'Holy jumping!' I said, 'they've finally come!' So he says: 'What do we do?' I said: 'Well, the first thing we ought to do is go down and get our ammunition again.' We had turned it in on December 6.

"This other fellow, the communications sergeant, came out and said: 'What's going on?' I said: 'Don't go out the door.' He said: 'I hear machine-gun fire.' I said: 'Yes, the Japs are bombing Pearl Harbor! You can see it from here!' From my house—it was on the edge of the beach—I could look right into Pearl Harbor. At Fort Kamehameha we were what was called the harbor defense of Pearl Harbor as well.

" 'Well, boys,' he says, 'what do I do?' I said: 'Where's your command post?' He says: 'I got to go down to Selfridge!' I said: 'That's right. That's the communication section.' So he went down to Battery Selfridge, and we went to our usual places to go ahead and start plotting, to see if there were any ships out there.

"Well, we went down to our battery and took our position. But first, like I say, we went to get our ammunition, and then go up to the OP. We had a 14-inch mortar. When we got to where the projectiles were, all the women and children had come into our area. The wives of sergeants and officers and the children, they had come to where our projectiles were stored, because it was the deepest and safest place they had available.

"It was safe because the projectiles wouldn't blow unless they were fused. Now the powder, it was way down below. Definitely further underground where it wouldn't get wet. It's no good wet. We had to keep our powder dry. We just rolled the projectiles out after the attack was over.

"Of course, Fort Kam was under attack. The Japs were taking shots at it when they came in. They had to come in close to us to get to Hickam, and they had to come in close going the other way to get to Pearl Harbor. When they dropped their bombs, they dropped them close to us. They blew up the mess hall.

"Also, we found out afterwards that the marines were not cutting their fuses on their 4-inch square battery. It was four antiaircraft guns—four 4-inch guns, placed in a square. That's why we called them a 4-inch square battery. They were so fast that they didn't cut some of their fuses. If you didn't cut a fuse, naturally it didn't explode up in the air. It came straight down. Then it exploded when it hit something. Some of these fell on the fort.

"Then we shot down a Japanese plane. As a master gunnery sergeant, also in intelligence and in practically everything else, I had to go down with Lieutenant Twining and check the plane. Actually, when it came down, it hit against our icehouse. In those days we made our own ice. The plane hit the icehouse, and, of course, the pilot was killed.

"The attack was still going on when we drove down there in the jeep. We took everything we could out of the pilot's pockets. We found maps. Naturally, everything was bloody. Lieutenant Twining took the maps out. There was the usual stuff in the pilot's pockets, except for identification. There was nothing like that. But we found different types of maps. I knew maps, since I made them. The minute I saw them, I saw that everything they were going to hit was circled. One showed Kam; one showed Battery Closson at Hauula Point; and one showed a railway battery that we hadn't put in yet. I had done a map of the battery that was planned back in 1940, maybe 1941. They knew we were putting it in but not that it wasn't in yet.

"I could see the action at Pearl Harbor all along, but you

couldn't see much. You could see smoke and flames, very, very black smoke, but that's about all. You could see Hickam real good because we were right next to it. To get to Fort Kamehameha you had to go through Hickam. The tower we had, we put a .50-caliber machine gun on. I helped take it up there, and I could look over into Hickam Field. It was pretty well shattered—planes blasted all over. A couple were getting off the ground, though. They came right over the tower. They didn't care about the wind or whatever, as long as they took off. One that got off went into the drink. Then, like I said, I went over to Hickam to check the saboteur rumor that wasn't true.

"There were all kinds of rumors. 'They're landing here! They're landing there!' In the command post where I was we got all of that stuff, and we had to check it out. I had to check it out. 'Oh, they are landing paratroopers!' One pilot probably bailed out instead of getting killed. None of what we heard, the paratroopers, the saboteurs, the landings, was true. We did know there were Japanese communicating with the attackers. We found some of those.

"We got one of them. He was in a house, and we caught him up at what we called Aiea, which was behind Pearl Harbor. We took radios and radio receivers. The regular intelligence people got him before I got there. We just got the radios. We confiscated them. They were just ordinary stuff. In those days there wasn't the sophisticated equipment that you see today, but it was enough to radio two or three hundred miles and get answers back. They also had shortwave radio receivers but not senders.

"That night things got really noisy. Every time anyone heard something, he fired a burst, and then a couple of other shots would go off. But after a while the ones firing settled down. They knew if the Japanese hadn't come by that time they weren't coming. We did get some planes that tried to come into Hickam Field, but it was so bad they couldn't land. The planes were off the *Enterprise*.

"Some of our boys down on Hauula Point opened up on them. Of course, they weren't from my unit. They were infantry from Schofield Barracks. They took over our perimeter while we manned our guns. Our secondary purpose as Coast Artillery was to act as infantry, but our first purpose was to man our guns, and that's what we did. But those infantry people, naturally, they'd shoot at anything.

"I'll tell you, very truly, I seldom get emotional, for the simple reason that you've got a job to do, and you concern yourself about that. If you don't, somewhere down the line something will break down. I don't think any of our soldiers had any thought of breaking down—no fear, no thought that this was going to be the end. We had a job to do, so let's go do it. Let's put up our defenses as we were taught to do. Go out and man our guns, get ready. When we were needed, we were there. That's what we thought we should do, and that's what we did."

Frank Luciano spent the remainder of World War II in Hawaii and the United States. He was commissioned as a second lieutenant during this period, and, before his retirement from the Army in 1963, he rose to the rank of major. After a brief career in the Civil Service at Fort Bliss, Texas, he retired following a massive heart attack. For the next score of years, he remained in El Paso, where he died at the age of sixty-three on January 9, 1985.

32
Second Lieutenant Revella Guest
Tripler Army Hospital

"Beautiful," "exciting," "gorgeous," and "really great" are ways Revella Guest described how Hawaii appeared to her on the eve of the Pearl Harbor attack. She had been there since March 1941 and thoroughly loved the islands. The social life she enjoyed helps explain why.

"We just had a lot of fun. I wasn't at all bored. We had our own friends and our own group. If we had dates, that was fine; a lot of times we doubled-dated, or we'd go on picnics or on a tour of some sort. There was always enough to keep you interested. There was a lot of formal entertaining. You had the opportunity to go to the club, and they always had dances. They were formal affairs that you'd get dressed up to go to. If you didn't want to go to them, you didn't have to. The choice was yours, but at least they were available."

* * *

Lieutenant Guest had joined the Army Nurses Corps in 1938 but did not receive an assignment until January 30, 1939, when she reported for duty at Fort Jay, New York. After twenty-one months there, she requested a transfer and was sent for five months to the Plattsburg, New York, barracks. Then, on March 15, 1941, she sailed on the *Chateau-Thierry* for Hawaii.

Guest was born in Brownville Junction, Maine, forty miles northwest of Bangor, on November 8, 1912. Her parents were immigrants from England and Canada. After high school she studied nursing at the Maine General Hospital in Portland, where she received a nurse's diploma in three years. She entered private nursing but "got fed up with it." She grew "restless" and decided to join the Nurses Corps to see the world.

In Hawaii she was assigned to Tripler Army Hospital but first lived in a duplex at Hickam Field. On December 5 the nurses moved into a new barracks built on the site of an old tennis court at the hospital. Guest had a rank equivalent to second lieutenant but was paid only seventy dollars per month since nurses were not part of the regular Army until 1947. Her work schedule involved a variety of daytime shifts, but periodically she worked an eleven-hour night shift for a week. She was on duty at her post, the surgical orthopedic ward, when the Japanese attacked.

She did not pay much attention to international affairs before December 7 because "we were too busy having fun." She said that "we thought: 'Well, our leaders in Washington will take care of it.' It didn't matter to us. We were in Hawaii having a good time." On the Friday before the raid, Guest attended a dinner party aboard the USS *West Virginia* and watched a movie afterward. On Saturday she and another nurse had dinner with friends in Honolulu. She left that engagement early because she would be on duty Sunday morning at 7:00 A.M.

"The next morning I was on duty. I went to the dining room, had breakfast, and then went on duty. I was on my ward, ward five, the orthopedic ward. Everything was fine, lazy, not much to do. Some of the patients were out on pass. There were just routine things to do.

"All of a sudden the radio started blaring for all military

people to report back to their stations. We had porches on the hospital, and I was looking off in the direction of Pearl Harbor from the back porch, and I heard guns and saw smoke, black smoke, coming up. I thought: 'My goodness! I've never seen that before!'

"Then the radio started to blare that we were being attacked by the Japanese. I telephoned down to my friends where they were, and I told them to get up and get dressed because everybody was going to be working, because we were being attacked by the Japanese. Shortly after that, our chief nurse had called down there, and everybody was alerted and on duty.

"Since it was the weekend, the staff was more limited with more people having time off. That was like any hospital; you try to get patients in and out before the weekend occurs. Things were just routine. Doctors would come in and make their rounds. If they had somebody there that needed attention, they would be there to give it to him. It was routine. The only things that wouldn't be were emergencies. For routine stuff, if anything came up, then it would wait until Monday morning. That was nothing unusual; it was done that way all the time.

"When we got word of the attack, people got back, got on duty, and got things ready. We knew that we were going to have casualties, because we were the largest general hospital on the island. In fact, we were the only general hospital.

"First thing I did was to get my ward emptied out of patients that were there. These people were not acutely ill or seriously ill, or ill or anything. We used to call them goldbricks back in those days; you know: 'Go to the hospital so we don't have to do any duty.' Kind of easy. So we got rid of all those fellows. I only had two people left on my ward, who were up in traction. I had to watch those guys like a hawk, because they were going to cut themselves out of traction and go to war.

"We didn't know what was going to happen. We didn't know. We were ready, but we didn't know what the assignments of the ward were going to be. At the ward down below, which was ward three, it was emptied out, and they were the preop ward, where patients came in from the emergency room and were put until they could go into the operating room. Then, about 12:00 or 1:00 P.M., my ward was postop. Every patient that I received had been to surgery. There was no sorting out of patients. You had amputees, abdominal wounds, head injuries. You name it, and it was there.

"Most were from the Navy, from Pearl Harbor. By nightfall, about 5:00 in the afternoon, maybe a little later, I know by the next morning, I ended up with sixty-five fresh postoperative patients. We were designed to handle about fifty. We had beds out on porches where we used to put the ambulatory patients. We never put any bedridden patients out there, but they were out there that day. Any place they could get, they were put there.

"In postop we had to watch them and see that they were coming out of anesthesia all right. We also had to start IV fluids, but we didn't have the modern equipment that we do today. Our IV bottles were the glass type where you pour the solution in, and you had to be very careful to keep it sterile. I had three of those in my ward, and we went from patient to patient giving them one thousand cc. of fluid. The only thing that we did was be very careful in changing the needle, and then we'd go to the next one to start. We were fortunate, the Lord was on our side, because not one—not one—ever got a chill or infection.

"That morning only one other nurse was working with me. I often look back and wonder how I did it. How I did it, I don't know. But I did. As they came out of anesthesia, you had to be very careful. You had to watch them and see that they were getting oriented. I never left my own little area; I didn't have time. I couldn't worry about what was happening elsewhere; I didn't have time for it.

"In the first place, at night we had no lights. We had a flashlight, and a piece of blue carbon paper was put over the flashlight. That was practically like working in the dark. I can remember going out on the porch and giving a shot to a patient who needed a pain injection. I'd take that carbon paper off, and some guard would holler: 'Put out that light or I'll shoot!' I'd yell: 'Shut up until I give this shot!' It is amazing that more people weren't killed.

"I didn't get any relief until four or five days later. I can't remember exactly, because we never thought about time; we had so much to do. I did get back to my barracks to change clothes, get into a clean uniform. That Monday, about 6:00 in the morning, I went to the barracks—no lights. The only light was a blue light in the bathroom. One of the girls had a radio there, and we tried to get some news from the States, but we couldn't. So we gave that up and went back to work.

"I had an interesting experience. We had one small central supply that was issuing all of our supplies. I thought: 'Well, I'll help them out.' We had other people who came in to volunteer to help, so I had them make bandages and roll them. We had an old gas stove. So I thought: 'Well, I can fill that oven with these things, and, if I can get it filled and keep it on for at least eight to ten hours, then they would be ready for when the day came for the first change of dressings for these patients.' I didn't have any muslin to wrap the supplies in, but we had some brown paper, so we wrapped those in that. I did this. We just had the fire lit, you know. It was an old building.

"Pretty soon I was out in the ward doing something, and another nurse came to me and said: 'There is a fire!' I said: 'Where?' She said: 'In the kitchen!' Brother! I went off, and here I am—all my dressings were in flame. I put water in the sink, got a pair of forceps, and was running back and forth taking all my flaming dressings and dumping them into the sink in the water. I thought: 'Wouldn't you know it! All that time and effort gone!' But at least I tried.

"I've heard that prostitutes from town came out and volunteered to help at Tripler. I don't believe it. They are not that type of individual. They might have gone somewhere else. I can't say. It makes a good story, but I can't verify it. I don't know.

"Later, a friend of mine who had a car—at that time I didn't drive—was working, so she gave me the car keys. I found somebody that could drive, got permission, and I got a gal who wanted me to send a telegram back home. This was about four days afterwards. We went down to the telegraph office, and all we did was sign our names—'Revella.' Some people would have known me by that, and some people who got the telegrams would have wondered who in the world that was, but at least we got telegrams sent off, saying we were safe and sound.

"Another thing we did or didn't do was much charting, because we didn't have the time for it. All we did was put a piece of paper up and tape it to the head of the bed, and we kept track of the last time they'd had any injections. Also, the pharmacy made up a vial of a quarter grain of morphine to use for pain. We carried that in our pockets. We didn't have to record it there, but we just kept it in our pockets so we would save time. All we'd have to do is use it, and, when we were through, we'd get another bottle. Each nurse that was on duty had a vial of that in her pocket and would just go ahead and do it. We just kept track of it at the heads of the beds. We didn't think about charting until about a week afterwards. Then that was a mess, trying to get those records straight, you know.

"We got the first shipload of casualties ready to be shipped back to the United States on December 24, 1941. I know that in my ward we were up all night and all day plastering—getting these people in shape for transportation. They sailed for the United States on December 25, 1941.

"We didn't have all that modern equipment that they have now, but we did very well with what we had. For a small staff with a big job, it was well done. I was in the military for twenty-five years. I am retired as an Army major. I've had many interesting assignments through my career, but Pearl Harbor was the highlight. It had its tragic moments, and it had its great moments."

Revella Guest stayed in the service for twenty-five years, until 1963. During this time she spent three and one-half years with the occupation forces in Europe and later served at Walter Reed Army Hospital in Washington, DC, and Brook Army Hospital in San Antonio. After leaving the military she spent the next eleven years as an office nurse for an internist in Santa Maria, California, where she still resides. Of the air raid, she has said: "I don't hold grudges, but it's an experience I will never forget."

Chapter VI

Schofield Barracks and Wheeler Field

Schofield Barracks and Wheeler Field are situated adjacent to each other on the Leilehua Plain near Kolekole Pass, which runs through the Waianae Mountains, in what Rear Admiral William W. Drake called the "back country of Oahu." To the east is the Koolau Range and to the west, Kamaileunu Ridge, with the bases slightly northwest of the island's center. Schofield Barracks was named for a Civil War hero, Major General John M. Schofield, who had been involved in acquiring Pearl Harbor as a naval base in the 1870s and was a force in the annexation of the Hawaiian Islands during the McKinley administration in 1898. At the time of the attack, the installation was the largest U.S. Army outpost.

Wheeler Field, just south of Schofield Barracks, was built in 1922 and named for Major Sheldon H. Wheeler, who had been the commander at Luke Field, Ford Island, when he died in an airplane crash in July 1921. In 1941, Wheeler Field was the largest American fighter plane base in the Pacific. It had become a permanent military installation only a few years earlier, in 1939. Its major tasks were to provide protection for Hickam Field and later for the Pacific Fleet, which was shifted from the West Coast of the United States to Pearl Harbor in the summer of 1940.

Hostilities began in this area at 8:02 A.M., when twenty-five dive-bombers led by Lieutenant Akira Sakamoto attacked the hanger line at Wheeler Field and planes that were parked wing-tip to wingtip in a series of parallel lines on the aprons in front of the hangars. This first phase ended at about 8:20, and a second attack, by seven Japanese planes, began at 9:00 and lasted five minutes.

During both the second attack and the first, Japanese aircraft strafed the area, including not only the hangars, fuel dump, and airplanes but also enlisted men's tents, which served as temporary quarters, and military personnel. The planes destroyed the post exchange, badly damaged a barracks, hit a mess hall and a fire station, and bombed the baseball diamond. The purpose behind the attack on the airfield was to deny protection by Wheeler's fighter planes for the naval vessels at Pearl Harbor.

The assault on Schofield Barracks had no such logic. Arriving from the northwest, Japanese gunners hit Building 1492 first and bombed and machine-gunned Quadrangle C, a main barracks, as well as the library. Men standing in the Sunday morning chow line on one of the five big quadrangles that made up Schofield were strafed. The Japanese finished attacking the barracks by 8:17, leaving behind fire, smoke, death, and destruction.

33
Sergeant Emil Matula
Schofield Barracks

Emil Matula was born in the Czechoslovak-American town of West, Texas, on April 4, 1918. While he was still a boy, his family moved eighty miles south to the neighborhood of Granger, where his father farmed. Matula attended a Catholic grammar school, Saints Cyril and Methodius, and later the Granger elementary school, which he was forced to leave in the seventh grade because his father was seriously ill. After working the family's land for several years, on January 3, 1937, Matula joined the Army at Fort Sam Houston in San Antonio as part of a dare that involved five other boys. He chose the Army because "one of my friends from my hometown was in it." When his first tour of three years ended at "Fort Sam," he reenlisted for foreign service, to earn a 20 percent pay hike, and "to investigate" stories he had heard about Hawaii.

As a result, he arrived at Schofield Barracks in March 1940 and joined D Company, Thirty-fifth Infantry Regiment. The ability he demonstrated as a football player while at the San Antonio post caused the Thirty-fifth Infantry's commander to assign him to that unit's team once he arrived in Hawaii. Matula's regular duty was as a section leader of the 81-millimeter mortar platoon, spending morning hours training with his gun team and the afternoon on odd jobs around the barracks. According to Matula, morale was high among the soldiers at Schofield, one of the largest and prettiest posts garrisoned by the Army.

The day before Pearl Harbor was attacked, Sergeant Matula played in the post's championship football game. Before a crowd of thirty thousand spectators, his team, usually the victor, lost 13 to 6 to the Twenty-first Infantry, which had received "a lot of ex-college football players" through the draft. After the game he and the other players were given ten-day passes. Putting them to use immediately, Matula said, "all the football players from the Twenty-first and Thirty-fifth Infantry wound up down in Honolulu. Of course, we fought the football game all over again inside the Honolulu streets, and, about 4:00 in the morning, things started to close down, and three or four of us boys from my company went back to Schofield Barracks. We caught a taxi, and each one took an extra fifth of whiskey along with us so we'd have something to start off the next day with because we had ten days to go."

Matula was in bed by 5:30 A.M. and sound asleep when the attack began at 7:55. He and others assumed an earthquake was occurring because the ground shook. Ordered out of his barracks and onto Schofield's quadrangle, he soon learned otherwise. In the first part of the interview, he tells of men standing in their underwear, witnessing the early phase of battle, and then returning to their bunks to dress, arm themselves, and join the fight.

"About 7:45 or 8:00 in the morning, I woke up. My bunk was jumping up and down with me, and I couldn't figure out what was going on. I woke up my buddy next to me. I said: 'Claude, what's going on?' He said: 'Matula, hell, go to bed!' So we reached under the pillow and took a shot of whiskey and went back to sleep, and, about five minutes later, this thing just rocked a little bit more. About the second time that this bunk shook, the whistle went off, and the charge of quarters yelled: 'Everybody out of the barracks! It's an earthquake!'

"The drill for earthquakes was for everybody to get out of the barracks because the barracks were concrete, and, for the safety of the soldiers themselves, everybody was ordered out of the barracks onto the quadrangle. So, when we got this order to get out of the barracks, everybody went out, and there we were, in the middle of the quadrangle with the earth shaking. At that time we didn't know what was going on. The Japanese were, of course, bombing Navy installations in Pearl Harbor—Ford Island and Hickam Field and Fort Shafter.

"When they got through, they would come out to Wheeler, and they would strafe Wheeler Field with incendiary bullets. All the planes on Saturday were lined up, and there was at least 150 planes wing to wing in a straight line in two different rows. All of these planes went up in flames because the incendiary bullets set them on fire.

"But anyway, getting back to the barracks, we were standing in the middle of the quadrangle, and the first knowledge that we had of any attack was when these planes came over the top of the barracks, and we looked upstairs and saw the rising sun. That was the first time that we really knew what was happening. About the time that we looked up and saw the rising sun, one of the Japanese dropped a bomb on the flagpole in the general quadrangle, and at that time [what was happening] hit everybody. To myself, I said: 'My God, this couldn't happen to the United States or the American Army!' It was just unbelievable to think that, with all the precautions that were taken and all the guarantees that we had that we would have at least thirty minutes' or maybe an hour's knowledge of any attack that might be coming, that we could be surprised.

"We finally decided that this was an attack, and, of course, we all headed into the barracks and got dressed. The first thing we needed was our guns—to get the guns into action. We went to get the guns at the supply room, and the supply sergeant was gone, and there were no keys available. The charge of quarters didn't have the keys. They were locked up in the supply sergeant's quarters. So we took fire axes and chopped down the doors to the gun storage room. After we got into the gun storage room, we had to chop open the machine-gun racks, so we had to break all the locks on them. Then after we got the machine guns, we had to break down the ammunition storage room to get to the ammunition. We got the machine guns out, we got the machine guns up, we got four or five guns up on top of the barracks, but we only got to fire at the tail end of the last squadron of Japs that came to strafe. Outside of that, that was it.''

Matula pointed out that Japanese planes made six or seven passes and that, after strafing and bombing Wheeler Field, they would strafe the barracks. Below he expands upon his role during the attack.

"I think there were only three sergeants that were in the barracks at that time, and I was one of the sergeants that gave the orders to break down the doors. That's the only way that we could get to the guns, and, when you're under attack, you start fighting for your life.

"I had a BAR. It didn't do me any good to have the BAR because they weren't very effective against airplanes. I would say that I emptied four clips, which amount to fifty rounds to a clip, so I fired approximately two hundred rounds. I think the reason I done it was because that was part of our training. In case of an attack we knew what we should do, and I think this was just an automatic response due to my training.

"At Schofield Barracks, I would say the attack lasted about thirty minutes, but, as far as I was concerned, if felt like it lasted an eternity. There wasn't any panic, because, once the alert was given, all the men went up to their quarters. They dressed and were directed by their squad leaders. I presume that the training we always bitched about or griped about and stuff like that, because we didn't see that it was doing us any good in peacetime, actually paid off on that day because everybody really went to town and cooperated and got things done.''

* * *

After the attack, the Thirty-fifth Infantry soon took up positions near the Marine air base at Ewa. Matula's unit was involved in some of the confusion resulting from an anticipated Japanese paratrooper and amphibious invasion, which at times overzealous soldiers reported was occurring.

"Following the attack, I would say that it took fifteen minutes for the trucks to get to the barracks and forty-five minutes for us to get everything loaded and on the trucks, and within three hours we were in our positions in the Ewa subsector, which were our prearranged defensive positions.

"When we got to the Ewa subsector, we went into alert precautions. In other words, we opened foxholes initially and then trenches and whatnot. The first three nights after the Pearl Harbor attack there was no sleep. There were around-the-clock fortification jobs to be done; there were patrols that went out twenty-four hours a day. There were so many crank calls coming in to the regimental CP [command post]: There were Japanese being parachuted all over our area, and, every time we got a call, we had to send a detail out to check it out. Nine times out of ten, when we got there, it was nothing but a Filipino working in a cane field shaking a cane pole out there. I would say there were a few trigger-happy people the first few nights because of the fact they didn't actually know what was happening. Whether the enemy had landed or hadn't landed, we didn't know. If anything would move during the night, it got shot at. . . .

"As far as [damage to] Schofield Barracks itself was concerned, outside of some of the machine-gun bullets that went into the barracks, it wasn't damaged very much. However, a half mile from us where Wheeler Field was, as we were going out to the Ewa subsector, we passed by, and the main hangars of Wheeler Field, where they repaired the airplanes, were completely collapsed, and all the airplanes that were lined up for inspection were destroyed on the ground where they inspected them on Saturday. What casualties there were at Wheeler Field, we didn't know because what you heard were rumors.

"I don't think we had very much emotion, because the thing we were concerned with was to get into our positions and be able to defend the island. That was our job. Actually, it shook me up to see all these airplanes destroyed, but it never occurred to me in the second thought that these were the planes destroyed on the ground that were supposed to give us the protection while we were out in the field.''

Sergeant Matula went on to serve honorably for the remainder of World War II. He was involved in the battles for Guadalcanal and other Pacific islands, including the Philippines. He was twice wounded, and, in the battle to control Highway 5, near Bolong, just south of Balote Pass, Luzon, he won the Bronze Star for valor. By then he had received a battlefield commission and was a second lieutenant.

Emil Matula left the Army at the end of World War II and worked at various low-paying jobs for the next four years. In 1949 he was employed by Jewel Home Shopping, and he stayed with them until his retirement in 1981. He now lives in San Antonio, Texas. He said recently that he felt ''very lucky not to have been killed in the Japanese strafing on December 7, 1941.''

34
Chaplains Marcus A. Valenta
and Herbert C. Straus
Schofield Barracks and Fourteenth Naval
District Headquarters

Rabbi Herbert C. Straus and Father Marcus A. Valenta were assigned to military ministries in Hawaii during the buildup of forces there in 1941. Straus, a Navy chaplain, arrived in January, and Valenta, a member of the Army, came in July. Both men had entered the military years before these assignments, but this was Father Valenta's first regular Army service. Receiving a five-year commission in 1933, he had served only one year on active duty, and that with the Civilian Conservation Corps. From 1933 to 1940 he was assigned to a division in the National Guard. He had renewed his commission when it expired in 1938 but remained in Saint Anne's Parish in San Antonio until called to active service in October 1940.

Marcus Valenta was born in Sweet Home, a small town in

south Texas, on July 26, 1905. He attended elementary and high school at Saint Louis College and then began his training for the priesthood at Saint John's Seminary, both of which were in San Antonio. He finished his studies at the North American College in Rome and was ordained on December 21, 1929. Assigned to Saint Anne's Parish, he there met an older priest who persuaded him to join the Army's Chaplain Corps. Father Valenta was called into the service in October 1940 and was sent to Maxwell Field in Montgomery, Alabama. He left there in July 1941 when the Army assigned him to the Hawaiian Department, where he became a member of the Twenty-seventh Division at Schofield Barracks. In addition to holding religious services and counseling soldiers, Chaplain Valenta acted as the recreation and morale officer.

Rabbi Straus, on the other hand, served continuously in the Navy after 1931, when he was first commissioned into the Chaplain Corps. Born on September 6, 1895, in Denver, Colorado, he graduated from Haver Union College in Ohio and assumed his first congregation in 1916 at Lima. During the ensuing years, assignments to other congregations followed, and in 1931, while at San Diego, he became one of the first Jewish chaplains in U.S. naval history. When told that he would have to wear the corps insignia, which was a cross, Straus refused, offering instead to resign. But communications with the Navy command in San Diego and the chief of chaplains in Washington, DC, led to his being authorized to use a shepherd's crook instead of the cross. Straus thereafter often introduced himself as the only "crook" in the Navy. In 1942 he was allowed to wear the same insignia as the Army's Jewish chaplains: a tablet of the Ten Commandments and the Star of David.

The scarcity of Jewish sailors meant that he often held services with two or three men rather than the required minimum of ten. Because he was also the only Jewish chaplain in the Pacific, he traveled frequently to various naval outposts. At the time of the Pearl Harbor attack, the rabbi was assistant district chaplain, Fourteenth Naval District, and lived with his daughter, Selma, in a private cottage on Waikiki, one block from the Royal Hawaiian Hotel.

Each chaplain presents brief reminiscences of the air raid.

Rabbi Straus begins his recollections by trying to recall what he did on December 6 and he follows by describing how he set up a temporary hospital and his actions on the night of December 7.

"First of all, December 6 was a Sabbath, and that morning I held services. I don't know where, because I'd go to different parts of the island at different times on different weekends to hold services. I did that for the Navy, the Army, and the Air Corps because I was still the only Jewish chaplain in the Pacific. Then in the afternoon I traveled to some other point and met with the men. That evening I had supper at one of the bases with a group of men. Nothing unusual. I turned in at about 10:00 or 11:00, and I slept fairly well.

"I got a telephone call very early the next morning. The caller said: 'Get out to Pearl Harbor!' That was all. I left my daughter at the cottage on Waikiki Beach, and I jumped in my car. At a place where I had to stop for signal lights, either four or five servicemen jumped into my car without my knowing it, and they didn't get out until I got to the gate at Pearl Harbor. They got out, and I went on to my office.

"I didn't see much because the attack was primarily out at the waterfront. The *Arizona* and several other ships had already been hit. They were on the other side of Ford Island. So I didn't see much until I got to the office and went out into the field itself.

"My primary concern was to set up a hospital there on the base, and we kept the men there until we could put them into the regular Pearl Harbor hospital. This temporary hospital was at the receiving headquarters in a new barracks. The barracks was incomplete—no water, beds. I had to send out to get all of that stuff and a doctor and a nurse.

"A young marine came to me and helped me an awful lot. He worked outdoors with me at the time the attack was taking place, and one time I called to him to come to me. I yelled: 'Come on the double!' As he started on the double, he tripped and went sprawling. He came over to me and said: 'Chaplain, thank you.' I said: 'Thank me for what?' He said: 'You just saved my life.' I said: 'What are you talking about?' So he picked up the heel of his shoe and showed me two bullet heads in the heel that would have gone straight through him if he had been standing up.

"We had about forty patients in that little hospital I started. I got a doctor and a nurse to help out, and, while this was going on, let's say about 11:00 that morning, the doctor said to me: " 'Chaplain, I wonder if we could get a bottle of liquor. It might help some of these boys.' Unconsciously, I put my hand back on my hip, and there was a bottle. Somebody had stuck it in my pocket during the morning. Who it was or when it was, I have no recollection. He said: 'Good! Then we've got some.'

"I started that hospital within an hour or an hour and a half after I got to Pearl Harbor. I was getting word that there were wounded around there and no place to take them because the main hospital at Pearl was completely loaded. So, with no authorization at all, I took over this new building, the barracks, and I got several men to help me with it. I sent them out, and we got some beds and linens.

"I just pulled the men off the field. I had set up an information desk in the reception room of the receiving barracks with yeomen running it, and survivors came there and signed in so that we would know that they were survivors. There were crowds of men in there. I went and got half a dozen men. Who they were, how I got them, I don't remember, but I sent them out, and they got cots. Where they got them, I didn't ask. They got bedding linen. I sent somebody over to the main hospital, and we got a doctor and a nurse over there.

"I'll never forget one young fellow that they brought in. He had several bullets in the belly. I sat down on his legs until the doctor came in and gave him a shot. He wanted to get back out there. The men coming in suffered mainly from bullet wounds. There may have been some burns. Whether there were and whether they came off of ships, I don't know. I didn't ask where they came from.

"Despite water problems at Pearl Harbor due to the attack, as it happened the receiving station had plenty. I got these real tall milk cans and filled them with water and brought them over to the hospital, which was about a hundred yards away.

"We had around forty or forty-five patients that were trans-

ferred to the new hospital up at Aiea Heights. We took all of
them up there that night. It was done very quickly. It was a new
temporary hospital at Aiea Heights. When it was being dedi-
cated, later, Admiral [Chester W.] Nimitz was in charge. I had
known Admiral Nimitz from 1931, when he was in command at
the destroyer base at San Diego.

"That night, a number of young sailors came to me and asked
me if I could get a telegram home to their families. I said: 'Yes,
I'll try.' So, about 5:00 in the morning on December 8, I started
to go into Honolulu with all of these telegrams. From the entrance or exit of Pearl Harbor to the entrance or exit of Hickam
Field, you go right straight down a road. About 5:00 I was going
down that road and had just got beyond Hickam when BOOM!
I didn't know what had happened, but there was a big flash in
front of me, and my car was picked up and turned back 180
degrees toward Pearl Harbor. I threw on my brakes, nothing
more happened, so I turned back around and went into Honolulu
and took care of all the telegrams.

"That noon at lunch, I happened to mention the incident, and
one of the officers I was eating with said: 'Oh, that was you,
was it?' I said: 'What do you mean?' He said: 'We had a plane
flying over there, and it accidentally dropped a bomb, and as it
exploded, it exploded in a V, and we saw a car going into it.'
They said: 'How lucky can you be?' I wasn't injured or anything.''

At the request of Admiral Nimitz, on May 30, 1942, Rabbi
Straus conducted the first services to be held aboard the USS
Arizona in commemoration of the attack and of those who died
there. In the following passage he describes the ceremony.

"I was away for a three-day rest. I got called back by Admiral
Nimitz in order to handle this memorial service. Admiral Nimitz
prefaced his remarks by telling me there would be no pictures.
However, the admiral in charge of Pearl Harbor, District Fourteen, insisted on photographs, some of which I still have.

"But we held the service aboard the *Arizona*. I had two other
chaplains with me so that we had all three denominations. We
had the bugler, of course, and we had the volley, and I had a lot

of flowers that were sent to me by relatives of the boys that were down in the bottom of this ship. I said there were 1,100 dead. It was a little bit more than that. We held our service with a complete floral display. Oh, it was tremendous. The three chaplains all took a part in the service, and we had taps and our volley.

"Anybody could come aboard. Remember that the deck of the ship was only a few feet above the surface of the water itself. I took one of the wreaths that had been sent to me and threw it down a manhole in the center of the ship. It was flooded, and there was a lot of oil. Believe it or not, when I threw this wreath in—which was one that would float—it sank! Just as if some of the boys rose up and grabbed it by their hands and pulled it down! Don't ask me why or wherefore.''

Father Valenta's interview begins with church services he was conducting Sunday morning at the post chapel at Schofield Barracks. He had spent Saturday preparing for the next day's Mass and had retired around 10:30 P.M.

"Services began at 6:00 and then at 7:00. When I finished the second service, it was about five minutes until 8:00. I heard this rumbling and all the racket, and I remarked to the soldier who was assisting me—serving—I said: 'Say, John, what's all that racket?' He said: 'Oh, that's a maneuver between Hickam Field and Wheeler Field.' I said: 'Well, that doesn't sound like our planes.' I had been stationed at Maxwell Field, in Montgomery, Alabama, before I was sent to the Hawaiian Islands, and I had heard different planes and their sounds.

"So I rushed to take off my vestments that I'd been using, and I went outside of the chapel. About that time, a group of planes flew over, just a little higher than the steeple of the chapel—about 1,500 feet—and about a hundred yards distant from where I was standing.

"I saw one of the Japanese pilots looking down from the cockpit as I was looking up. They hadn't dropped any bombs—the group I saw—due to the fact that they were waiting until the other groups that were going to work on Hickam Field and Pearl Harbor had time to get to their destination so that they could strike simultaneously and without any disturbance. There were about eight single-engine planes; it was a small group.

"They came by where I was standing, and then they circled and went over to the artillery area and were just delaying time in order to give the other group that was going to work on Hickam Field and Pearl Harbor time to get to their destination so that they could all strike at once. It was only about a three- to five-minute flight from Schofield to Pearl Harbor. So, when those who were working on Pearl Harbor and Hickam Field got to their places, why, that's when this group I'd been watching came back and began dropping their bombs.

"About that time a bus pulled up with children on it. They were coming to service, the one we called the children's service, at 8:00. I saw the bus pull up in front of the chapel, and I ran around and said: 'Come into the chapel, children, and let's say some prayers.' They came in, and we went into the chapel and said some prayers.

"In the meantime, the chaplain, Father O'Brien, who was going to have the 8:00 service, arrived. He said: 'What am I to do now?' We heard the bombs bursting. I said: 'Well, I don't know, Father, but I'm going over to my outfit,' which was just across the road, in the Twenty-seventh Infantry Barracks.

"I don't know what he did then, because I ran over to my outfit. By then I saw the commanding officer, the colonel—he had already heard the attack—and he was standing on the second floor of the barracks there at Schofield Barracks. I ran up, and from there we could see the bombs flying in the air at Wheeler Field. They were big bombs, and they'd come in and, BOOM, up goes a hangar. So I said to the colonel: 'Well, I can see they're not bombing our place, and I would like to go down to Wheeler Field and help out.' He said: 'Go anyplace you can, Chaplain!' So I ran down, and this car came along. I flagged him down and told him to take me to Wheeler Field.

"There was confusion but very little damage to Schofield. Let me give you an example. One of the doctors at Schofield was telling me later on—a couple of days later—that he heard this call for doctors to report to their stations. He thought that it was a maneuver, so he was up on the top of his house taking pictures of this maneuver. He thought it was just a bunch of duds dropping, you know.

"So, anyway, just as we got to Wheeler Field, why, they were already beginning to close the gate. So then the driver left, and I went in. I helped give the sacraments to the dying and aid to the suffering. They had the boys lying out on the lawn in front of a little first aid station. That's all they had there at Wheeler Field. The attack was still going on. In fact, after the first wave came in and dropped all their bombs, they went back to their carriers, and another group came in with more bombs. Then a third attack came.

"I was just off from the runway. First, the Japs came in and dropped the bombs and blew up the hangars. They knew where everything was. They would fly over this hangar because it just had a bunch of junk in it and hit the next hangar that had all the machinery and equipment for repairs and all. After they did that, when they came back, they'd go right down that runway and machine-gun our planes, though I think one or two got off the runway. All the others were knocked out.

"I talked to some of our pilots afterwards. They told me that they could not have taken a group of our own pilots and done the job that the Japanese did, because they did not know where all these vital parts were in these hangars. But the Japs did.

"Then that was it. We had our ammunition trucks going up to Diamond Head to get ammunition. It was all stored at Diamond Head and places. They got up there, but they got stuck in the tunnel. So that was a delay, also. Anyway, the attack was going on, and shortly after that the rumor was out that 'the Japs are landing on the north end; they're landing on the south end of the island,' and we didn't know what.

"So, anyway, that's about all [that happened] there. Whenever the other chaplains arrived at Wheeler, then I went back to Schofield. I was put in charge of evacuating the women and children from Schofield, because the military was just almost certain that the Japs were going to invade the island.

"The officers and all had their families there. There was quite a contingent of civilians. We took them down to Honolulu and put them in the schools and wherever space was available and set up field ranges to fix a little meal for them. That's what happened. Of course, after we realized that the Japs were not making an attack, they went back to their different quarters.

"I returned to the Schofield hospital, the main hospital, and administered to the dying and helped those who were wounded and all. I was helping the nurses and doctors, handing them what they might need when they were working with someone they were sewing up or bandaging up and so on. I'd hand them gauze or whatever. Later I was in the hospital roaming around and visiting with sick and injured people. I stayed there and hardly left the hospital for three days because of the number of casualties. Like everybody else, I was overwhelmed. You know, when you look back, you just wonder: 'What in the world! How did this happen? Was I even there?' "

Both Father Valenta and Rabbi Straus continued to serve after Pearl Harbor. Father Valenta was sent to Canton in the Phoenix Islands, which was used as a landing field for B-29 bombers. After one year he went on to Saipan and from there to Okinawa, where he was stationed when the war ended. He remained in the reserves after the war, retiring in August 1965. On April 1, 1946, he was appointed pastor of Saint Philip's Church, El Campo, Texas. He served the Saint Mary's parish in Praha, Texas, from September 1974 until December 1979. Father Valenta died in 1984.

After leaving the Navy, Rabbi Straus lived for a time in Columbus, New Mexico, before moving to Arcadia, California. He died there in early 1982.

35
Second Lieutenant Ada M. Olsson
Schofield Barracks Army Hospital

On December 7, Ada Olsson lost her lover, Lieutenant Gordon Sterling, an American pilot shot down by Japanese aircraft during the Pearl Harbor attack. His comrades named the Veterans of Foreign Wars post at Wheeler Field in his memory, and citizens of his hometown in Connecticut called their new ballpark Sterling Field. Ada never forgot him, and she never married.

Second Lieutenant Olsson was one of only twenty nurses as-

signed to the Army hospital at Schofield Barracks in 1941, and
she liked the duty. The facility was beautiful, with several tile-
roofed, two-story stuccoed buildings connected by ramps. The
nurses' quarters were even more pleasant: "We had a house
mother. Our chief nurse was a captain. We had a lovely, great
big living room with a big fireplace, and we had a back stairs
and front stairs to the second floor, where we lived. We had a
spacious dining room, and we were served by Japanese servants.
We had houseboys, who were Filipino; they cleaned our rooms
and made our beds. It was nice living.'' Soldiers called the
installation Vassar because they felt the personnel were so
snooty.

Olsson's normal work schedule was from 7:00 A.M. until 9:00
A.M. and then from 1:00 until 7:00 P.M., with one-half day on
Wednesdays. For one month each year she had night duty, which
lasted from 7:00 P.M. to 7:00 A.M. She spent a lot of time at the
beach and was a participant in the formal party circuits at both
the Wheeler Field and Schofield Barracks officers' clubs.

Her life-style was a far cry from what it had been at home.
Ada Olsson was born on September 7, 1916, in Junction City,
Kansas, just south of Fort Riley and about seventy miles west
of Topeka on U.S. Highway 40. After high school, she attended
the Asbury School of Nursing in Denver, Colorado; returned
home; and, after a time, was employed as a private nurse at the
military hospital at Fort Riley. Officers there convinced her that
she should join the Army, and, although she signed military
papers, she was not officially sworn in until June 5, 1940, when
she reached Fitzsimmons General Hospital (now an army medical center) in Denver. After one year at Fitzsimmons she volunteered for duty overseas and was sent to Schofield Barracks.
She traveled first class from San Francisco aboard the Matson
Lines steamship *Mariposa*.

By the time of the Pearl Harbor attack she had worked in every
ward. As December 7 neared, she and others at the hospital
were issued gas masks and stood periodic alerts. At the formal
parties she attended at the Wheeler Field Officers' Club, talk
occasionally turned to the world situation, and some of the pilots
voiced concern over Japan, expecting war sooner or later. Of
course, no one suspected it would start at Pearl Harbor. In the

following interview, Lieutenant Olsson discusses her experience during the weekend of the attack, beginning with Friday the 5th.

"I had my last date with Gordon Sterling on Friday. He was based at Haleiwa, out along the beach. He never talked shop, and I have tried to forget that weekend ever since.

"On Saturday night I had to work. We were delivering a baby, so I had to stay on duty late. Thus, I didn't go out Saturday night; I didn't get to the club. Gordon and I had planned a picnic for the next day. We were going to have a beach party—take food, swim, and play ball.

"I worked from 7:00 until 9:00 in the morning on Saturday and then went home. I think I went swimming. I went back to the hospital at 1:00 and was supposed to work until 7:00, but I had to stay on until we delivered the baby. I think I finally got off about 9:00. It was too late to get dressed and go anywhere, so I went to bed.

"The next morning I went to work at 7:00 A.M. in the nursery. I was going to get off at 1:00; it was a half day for me. The baby that had been born the night before had weighed ten pounds. We had another baby in an incubator; he needed oxygen. Then I heard this terrible bomb and then another, and all of a sudden the building shook. I said: 'We're all going to be killed! Something has blown up!' Then we saw corpsmen running through the ramps between the buildings, and they said: 'Stay away from the windows! The Japs are bombing!' Then the planes came over, and we could hear them strafing us with their machine guns. They flew low. You could see the men in the cockpit.

"Between the buildings we had a lot of flowers and plantings, and I looked out. I went to the front where the ramp was and looked up, and they flew low. It is a wonder they didn't crash. I could see them. They had helmets on, and they were yellow skinned. They had rising suns on their planes. They dove and climbed, up and down. They were coming past very fast—like they do in dogfights.

"On one of the floors there was a fellow in a cast, and a bullet came through the window and went through his cast. It didn't hit him. The strafing must have lasted about fifteen minutes. Then you could hear more bombs being dropped. Later, we

found out that they were bombing the mess hall at Wheeler
Field. They'd drop a bomb, and the fellows would run out of
the mess hall, and then they'd shoot them down.

"At first everybody was running around. Then somebody
came down—I don't know who—and told the nurses to take all
the babies in the baskets to their mothers and tell them to take
care of them. They sent me up to the surgical floor, which was
above the nursery, and the doctor there sent me to the pharmacy
to get some morphine. The pharmacy was in a building in front.

"When I left they were bringing the wounded in. I had to wait
while the pharmacists mixed up the morphine because it came
in liquid form. When I got back they had the wounded on hospital litters up and down the hall, and it was all red, nothing but
a bloody mess. They had a nurse going down the line, giving
them all shots of morphine and marking a red *M* on their fore-
heads, so they would know they had been medicated.

"Everything seemed organized. Patients got out of bed and
helped us. We got extra cots and put them down and put the
beds close together so we could hold more patients. In time of
disaster, you'd be surprised how people will help out. We had a
lot with their legs shot and with abdominal wounds caused by
bomb fragments.

"After I got the morphine, I went back up to surgical, and
they were bringing the ones in that were critical. The ones that
had broken legs and things that they couldn't set, they sent them
over to surgery, and they did amputations right away, which is
the wrong thing to do. They should be treated for shock first,
but they didn't know that in those days.

"They had these two rooms and a great big ward. The people
that were really hurt they put in a room away from the other
fellows. I stayed there and ran the IV injections, and I stayed
with them until they died and then fixed the bed up for another
patient. I did that until 9:00 that night. They were all young,
good-looking kids. I noticed that most of them had beautiful
teeth. We were treating them for shock; that's why you start the
IV feeding, and you give them something for the pain.

"I was busy, but I was scared. I really was scared. In the
afternoon they told me that Gordon Sterling was lost. He'd gone
up when the Japanese came over. He saw the rising sun, so he

and the other fellows just jumped in their suits and went up. I think he shot down four before they got him. They never found his body or anything. It may still be up in the mountains somewhere. When you're scared your insides quiver, and you have to go to the bathroom all the time. Your kidneys overwork. It's a terrible feeling. I'd never been around anything like this.

"Gordon and I would have been married in the spring. I didn't want to get married right away; I was having too good a time. One of the girls dated a friend of Gordon's who was in the same pursuit squadron, and she came and told me. She said he was lost, so he was presumed dead.

"I had a terrible headache, and I was scared. One of the assistant chief nurses gave me a sleeping pill. I couldn't sleep, but she poked a couple of sleeping pills down me. During the night we had to get up for an air raid. We had to go to the basement of the nurses' home, which was made of concrete and steel.

"That night the guards shot at anything that moved. You'd hear them yell: 'Halt! Who goes there? Advance and be recognized!' We heard that one plane landed on our smallest island. The only family that lived there were pure Hawaiians, and they supposedly were beaten to death.

"They gave us blue paper to cover our flashlights. We all had to have flashlights, and then we all had to buy pocketknives to carry. In case we were captured, we were to slit our wrists. They knew the Japanese would treat us terribly.

"Our cook was Japanese, and they got rid of him. He went to cook for the governor of the islands. His son was an officer in the Japanese Imperial Navy. His name was Hato. He was good to the nurses. But, because he was Japanese and our servants were Filipinos, and they hated the Japanese, they got rid of him. The Filipinos used to chase him around the basement with knives—they all had living quarters in the basement of the nurses' home. His daughter used to wait on tables. They say his son participated in the attack.

"I tell you that time was just like a dream—a terrible dream. In the days after the attack, I just worked. I stayed in the surgical area. I finally got out of the Army, but even today as a private nurse I'm still taking care of soldiers."

* * *

Ada Olsson is now retired and lives in the town of her birth, Junction City, Kansas.

36
Staff Sergeant Stephen Koran and Flora Belle Koran
Wheeler Field

Stephen Koran was older than most enlisted men at Pearl Harbor on December 7. He was born on December 18, 1913, in Chicago, and, after two years at Northwestern University in nearby Evanston, he joined the U.S. Cavalry in 1933. He was looking for "economic security" and was attracted by what he believed was a "good opportunity for promotion, education, and retirement."

After two years in the cavalry, Koran transferred to the Air Corps because he had grown tired of "eating dust." He had been a communications sergeant but in his new assignment learned to be an aerial photography expert. During his time in photography school at Lowry Air Base in Denver, he met his future wife. Flora Belle Koran was born in Omaha in 1912 but claimed to have been reared in the West because her family moved about the area several times during her childhood. In 1929 she became an employee of the telephone company and was a supervisor at the central exchange in Denver when she met Steve in 1938.

Lack of money kept them from marrying until 1941. Steve was sent to Wheeler Field in 1939. After their wedding the couple began housekeeping in a "beautiful, two-bedroom, new duplex" in the noncommissioned officers quarters about one thousand yards from the aerial photography lab, which Steve ran at Wheeler. A staff sergeant, he was chief aerial photographer for the Eighty-sixth Observation Squadron.

The Korans spent the day before the attack at home, enjoying their first child, a daughter born eighteen days earlier. Mrs. Koran had sterilized milk bottles and seen to other family chores during the day, while Sergeant Koran had worked around the house, "proud of the little bundle we had just had." They went to bed at 9:30 P.M. They were in the bedroom, with Flora rocking the bassinet, when the bombing began the next morning. In the following passage, Steve Koran recalls his reaction to events during the first attack.

"We heard the aircraft coming in. We didn't give it too much thought because, prior to the December attack, what the Air Corps used to do is periodically go over unannounced on a Sunday morning and put a mock raid on Pearl Harbor to see how fast the Navy could get up, get out of bed, and get their aircraft in the air. It wasn't on any schedule. Maybe two or three weeks later, the Navy would do the same thing to us. Of course, we didn't know which week it would be because it wasn't supposed to be run on a scheduled basis. It so happened that, just a couple of weeks prior to December 7, we had done our buzz job on the Navy, and it was their turn to do it to us.

"So we gave it no thought. I thought it was the Navy coming over, and I wasn't scheduled for any duty on the flight line, so I just laid there, and then I heard one plane that seemed like it pulled out and went into a screeching dive. I mentioned to my wife that 'if he doesn't pull out of it, he's going to crash.' I no sooner got the word *crash* out of my mouth than I heard a great big explosion. Well, I was in such a position that I leaned on my elbow on the bed and looked out of my window. I could see the engineering hangar off in the distance. I saw black smoke coming out of it, and I remarked: 'My gosh, he's crashed into the engineering hangar!'

"About that time I saw another plane pull out, and I saw a little black object drop down. When he dropped the object he pulled up, and that's when I noticed the red disk around the aircraft. I yelled to my wife: 'Let's get out of here! It's the Japs! It's not the Navy!' Then all hell broke loose.

"Our quarters were built of cinder blocks, with stucco on the outside, and the inner walls were also cinder block. So my first thought was to get my family into the inner room, away from the bombs. This was all well and good until in the course of the bombing they must have dropped a bomb in the rear of the quadrangle where we lived, and a back window frame in our back bedroom blew out.

"When that happened, I figured that this was no place for us to be. I remembered that up the street, a block from us, there was a great big banyan tree. Underneath this banyan tree there was an abandoned cesspool which we knew was dry. My main object was to try to get my family out of the house and down into this abandoned cesspool.

"So my wife grabbed the baby, and we started out of the house. There were a couple of other couples running down the street, heading for the same place. About that time, I heard a plane coming pretty close. I managed to stick my head out from under the porch's roof, and I could see he was coming right down on the quarters. Evidently, he saw these people running down the street, and he was going for them. When he started getting real close, I gave my wife a shove. She had the baby, and she landed down on the street by the curb. I took a flying leap on top of her. Just as I did that, he started machine-gunning into the roof of the porch that we had been underneath. As a matter of fact, she got dust in her eyes from the machine-gun bullets. They were that close to us as they went down the line.

"We finally got back up again and headed down the block. My main object was to get them out of the house because, after the Japanese got through bombing the flight line and had done all the damage they could down there, they started to work on some of the quarters. When they started bombing and strafing the quarters, I knew that was no place for us."

In the paragraphs below, Mrs. Koran remembers the period before they made their way to the cesspool and then what happened following their arrival there. She explains that the choice of the cesspool as a place of security was a bad one, because gasoline trucks with aircraft fuel were parked nearby.

"It seemed like there was a bomb dropping every five seconds. My first thought was the baby lying in the bassinet. I thought: 'Oh, my, she's going to have her eardrums punctured!' I grabbed a down comforter and threw it double over the bassinet, and, when my husband said: 'It's the Japs! Get your clothes on!' I started to dress. In between grabbing things to dress, I thought: 'Oh, my goodness, what if they've poisoned the water!' It's very peculiar what you think of at a time like that. I must have had an arsenic bomb in mind. I had read someplace where that had been done.

"While I was dressing, there was a young man outside our house hugging the wall right next to the window. I rushed over and screamed out the window: 'Come in out of sight!' I screamed and screamed, and he absolutely did not hear me because the din was so loud.

"There was a little pause after the first wave went over. We went across the street to Shorty and Marge. Shorty was laughing to beat the band. You think of some funny things. During the middle of the bombing, Marge was dancing up and down and clapping her hands, having a conniption fit, saying: 'Oh, what'll I wear, what'll I wear?' She had dozens of things in the closet.

"But then a second wave came over, and we made it to the cesspool. There were about three high-test gasoline trucks that they had brought in there, and they parked them so that there would be some fuel left if the main supplies got blown up. So we—Marge, the baby and I, and her little Scottie dog—squeezed ourselves into a space about 3 feet by 4 feet and about 2 feet sunken under the ground. It was concrete lined but open at the top.

"We were under the banyan tree, and the trucks were parked there because banyan trees are so thick that from the air you cannot spot things underneath them. If one tracer bullet had hit those . . . I didn't think about it at the time."

Sergeant Koran discusses below the variety of events he witnessed before, during, and after the second attack.

"Between the first and second attacks there was a little incident that happened that irritated me quite a bit. I think, if they wanted to, they could have court-martialed me.

"The boys were gathering around one of the hangars which was our ordnance depot, and all the machine guns were behind the fenced-in area back of the hangar. A young second lieutenant, a shavetail, was the ordnance officer, and the boys were trying to get the machine guns out, but he refused to give the guns up because they did not have a damned requisition. Well, I came down there, and, being one of the senior noncoms, they came over and told me about it. So I went in there, and the lieutenant started to give me some guff, and I pulled out my .45 and told him: 'Lieutenant, if you don't open up that damned cage, I'm going to put one right between your eyes,' and he opened the cage, and we got the guns out.

"The way I looked at it, if you've got bombs falling around you and people getting killed, and you see a bunch of guns, the first initiative of any normal human being is to grab one and see what he could do. It just irritated me to see some young lieutenant guarding the damned thing with all the guns back there and saying: 'You can't have them because you don't have an order to get them.'

"When the second attack began there were an awful lot of bombs blowing up around the place. I got down to the flight line, and I could see all these aircraft. Their nose and tail would be sticking up, because the incendiary bullets had gotten right down the middle and had burned out the center of the aircraft. Of a total of all aircraft we had out there, we had 120 that were burned up on the field. They were all pursuit ships. Bear in mind, the Japanese hit our base first, before they hit Pearl Harbor, because we had the fighter aircraft.

"But fortunately we had one of our squadrons that happened to be at Haleiwa, on the north shore, having gunnery practice. Of course, that Saturday there was a party going on at the club. We had Lieutenant George S. Welch, who was a youngster at that time, Lieutenant Kenneth M. Taylor, and Lieutenant Philip M. Rasmussen, who happened to be living in the BOQ [bachelor officers' quarters] there. They were still half asleep and still had their tuxedos on from the previous party.

"Lieutenant Taylor had a little MG. When the first bomb dropped, they jumped into that MG and went the eleven miles from Wheeler Field to Haleiwa, where their airplanes were parked underneath trees. They traveled that eleven miles in less than six minutes. While this was going on, their crew chiefs had loaded their P-40s, and, when they got there, they jumped into their aircraft while they were still in their tuxedos, and they got down the sand runway and were airborne. In order to get airborne, Lieutenant Welch had to waggle his wings to knock the ammunition boxes off each wing. Welch landed and took off at least three times and during the process managed to shoot down five Japanese. I think Taylor got three, and Rasmussen, two.

"I knew all of them well because they all had to report down to the photographic laboratory to take their official portraits. I got acquainted with Lieutenant Welch there, and we did a lot of work together before the war. I jokingly asked him, when he first came down there, when was the last time he shaved. He looked like he had just a little peach fuzz on his cheeks. He was one of the type of boys that nobody cared to fly with in formation. He was a poor formation flyer, but you could put him in a P-40 and let him fly by himself, and he'd turn that P-40 upside down, inside out, turn on a dime, and give you nine cents change to boot.

"We had to make confirmation of the planes shot down. The reason we were able to officially certify this is that, when they have gunnery practice, they have the machine-gun cameras attached to the aircraft at the same time. So the cameras were automatically turned on when the machine guns started to fire, and they automatically started to take photographs. After the film was sent down, and the file was processed, we had official confirmation from all the aerial machine-gun film. There's where we got the official confirmation.

"During the attack on Wheeler Field proper, there were a few planes shot down that crashed in the pineapple fields. One of our machine guns on top of the barracks managed to get one. After the bombing was all over, and things settled down, I was sent out to the pineapple field to locate this crashed Japanese plane and photograph it. It was a twin-engine, torpedo-type aircraft that they used as a dive-bomber.* There were two bodies still in the aircraft—the pilot and the observer. They were burned pretty well beyond recognition. The one in the rear cockpit was leaning over with his arm sticking out of the side of the cockpit, and I noticed something peculiar that was on his hand. So I took a photograph of that hand with infrared film that I had. I also took photographs of the engine. When I processed these photographs, I blew up his hand to a 20-by-24 size, and we discovered that the ring that he was wearing happened to be that of a

---

*The Japanese did not use twin-engine planes in the air raid.

graduate of the Punahou High School, which was one of the high schools in Honolulu.

"Another thing that struck me and made me all the more angrier and teed off was the fact that, after we blew up the prop, the manufacturer's plate on it, believe it or not, happened to be of an American engine they were using in a dive-bomber. It was a Hamilton-Standard prop. This was some of the aircraft equipment and iron and stuff that we had sent over to Japan prior to the attack. This burned me up a bit more.

"During the attack, I grabbed my camera. It just came as second nature. I figured I couldn't do anything else, so I thought I might as well try and get some sort of record of the attack. I photographed all the various flight lines—the ships that were burned out right in a beautiful row. I photographed the damaged hangars and took some general photographs showing the overall damage to the field proper.

"I was photographing one particular area, and I saw one of the fellows running out for one aircraft that was still on the flight line that hadn't been damaged. Before he got there, the Japs got him. They dropped another bomb, and the concussion knocked me against the flight hangar. The reason I know this is because I unconsciously held the shutter trigger on, on the motion-picture camera I had. When we processed the film, that particular film showed the sky and the top of the hangar. After that bomb, all I found of him was his undershirt in a big hole out there, that's all.

"After the second bombing was all over, everybody got as much armament and ammunition as they could get in their arms. They had a slight rumor that paratroopers had landed on the island of Oahu and that they were dressed in blue coveralls. Well, in those days the military had blue coveralls. So an order was issued that everybody in blue coveralls was to get out of them—wear anything, but get rid of the blue coveralls.

"We had a perimeter set up at that time. After that things kind of settled down a bit. I went down to find out how my wife and daughter were doing, and she laughed when she saw me, because I figured, if something was going to happen, I was going to be prepared. I had taken about four bandoliers of .30-caliber shells wrapped crisscross across my chest. I had a Springfield rifle across my shoulder. I had a .45 on my hip, and I had about half-dozen grenades attached around me, and I was carrying a Thompson submachine gun in my left hand, and I had a steel helmet and gas mask on. I don't think I could have run a hundred feet if I had tried.

"With the excitement and everything, I wasn't too frightened, but, when I saw the situation under that banyan tree, and I saw those high-test gas tanks over there, then I got frightened. I could just imagine what would have happened if just one tracer had managed to get in. There would have been nothing but a hundred-foot hole.

"There were a few tragic things that might have happened. I noticed one boy sitting down on the curb, just crying. When I told him to get out of the street and go into the basement of the barracks over there, he was a little hysterical. He was just a young fellow, not more than eighteen. I ran over to him, and, not giving too much thought, I grabbed him by his shirt where his tie was and more or less picked him up and slapped him across the face three or four times and told him to snap out of it. He lost some of his hysteria and managed to stagger over to the barracks and go in the door and get under the staircase.

"I noticed the tent city we had between the hangars [an area where pyramidal tents were set up as temporary quarters]. There were a lot of dead bodies there. A lot of people got shot. But, as far as individual heroism, there was none of this individual stuff going on. There was very little hysteria. Everybody was anxious to do their bit. Nobody slacked off. As a matter of fact, a lot of them gave us a lot of things on their own without being told what to do.

"A peculiar situation of this whole affair is that we had eight hangars on the flight line plus the engineering hangar, which was a large hangar separated from the flight line. Prior to this time, we had notification that there was one squadron that was going to be transferred from Wheeler Field to the Philippines to Clark Field.

"All right, in the meantime their supplies and stuff was in crates, which were stored in these hangars. Well, it so happened that we had two hangars adjacent in sets of threes—two hangars, two hangars, two hangars. These crates that the supplies were in were in the second and fourth group of hangars. Well, strange as it may seem, when the bombing was going on, those two hangars plus the engineering hangar were the only three that were bombed. We surmised that the Japanese had already had information that there was somebody going to be shipped out and that these hangars contained critical military supplies.

"It broke your heart a little bit after the attack was all over, and things calmed down. The next day, a fellow could sit out on the flight line and cry to see all those bulldozers come out and push the planes—what formerly were P-40 aircraft—together in three piles that averaged maybe 30 or 40 feet high when they got them squared away. We spent the rest of the day and the following days getting the debris off the airfield, because we expected new aircraft to come in.

"It wasn't more than a few weeks after that that we had some aircraft carriers come in, loaded full of crates with planes aboard. In order to get planes over to our area, it meant that a lot of them were brought over in crates, and they had to be reassembled. We had gotten our engineering hangar cleared, and the crates were all unloaded. Then we got our engineering officer, and they started putting the planes together. Of course, every time a new aircraft came out of the hangar, why, it was kind of an elation and a little better feeling.

"Finally, when we got them all rolled out and squared away, as we got them on line, we sure as hell didn't line them up wingtip to wingtip anymore. After a short time we had our complement of aircraft back, and we were ready for any eventuality that might come."

Following the attack the military ordered servicemen's dependents back to the United States. Mrs. Koran and her baby daughter traveled aboard the *President Taft*, which the War Department had commandeered. In the concluding portion of the interview she tells a heartrending story of burned American soldiers and sailors on board the ship.

"People who perform heroic acts don't realize that they're doing heroic acts. I had to go up to the sick bay and get some aspirin for the baby when she came down with a very heavy cold, and, being a new mother, it frightened me to death. Well, I waited for the doctor or the nurse to give me the aspirin, and, while I was waiting, I could look into the sick bay, and there were stacks and stacks of boys in bunks with burn cases, eyes and faces and hands. There was one boy that was there waiting on others, giving them cigarettes and water and all, and I have never seen a boy on two feet that was burned as badly as he. He was bare to the waist. His arms were swollen, but he could manipulate his hands. He had ears that were so swollen from being burned that you don't know how he could keep going. But yet he was willing to help his less fortunate fellows.

"One little boy was blind. He was burned so badly that it destroyed his sight, and the doctor or nurse had told my neighbor who helped feed him that he would never see again. But, when she went in to feed him, they were introduced, and he said: 'Oh, Mrs. Leahl, do you think my hair will ever grow back in?' That broke her heart. You have never seen so many tears in your life, and men cried as well as women, and it was not a sign of weakness to cry. It was a sign of strength."

During World War II, Steve Koran flew in reconnaissance aircraft in the Pacific theater, was shot down on three occasions, and supposedly rescued by the same destroyer each time. He stayed in the military after the war, making the transition from Army Air Forces to U.S. Air Force. In the 1960s he retired and went to work for the National Aeronautics and Space Administration (NASA) in Houston, Texas. He died on December 20, 1978. Flora Belle, who was always a homemaker, moved to Washington state soon after Steve's death, but she has since returned to Texas.

37
Lieutenant Everett ("Stu") Stewart
Wheeler Field

That the American military had more to fear from sabotage than from a direct attack seemed to be the common opinion of Army commanders at airfields near Honolulu in December 1941. Lieutenant Everett Stewart, who was at Wheeler Field, remembered that, on "the 6th and a few nights before, we were on sabotage alert. We figured mainly: 'Well, they might blow up our airplanes from within Hawaii.' " Consequently, the planes were parked close together in neat rows on December 7, when the unexpected Japanese attack occurred. A formal military review on Saturday morning was the main reason why they were lined up. Having been in the Air Corps for about two and one-half years at the time, Stu Stewart was operations officer for one of the newer squadrons that had been formed at Wheeler.

Stewart, a native Kansan, was born on July 18, 1915, in Talmadge, a small town about thirteen miles northeast of Abilene. He was twenty-six years old when the Second World War began. He had been commissioned in the infantry reserve following graduation from Kansas State University in Manhattan but wanted to be a fighter pilot. From late 1938 until mid-1939, he attended flight school, finishing just prior to his marriage in June 1939. Before transferring to Hawaii, he served at Barksdale Field near Shreveport, Louisiana, and Moffitt and Hamilton fields in California. In February 1941 his group boarded the USS *Enterprise* and sailed to Honolulu. He said they actually flew off the carrier and landed their planes at Wheeler.

Stu's wife joined him in newly constructed housing on base that March. Together they enjoyed the relaxed island atmosphere, although the Army made sure that life in public appeared formal. Stu wore his dress uniform, and his wife, a long gown to football games, boxing matches, movies, and parties after 6:00 P.M., and even when more than four military people gathered at home for an evening. Still, Mrs. Stewart remembered life as "lovely."

The duty schedule was light. Stewart worked from 7:00 A.M. until noon, usually involved in a "regular fighter training routine," which included dive-bombing, aerial and ground gunnery practice, and sometimes mock raids on the Navy, first in the Air Corps P-36 and later in the P-40. Preparing for a Japanese air raid was about as far from Stewart's mind as a notion could be.

On Saturday, December 6, Stewart took part in the review, and that evening he and his wife went to the squadron commander's home. There were four couples, and they played bridge rather than go to the officers' club as they most often would have done. They had a couple of drinks and went home about midnight, earlier than usual. Mrs. Stewart said: "I didn't feel too well. We parked our car out in front. The next morning it wouldn't start. There was a bullet hole in it!" In the first part of the interview, Stewart discusses his reaction during the attack the following day.

"We were in bed. I guess Mrs. Stewart woke up first. The first thing I heard was at nearly 8:00, which I found out later. I heard the wind up of an airplane. I thought: 'Uh-oh! The Navy's hitting us,' because we used to go back and forth, you know, beating up each other's airdromes. We'd made mock attacks. I thought: 'Well, here comes the Navy again,' and then all of a sudden I heard a big explosion. I said: 'Uh-oh! We got one.' I figured: 'Well, one went on in somehow or another.' Pretty soon there was the same thing—another explosion. I thought: 'My God! We're getting a bunch of them this morning!'

"At this particular point, I was getting out of bed. I guess after about the third one, I figured, 'Well, this is too many,' or something like that. Mrs. Stewart had already gotten up, gone out to the window, and said: 'My God! There are Japanese out there!'

"I don't know whether I was in the backyard or looking out the back, but I could see the rising sun on the airplanes. I knew then what it was. Then I looked out at the flight line. I could see the eastern end, and I could see all eleven airplanes in our squadron. When I looked out there, I could see ten of them burning, including my own personal airplane. The only one that didn't burn was the one we had for spare parts. It was up on jacks. It had the prop off and the instruments out and wheels off. I could see all of that.

"I wanted to get out there and get up at them. Then I thought: 'Hell, I don't have an airplane, so what can I do?' So I went back in my quarters, and I called the squadron commander whose house we had been at the night before. I said: 'Are you still there?' He said: 'Yes.' I said: 'What are you going to do?' And he said: 'I'm going to stay right here until they quit attacking us.' I said: 'Good. I am going to, too,' which really was the only smart thing to do because, if we'd have gone down there, we'd have probably gotten ourselves shot.

"Along our particular set of quarters—line of quarters—they didn't actually strafe, but the sidewalks in back were pockmarked with bullet holes. Some of the BOQs and some of the apartment quarters were hit. As a matter of fact, Lucille Toole, the wife of Lieutenant Dick Toole, was in the bathroom, and the bullets came in there and just went all the way around the place and fortunately didn't hit her.

"Then, of course, they were strafing the barracks and the tent area where our enlisted personnel were living in tents between the hangars. That's where we suffered some casualties—in there. They were strafing all up and down there as well as the flight line, the airplanes, and so forth. They did quite a bit of strafing, but our own particular quarters weren't actually hit, but they hit right alongside of us.

"I went back in to get dressed and then get ready to go down, and, as soon as the first wave was over, then I drove down as quickly as possible to see if we could salvage any airplanes. This could have been anywhere from ten minutes to thirty minutes after the attack began. It seemed like several hours, but it was probably in the nature of twenty minutes plus or minus.

"I didn't go down until there was a lull in the attack on our place. Then I kind of hurried to get down there. The attack might have still been going on down at Pearl Harbor with the torpedo bombers and so on. I'll give you an example of why it was best to stay in the quarters. A former squadron commander, Captain Bill Steele, and, I believe, Major Bill Morgan and a couple of others had started down there during the attack. They finally decided that wasn't very smart. So they ended up hiding under the church steps until the thing was over, because it was just too strenuous down there.

"But, anyway, a bunch of us started to gather down there to try to see what airplanes we could salvage, or if there was anything flyable, or if we could get them out to the revetments on the edge of the field. There wasn't too much panic—a little bit but not too much. We said: 'Well, here's what we've got left. What are we going to do with it? What do we have left?'

"That was the big question: 'What do we have left?' If anything looked like it might be able to fly, we'd tow it out across to the revetments. Well, we were in the process of this when the second wave hit at Wheeler. I recall that down near our squadron area was where my car was. When they started coming in again, I jumped in the car. About that time the car filled up with people, and they were standing on top of it and around it. We drove up the field, and up there was a great big flatbed truck for some reason. I don't know why it was there.

"I was afraid they were going to hit the car. It was full. I don't know how many people were in it. We drove by this flatbed. I said: 'Boy, this is the safest place in the world.' I skidded to a stop. By the time I got stopped and was ready to get out of the car, everybody was out, and the car just sprung up. When I got ready to get under the flatbed, there wasn't any room. The thing was packed and not just with people from my car, but from all around. So I went around to the opposite side from where the Japs might be coming in and stayed on the outside.

"The second attack, from what I could tell, was more sporadic. It wasn't as concentrated. In the first attack, the Japs would come in and make their pass, and they were going way up high because they didn't know whether we had any defenses down there or not. And, after their first pass or two, they got to where they'd just barely come back up over the hangar, just make a pass as fast as they could—dive-bombers and strafing both.

"By the second attack, they'd expended a lot of their ammunition and a lot of their bombs. Most of their bombs were gone. The second attack was primarily strafing and many less airplanes, really, just kind of a haphazard type of thing. They were right on the deck—as low as they could and be effective in shooting. They didn't do so much damage in the second attack, but they'd already done enough in the first attack, so it didn't make much difference. They might have shot a few more people or something like that, but not too many. The second attack lasted probably ten or fifteen minutes.

"When the first attack was going on, we didn't have any rifles or guns or anything at Wheeler, so somebody went up to Schofield Barracks to get some rifles and whatever. I am told that they were told: 'We can't give you any guns because we don't have any official declaration of war. We can't give you any guns.'

"But somehow or another, there were some guns around. I remember on the second attack—he might have been doing this on the first attack—but on the second attack there was one of our squadron's sergeants, Sergeant Hammer, either in a little depression, or he dug a little one, lying with this rifle and shooting at the Japs as they were going by.

"He was shooting at them, and he said: 'I'll get you, you son of a bitch! I'm going to get you!' And he was shooting like hell. Somebody said they thought he shot one down. Now, whether he did or not, I don't know. Nobody knows for sure. A rifle or a machine gun probably brought down one of our leading aces in Germany. So a rifle can be effective against an airplane, but it's awful lucky. But this was the main kind of resistance we had.''

In the next portion of the interview, Stewart comments on the activities of Lieutenants Kenneth Taylor and George Welch, who both became famous for their actions on December 7, and recounts the arrival of a flight of B-17s from the United States that reached Wheeler Field during the attack. Stewart then offers an opinion regarding another of his acquaintances, Lieutenant Kermit Tyler, the young officer on duty at the Fort Shafter Aircraft Warning Service's Information Center when the report came in a little after 7:00 A.M. of multiple aircraft sightings by the newly emplaced mobile radar station at Opana, located near Kahuku Point, on the northern tip of Oahu.

"I knew Lieutenants Welch and Taylor well. Neither one was in my squadron at that time, although Taylor later was. They were a couple of good, young, and new fighter pilots in the outfit. They were good pilots in their training and so on. At the time, most of us were flying P-40s. We had a few P-36s intermingled in. On the morning of the attack, as I recall, they were back at Wheeler when it hit, and they called out to Haleiwa.

"It was one of our gunnery bases out there. They called out and said to get their planes ready, that we were under attack, and they were going to take off as soon as they could. They raced out there. This was brought out very well in the movie *Tora! Tora! Tora!* [1970]. That part was quite true. They tore out there real fast and jumped in their airplanes. They and Lou Sanders, who had the squadron at Mokuleia, and three or four more got in the air that morning.

"Anyway, Taylor and Welch fairly had them a good time that morning. Then they came back into Wheeler. I don't recall whether it was in between attacks or after the second attack. I don't remember now. I believe it was Taylor that I helped get reserviced when he came back in. He had a little nick in his left arm. I jumped up on the wing. I said: 'Come on, Taylor!' He said: 'I'm going to stay in here because, if I get out of here, you'll take my airplane!' I said: 'You're right! That's what I wanted!'

"We helped them out as much as we could. He had a little nick in his arm and a slight bleed there. It didn't hurt him any. I was going to try to talk him into going to the dispensary and get something put on it, but I didn't. So he went on. I wasn't going to throw him out. Besides, he was bigger than I was.

"He got two that morning, and George Welch got four. A couple of the other people got one apiece, and then Lieutenant Gordon Sterling got shot down somehow or another.[*] I don't know whether Sterling was flying a P-36 or a P-40.

"Now I also saw the B-17 that landed during the attack. I was busy doing other things—I don't remember what now—when the B-17 landed. It pulled up toward one of the hangars and the ramp in front down there. I don't remember whether more than one landed there or not. But one of our commanders, Major Bill Morgan of the Fifteenth Group, well, he scurried around and got that thing refueled somehow or another, and he got himself a little crew together, and he took out to the northwest somewhere trying to find the fleet so he could spot it and then direct whatever bombers they could get together to go out and maybe make an attack on it. Of course, they were unarmed.

"Well, let me digress a bit about their arrival. If you'll recall, we had a radar out on one of the western mountains. A young soldier or airman or whatever by the name of [Joseph] Lockard

*See also Olsson interview, pp. 253–258.

and another guy or two were out at the radar site. Kermit Tyler, a lieutenant, was down at our control post. They were all supposed to go off duty at 7:00 in the morning.

"They were at Shafter at the time. Tyler had gone over to Hawaii in the same flight I did—off the same carrier. We had both gone out of Hamilton Field in California. He happened to be the practice control man at that particular time. I knew him very personally for a couple of years. So he was on duty, but he was getting ready to leave. He was supposed to have gotten off, but he was sticking around and fiddling while guys were sending in reports. They were getting ready to close up when Lockard reported this flight from the northwest. Well, Tyler thought about it a little bit—now this was his personal account to me later on of what happened—so he called the Navy and said: 'Hey, we've got a bunch of airplanes out here somewhere.' He told me that the Navy told him: 'Well, don't worry about those. We've got a flight of B-17s coming in from the States, and they're lost. It's got to be them coming in from the northwest.' Well, we found out it happened to be the Japs coming in. And the Navy told him to forget it.

"The Navy was in charge of that particular phase of the whole thing out there. Tyler told me that whoever was on duty down there said: 'Well, forget that. That's the B-17s. They've gotten lost.' The timing was perfect. I see the logic for the Navy to assume that it was the B-17s. Nobody knew exactly. They said: 'Well, they've gotten lost. They've overshot, and they're coming back in, so forget them.'*

"Tyler was senior to me at the time, and he retired several years ago [circa 1974] as a lieutenant colonel. So, yes, he was definitely made a scapegoat.

"But, anyway, the B-17s were coming in from the east about the same time the Japs hit, and they scattered all over. One crash-landed at Kahuku Point on the golf course, and they crash-landed around the island at various places—Bellows Field and others.

*For a different version of this episode see Gordon W. Prange et al., *December 7, 1941: The Day the Japanese Attacked Pearl Harbor* (New York: McGraw-Hill, 1988): 97–98.

"I don't think the one at Wheeler was damaged to amount to anything, however. A great many of them were pursued, and some of them were shot up or shot down or scared the hell out of. They got to the ground in various stages. There might have been a couple of others that came in at Wheeler that taxied off the edge somewhere. I really don't recall. This one was apparently okay, because Bill Morgan got in it as soon as he could get it ready and took off to try to find the Japanese fleet, which, of course, he did not find."

In the concluding portion of his interview, Lieutenant Stewart discusses the period immediately following the raid.

"After the attack we continued trying to salvage what airplanes we could to see what we had. We were trying to clear the flight line and things like that, you know, whatever needed to be done—clear up the debris, check the wounded. Of course, we went down to check on our squadron personnel, who were pretty well shot up in tents down there.

"There were people laying around dead in the tents and in the area. But a good many of them had been taken out. By the time we got down there, the medical people had kind of cleared those out, taking care of the wounded and getting them out of there. Of course, they tried to get the wounded first. But there were mainly just riddled tents and so forth, and then they had bombed out two or three of the hangars. The maintenance hangars were bombed out. We had a few airplanes in there, and some of those were bombed. And there were burned airplanes up and down the flight line.

"I guess I felt: 'Well, it looks like we've had it for now, and what can we salvage and what can we do?' It's just a fact of life. You've got to accept it. 'Well, they got us.' I suppose there was a little panic down on the line, but nothing real great because we weren't right there in the midst of it at the time. Basically, we felt: 'Well, gosh. Here's what we've left. What can we do about it?' "

Stewart spent twenty-eight years in the Air Force, retiring as a full colonel in 1967. At some time after Pearl Harbor he transferred to Europe and flew the P-51 Mustang. He became an ace by the end of World War II and went on to fly jet aircraft during the Korean War. In the early 1970s he met with several Japanese airmen who had taken part in the Pearl Harbor raid, and they told him that they had not expected to meet so little resistance. Stewart, however, remained convinced that a lot of the Japanese success was due to their careful planning rather than the light defense. Although born in Kansas, he spent the remainder of his life in Dallas, where he died on February 9, 1982, at age sixty-six.

Chapter VII

Kaneohe Naval Air Station and Bellows Field

Kaneohe Naval Air Station and Bellows Field were located near each other on the east side of Oahu. The station was situated on Kaneohe Bay at the foot of Mokapu Point on the Mokapu Peninsula, while the airfield, an Army Air Forces fighter base, was in the southeast corner of the island on Waimanalo Bay, six miles north of Makapuu Point. Both were relatively new installations, with Kaneohe established in 1939 as a seaplane facility that was expanded into a naval air station the next year. Although it had barracks, hangars, and an administration building, it was in "a constant state of building," according to Yeoman First Class Kenton Nash. Bellow Field was more primitive. Some men were billeted in tents, and the runway was still earthen.

The first attack on Kaneohe probably began seven minutes earlier than the one at Pearl Harbor, since Japanese Zeros began strafing the runways about 7:48 A.M. The officer of the day at the air station called Bellows "to warn them and to ask for help but his call was regarded as a practical joke."* Immediately,

---

*Aviation Machinist Guy Avery, quoted in Gordon W. Prange et al., *December 7, 1941: The Day the Japanese Attacked Pearl Harbor* (New York: McGraw-Hill, 1988), 174.

dive-bombers joined the Zeros and did the lion's share of damage. This phase ended about fifteen minutes after it had begun.

A second attack by nine horizontal bombers, aircraft similar to the Navy's light bomber type, began around 8:30, and a small number of fighter planes returned briefly to join in. The damage caused by the two sorties was extensive, far greater than that at Ford Island. Hangar number one was hit on the southeast corner during the second attack, which destroyed the planes it held and created a fire that burned until only the steel framework was left. Hangar number three was also hit hard, as were the PBY Catalinas stationed there. Of thirty-six such aircraft, twenty-seven were destroyed, six others were damaged, and only three, out on patrol, were left intact. The second assault ended about 8:45.

At the time, Bellows Field, which was approximately six miles south of Kaneohe Naval Air Station, housed a squadron of fighter planes that were there "for a month's aerial gunnery practice," as Lieutenant Phillip Willis remembered. The twelve P-40s in the group were parked in a row at 10- to 15-foot intervals. Reconnaissance aircraft also were lined up but separated by greater distances.

The Japanese plan called for an assault on Bellows after the Kaneohe raid. At 8:30 a single Japanese fighter machine-gunned a tent area, causing little damage. Around 9:00, nine Zeros attacked, setting fire to a gasoline truck, shooting holes through roofs, destroying and disabling parked aircraft, and keeping American airmen from launching an offensive of their own. The Zeros also harassed one airplane out of a squadron of B-17s being flown to Hawaii that morning, as it was trying to land. By 9:45 A.M. the fighting at Bellows had ended, and restoration and salvage operations began.

38
Yeoman First Class Kenton Nash and Minerva Nash
Kaneohe Naval Air Station

Minerva and Kenton Nash were married in a Honolulu church at 7:00 P.M. on November 15, 1941. They had planned their wedding for one week later, but Kenton was told that by then he would be at an "advanced base" on Midway Island. He called Minnie on the 14th and said: "Let's get married." At first she was reluctant, since her family had already made arrangements for the 22d; but, when Ken said: "I won't be here. It's a military secret, and I can't tell you," she relented.

Ken and Minnie had met in January 1941 at a March of Dimes dance in the Alexander Young Hotel ballroom. One week later he began courting her in earnest, in a way that she described as "the bum's rush." He had plenty of time for romance. His unit, PBY Squadron VP-11, required that, as head yeoman, he be at his desk from 7:00 A.M. to 1:00 P.M. Otherwise, he had "unlimited liberty."

Although Minnie Nash was born on May 1, 1915, in Oakland, California, she was practically a native of Hawaii. Her father, who worked on a sugar plantation run by Alexander and Baldwin on the island of Kauai, had taken his family to attend the San Francisco Exposition. After her birth they returned to the islands. Minnie attended grammar school at Makaweli and high school in Waimea. After a few years during which she worked in various jobs, she studied to be a hairdresser at a school in Los Angeles. When she met Ken, she was working at a beauty parlor in Honolulu.

Kenton Nash was born in Dekner, Montana, on July 6, 1915, and graduated from the Sheridan, Wyoming, high school in January 1937. From 1933 until 1936, however, he had worked at a dude ranch and then had joined the Civilian Conservation Corps (CCC). One month after high school graduation, he enlisted in the Navy, hoping to begin a career and wanting "to put some money in my pocket." He chose the Navy because his CCC camp commander, whom he respected, was an Annapolis graduate, and because Nash had friends who were sailors. After boot camp in San Diego and a brief period at radioman's school, Nash was assigned to PBY Squadron VP-10. He first served at the Ford Island Naval Air Station; but, when Kaneohe was completed in June 1941, he was transferred there.

After the wedding on Thanksgiving Day, Ken and Minnie moved into base housing. Two weeks later, on December 6, they went from Kaneohe to Honolulu to attend a brother's birthday party and to return Minnie's bridesmaid, who had been living with them since their marriage, to her home. Minnie wanted to spend the night with her family in Honolulu, but Ken insisted that they go back to the base. He won the argument when he said: "Do you realize that this is going to be the first time we'll be alone? Let's go back." They arrived at their apartment at 2:00 A.M.

In the following interviews, Minnie and Ken explain their reactions to the attack. As Minnie notes, she, like many other Americans at Pearl Harbor, did not even remotely realize that the first explosions she heard were the opening of an enemy assault.

"It was 7:00 or a little after 7:00. We had been sleeping when we heard the roar of planes. Ken said: 'I wonder what's going on?' So I got up and looked out the window, and I saw this fire. I said: 'Ken, there's a fire in the hangar.' I didn't know the fire was in the bay. Ken came out and said, 'That isn't the hangar! That's the PBY on the bay!' Then he got dressed and came downstairs.

"Somebody came by and said: 'We're at war!' But Ken didn't believe him. Then he saw a Japanese plane and said: 'My God! They're really going all out! They've even painted the rising sun on that plane!' The planes were flying rather low in back of our place. As I've said to many, many people, if I had had a baseball, I could have hit that plane from my bedroom window. That's how low they were flying.

"Well, Ken got ready. He went down to the hangar. I said: 'I'll get breakfast.' As lousy a cook as I was, I was going to make hotcakes. So I put a pot of coffee on, and I started to make the hotcake batter. After a while I sat the batter down waiting for Ken to return, and he didn't come and he didn't come.

"There were a lot of people gathering next door, so I took my coffeepot over and said: 'Here, have some fresh coffee.' I don't even know their names today, and they've still got my coffeepot. Well, I waited and waited, and Ken never came back. Louis Hegwer came by, and I said: 'Hey, Louis, have you seen Ken?' He said: 'No, I haven't, but somebody told me he has an injured hand.' I thought: 'Oh! He is at the dispensary; he'll come back.'"

* * *

Ken would not return soon. After going to the hangar he was hit by shrapnel from an exploding bomb.

"Well, I had dressed hurriedly. This gentleman from next door came in and told us: 'We're at war!' Of course, I had to be convinced. He showed me the holes in his automobile sitting outside, and he had little flecks of blood on his dungarees. So I was convinced. About this time there was a break in the action. I drove down toward the hangar. About the time I got there the second attack started. Some people said: 'You better get out of this car!' I did. There was a civilian worker and an enlisted man from my squadron who were trying to man a machine gun that they had taken out of a plane. They had it laid up on top of a pile of reinforcing steel that was to be used in construction work on a third or fourth hangar—I can't remember which.

"So I stood in among some crated toilet stools that were to go into this hangar and sort of eyeballed the sky and tried to advise these people from what direction the planes were coming. My primary purpose in going down there in the first place was to go into the hangar and get hold of all the personnel records and throw them down on the floor of the hangar, because we had our sprinkling system in the hangar. I felt that, if they were down on the lower floor, they might not be destroyed; they might get wet, but they wouldn't be destroyed. As it turned out, the yeoman who worked for me had already had the presence of mind to do this. The records were all saved.

"The hangars had been strafed. They had small windows out from the strafing, plus fellows had machine guns stuck out of the windows. They had broken glass in trying to operate these machine guns. But the machine guns needed to be tied down; it was very difficult to do any shooting with them.

"Well, we came under attack again. In fact, there was a fighter plane that flew over about fifteen feet above our head, but he was strafing planes. The main thing they did was to destroy our planes. It was a terrible sight to see our planes lined up so well that all they had to do was go down Di-di-di-di, like that, like you were stitching cloth. The minute those tracer bullets hit gasoline, why, they just completely exploded. The gas tanks are in the wings. They hit the gas; they explode; fire comes out; and the wings just droop down. We had landing floats [pontoons] at each end of the wing, and when they were parked, these floats were down, perpendicular to the wing. They just dropped down on these floats, and the tires would crumple. It was pretty sad to see brand-new planes destroyed so quickly.

"I saw a few planes—they were strafing—and then the low-level bombers were in at more or less the same time. The strafers got into one position to do their work, and the bombers got in position to do something else. I think the bomb that hit me was dropped by a plane that was a little off target. I really think he should have been aiming at the hangar. I was a good 150 feet from the hangar. He came in at a glide about 50 or 60 feet off the ground, diving at an angle. I saw the bomb being released from his plane. The plane pulled up; the bomb hit about 60 feet away and exploded. I actually saw the windows pop out of my car—the windshield and back window. They popped out like breakaway windows in a movie. Before I realized it, I was hit myself.

"I was hit by shrapnel. I had my arm leaning up on top of one of these crates, and the shrapnel hit my arm and tore out the lower muscle and knocked out a bone in the upper arm. Everything from the elbow down was in perfect shape; it was only the upper arm that was damaged. The muscle tissue of the upper part of the arm held on, and I walked around into a contractor's shack. There happened to be a sailor in there who took one look at me and ripped up his shirt and put a tourniquet right up near the shoulder on my arm. It wasn't very long after that that the ambulance came into the area. A good friend of mine was driving it, and he got me out of there in pretty much of a hurry and took me to the dispensary. My ears were ringing a little bit, but I was conscious.

"I was in a passageway between the crates that were a good six feet high. The passageway was probably two feet wide. I was protected on three sides, but I was exposed at the opening. I was exposed to the bomb. I saw the bomb coming, but I really didn't realize that this was what it was. I probably had been trained to react sooner; I should have dived down and back into there, and I might not have been injured. I was watching a strafing plane at the time, and I was talking to these people who were only about six feet from me. It was very quick. I wanted to see what was going on. The general tenor of everyone around me was that they were mad. They weren't scared; they were mad. I've talked to a lot of people since that time, and that would seem to be their reaction.

"One of the fellows had a .45-caliber pistol, and I think he pierced the oil tank on a fighter plane, which I saw going away smoking. So I feel that he got one. But there was no antiaircraft batteries, and the only thing available was the .45-caliber pistols that they checked out of the armory."

Nash was taken first to a dispensary, but his wound was serious enough that he was then transferred to a nearby mental hospital, where, in an existing operating room, his arm was amputated. The next portion of Ken's interview begins with him in the dispensary.

"I had lost a lot of blood from an injury on my forehead, and I didn't know it. They had us laying on mattresses in the dispensary. They had given me a shot, probably morphine, for shock. I was still conscious, though. I heard them say: 'I wonder where the blood's all coming from?' So the doctor put a hemostat on this injury on the hairline.

"The doctors and the corpsmen were moving very fast. There were several injured—I wouldn't know how many—in the dispensary prior to me getting there. They had very little ward space. Those buildings were built with a lanai. So they had put down mattresses—probably broke them out from the supply department nearby—and laid them down. They took us off the stretchers and laid us down on the mattresses.

"Then we were loaded into ambulances, four of us, and taken to Kaneohe Territorial Insane Asylum, which was near the town of Kaneohe, just across the bay. It was about a five-mile ride. I had arrived at the dispensary at approximately 9:00 in the morning, and I think I got in on the operating table at the territorial insane asylum about 12:00 or a little after.

"The doctor-administrator had been there only six months. He was a Chinese fellow, and he had been involved with the

Chinese-Japanese war. He knew what to do in a hurry. He had a way of assessing which injuries to take on first. I was not the greatest injured because of the fact that one of my friends had been shot in the stomach.

"They had two operating rooms, and they had a Japanese doctor—woman—who was so short she had to have a stool to stand on. I didn't find this out until afterwards. This Chinese doctor moved things pretty fast, and they had good facilities and quite a few nurses. So I was placed on the operating table around noon. I was given a transfusion right there by one of the inmates, who was an alcoholic. He was in there for a drying-out period. I apparently have a low tolerance for ether, because that's what they gave me. I didn't come to until about 8:00 that night. This Chinese doctor woke me up, and he had a tin cup with ice in it and bourbon whiskey, and he said: 'Here, son, take a drink of this. It might not help, but it'll make the world look better.' So I drank it with pleasure. I knew my arm had to be amputated the minute I was hit. So I'm one of the few people that never went through the shock of waking up and finding part of their body gone. That was not a problem with me at any time.''

Mrs. Nash's story of what she did during the battle and after Ken was wounded provides information about civilian personnel at Pearl Harbor and how the Honolulu public reacted.

"Louis Hegwer came by and told me that he heard Ken had a hand injury and was at the dispensary. He said: 'I hate to say this, Minnie, but there is a Packard that has been bombed, and it's destroyed.' Now, on that base, there was a young ensign who had a car similar to ours, the same color. So Louis said: 'I don't know if it's your car or this officer's car.' I selfishly thought: 'Oh, my God, I hope it isn't mine,' but it was.

"I stayed in the house, but they came over and told us we would have to be evacuated. I wasn't going, being a bride. Two houses down and right on the corner, there was this flyer's wife who also was a bride of three months. I didn't know her very well, but, anyway, in this confusion you met all your neighbors. We decided we weren't going to leave; we were going to wait there for our husbands. Meanwhile, all the wives and children that lived there were being evacuated. They had the cars take them away.

"It was getting kind of late, and I went home. Somebody rapped on my door and said: 'You will have to leave, Mrs. Nash; it's an order.' All I ever heard was that, if you don't do things right, your husbands catch hell, so I wasn't about to get my husband in trouble. So I left. They took us up a hill—in the side of a hill. We got in this one place, and I can't recall what it looked like. There were more little children, and there were a lot of pregnant women that were due any minute.

"There was this one gal named Saul, who lived up on this hill, and she said: 'Why don't I go ask the Japanese owner if we can come up there?' He said we could, so four of us gals decided we'd leave the facilities for the pregnant women and all those children. So we left. We weren't too terribly far away, a couple of miles. We made a pact that we weren't to leave each other alone. We were going to stick together in case the Japanese came. In the meantime they kept saying that the Japanese were landing; the parachutes were coming down, especially on these hills. It was getting kind of dark, and the four of us decided we were going to stand watches. Two would stay awake while two would sleep.

"Before they took me away, I wrote a note to my husband. I said: 'They've made me leave. They have evacuated me, but I'll be back as soon as I can.' But, getting back to these gals, I told them I had a terrific headache. I guess I hadn't eaten. The girls were pretty nice. They said: 'Well, if you don't want to stand guard, you can lie down and get rid of your headache.' It was getting dark, and way out you could see the lantana, a bush that has a nice blossom, and some are six feet tall. Well, way in the horizon we saw this white thing moving the lantanas very slowly. They said: 'Oh, my God, the Japanese have landed, and they're heading for this house!'

"We kept watching at that window, and it got dark, and we couldn't see. So nobody slept, and we decided we weren't going to open that door come hell or high water, no matter who knocked. Soon as sunrise came we got up. We really hadn't slept. We looked out the window, and, not very far from where we were, there was an old gray mare that had come in to us.

That gray mare kept four women thinking they were going to be invaded by the Japanese.

"All this time, I don't know what's happened to Ken outside that he hurt his arm. We're into Monday morning now. You couldn't go out into the Navy Yard; you had to have permission. So Mrs. Saul called in to the officer in charge of the yard and said that I was coming in to work at the laundry. They wanted volunteers at the laundry or at the hospital. Well, I couldn't go to the hospital because I don't like blood, so I went to the laundry. The reason I volunteered was because I wanted to find out what happened to Ken. I was there all day, and about three or four times that day the air raid sirens went off, and that meant we had to make for safety. That's the first time I actually got scared. I wasn't scared during the bombing; it was the next day, when I volunteered my services at the laundry. When the sirens went off, I thought: 'My God, Minnie, now what did you do? If anything happens to you, it's your own fault, because you didn't have to be here, you know.'

"Late that afternoon, after they were about to close the laundry, about 3:00, I tried to get in touch with my brother, who worked on the base as a civilian. I wanted to find out about Ken, and I wanted to get hold of my brother to bum a ride back to Honolulu. I left the laundry, and I went to the hospital and said I wanted to talk to a doctor. I told him I was Mrs. Nash and that I was Kenton's wife, and I didn't know where Kenton was, and I wanted to know what happened. He looked at me and said: 'Mrs. Nash, Kenton's been seriously injured, and he is now at the territorial hospital, the insane asylum.' I said: 'What happened?' He said: 'He lost his arm.' My first reaction was: 'Which arm?' He looked at me and said: 'His left arm.' Before I could do anything, he said: 'Yes, I know. Mr. Nash was left-handed.' I probably turned white. See, Ken was left-handed, and that's why I wanted to know which arm he lost. He said: 'I will write a note to the doctor and see if they can let you in to see your husband.'

"My brother worked in the motor pool, so I went down there and got him to drive me back to Honolulu by way of the territorial hospital. Before I did that, I ran in and got some cigarettes for Ken; I thought this would ease his pain. When I walked in, it was a shock. I had been crying. Ken had never seen me cry, and he wouldn't want to see me cry. So I braced myself, and I went to the office. They told me what room he was in, so I walked in. As I came through the door, before he could see me, I saw him in a propped-up position. He still had dried blood in his hair, and he had a sandbag hanging for weight, for his arm. I thought: 'Oh, my God, I cannot cry,' so I came through the door smiling. I said to him: 'Hi! What are you doing here?' It was just something to get his mind off it. Later he told me that it did. If I hadn't come in there smiling, it would have been pretty bad. As it was, I took it pretty good. It was killing me, but I wouldn't let him know. So I stayed there with him for a while. I asked him: 'Would you want to see the others?' He said: 'I think I'll just see you today, that's enough.'

"I left because it was getting dark. We drove without lights. When I got to Honolulu, my sisters and everybody was so happy, because Mother and my sisters had been worried about us. They knew we were in Kaneohe. My brother told them what happened to Ken. I walked in the bedroom, and my mother was lying in bed. She started to cry. She said: 'What happened to Kenton?' I said: 'Well, Mom, I think Kenton's better off than you. What are you doing in bed?' The reason she was in bed [was that], a block from our home in Honolulu, they had been bombed; and, had the trade winds changed, it would have come right up to the block where we lived. So the shock of that got my mother, and she was all upset, so she went to bed.

"I spent the night in Honolulu. I thought: 'Well, I've got to get down to see Kenton.' So then I contacted the Red Cross and told them that I had no clothes. I was using my sister's clothes. I said I would like to go back and volunteer my service and stay in the hospital with Ken. So the Red Cross came over and picked me up and drove me back to Kaneohe. It was about three days later, and I stayed in the hospital. We say we spent our honeymoon in the crazy house! We stayed there until Ken got transferred to Pearl Harbor. When we got to Pearl Harbor Hospital, Ken knew he was going to come to California to Mare Island Naval Hospital, so he made it a point that I'd be on the same ship. He told me: 'Don't say anything, but you will be getting a call. When I leave, you will be leaving with me.'

"On Christmas Eve at midnight, I got a phone call. It was Pearl Harbor calling to notify me to be at the dock the next day by 1:00. It was Christmas Day. So on Christmas I said goodbye to my family and went down to the pier and boarded the ship. We didn't leave until the next day, but it was with Ken, and we were on our way to the mainland."

Kenton Nash was discharged from the U.S. Navy on May 27, 1942. For the next twenty years he worked as a civilian employee at the Mare Island Naval Shipyard. In 1962 he joined the U.S. Civil Service, working for the Naval Audit Service. After retiring in 1973, he and Minnie began to travel around the United States and overseas. Their home base, however, is Vallejo, California.

39
Painter Third Class Henry Retzloff, Jr.
Kaneohe Naval Air Station

People sometimes make important decisions for trivial reasons. For example, Henry Retzloff joined the Navy in 1940 because his brother and two friends were going to downtown Lansing, Michigan, to enlist, and he just "tagged along." They failed the exam, but Hank passed. Since he was seventeen at the time, he had to return to the recruiting office after his birthday, two weeks later, entering the service on April 16. He picked the Navy "because of the uniform." His friend had told him: "If you want to get into the Donald Duck suit, go down and sign up." Born in Lansing on April 9, 1922, Retzloff had just graduated from the public high school there when he joined the military. He did not have far to travel for boot camp, since he was sent to the Great Lakes Naval Training Center, near Chicago.

Retzloff had not followed world affairs to any degree and thus had not thought of fighting in a war when he enlisted. After boot camp he was sent to the Navy's destroyer base in San Diego and assigned to the USS *Schley* in Destroyer Division Eighty, which comprised three other "four-piper tin cans," including the USS *Ward*. The main order of business on all the destroyers when

Retzloff arrived was chipping and repainting these "relics of World War I."

In December, Hank sailed to Pearl Harbor in the *Schley*. Three weeks later, in January 1941, he and the majority of the ship's crew were transferred to Kaneohe Naval Air Station, a new facility then being constructed. A plankowner (a serviceman present when a station is commissioned), Retzloff stayed at Kaneohe for the next fifty-two months. As a painter in the Transportation Department of Public Works, he had a job "pretty much like a civilian's, like a seabee unit." When he left in early 1946, Transportation had eight hundred vehicles that he kept painted and lettered.

Like most servicemen in peacetime Hawaii, Retzloff enjoyed the duty. Work was light, and liberty regular. He was off on Wednesday afternoons, Saturday afternoons, and Sundays, when he frequented the beaches, "looking for girls for companionship," or boxed, played basketball or softball, exercised, or wrestled. He did not live the life of "Navy people, going out and getting drunk, boozed up."

On the Saturday before the attack, Retzloff went to Honolulu on his motorcycle, driving up and down Waikiki Beach and Kapilani Boulevard. Honolulu was a "quaint town," and he enjoyed the "quaintness." He returned to Kaneohe by 8:00 P.M. because he had "the duty." At the time, he was a section leader with the rating of painter third class. What Retzloff remembered most about the night before Pearl Harbor was the trouble he had with the officer of the day. Around 10:00 P.M. the OD called to request a ride to the Bachelor Officers' Quarters (BOQ), about one and one-half blocks from Retzloff's duty station. While he was leaving to pick up a truck, another seaman asked him where he was going. He replied: 'Well, some fucking officer is too damned lazy to walk up to the BOQ." Unfortunately, the phone was still connected, and the lieutenant overheard his remark. When Hank picked him up, the OD asked: "Who's the wise son of a bitch down there?" Retzloff feigned ignorance, but he was sure that, if the attack had not intervened, the officer would have had him "hung from a yardarm."

His duty ended, Rentzloff went to bed around 11:00 and rose the next morning at 7:30, when his interview begins. According to his recollection, the Japanese attacked Kaneohe slightly before the main assault on Pearl Harbor.

"I was getting ready to go to chow. The planes were zooming by outside; it sounded like maneuvers. We thought: 'Gosh, maneuvers on Sunday morning?' It wasn't likely that they would have maneuvers, but there were the planes. They seemed to be firing ammunition, but we assumed that they were blanks.

"Then we looked outside—our barracks was on the second floor above the dispatcher's office—and this gave us a view of Kaneohe Bay. A lot of PBYs and a couple of planes bigger than PBYs were anchored there. The Japanese were bombing, strafing, and setting them afire. A lot of guys had gone out on boats and spent the night standing guard on the PBYs. They were now swimming back. I remember seeing this while I still thought that it was a practice session. Then I looked up and saw that the PBYs were on fire. I said: 'Well, golly, this is unusual! They don't set planes on fire in an air raid drill!'

"The Japanese planes were flying so low that I swear you could have hit them with a stone. You could see the pilots. I don't recall that I recognized them as Japanese. I didn't even recognize the red ball. It meant nothing to me; it could have been a green square, and it would have meant as much to me at that particular moment. They were dropping bombs and strafing. One of the hangars was bombed, and we had a couple of men killed in the bombing. But we got hit primarily by strafing.

"The action didn't last very long. We ran downstairs, and everybody was going every which way. There were no battle stations; this made for a lot of chaos. Some people were saying: 'My gosh! What's happening?' There was no way to fight back. You just starting running in all different directions and wondered what is going on. I don't recall any siren going off.

"I know a bomb hit pretty close to the transportation department, and a lot of paint in my shop fell off the shelves, down to the ground, and was torn up. We had a fire engine sitting outside which was set afire. Some of the shells went through the wheel housing which were about three-quarters of an inch thick. These shells set the engine on fire. Somebody was telling me that my paint shop was all messed up: 'Hank, your paint shop is all screwed up, and your paint is spilled all over.' I said: 'To hell with that! We're at war!' This showed my stupidity. I thought, 'If we're at war, I don't need the paint shop. Give me a gun; I want to shoot!' I had no idea of what to expect.

"There were a lot of Japanese fighters and bombers. A lot of the land-based planes that we had were lined up on the apron, you know, typical Navy fashion. Well, one enemy plane could go down a line of planes, and, with every fifth shell being an incendiary shell, it could set most of the planes on fire. It could then come back and get what it missed pretty easily. I think we learned a lesson right there about lining planes up.

"After the first attack, somebody spread the word that they were opening a gunnery shack. Everybody ran over to it and got hold of a .30-caliber rifle and a couple of bandoliers of ammunition and ran back someplace. They found a hole, a tree, a log, or made a little dugout.

"We did have one .50-caliber machine gun on the base. We had one machine gunner—I think he was a gunner's mate second class. I don't recall the guy's name, but I picture him. He took the machine gun out of the gunnery shack and set it up outside and was firing at the Japanese as they were going over. These were the planes coming back from the attack on Pearl Harbor. One had been hit, and it came over the mountain range, over the Pali, and crashed straight into the hill on our base. This is the one Japanese plane that went down on the base. It was piloted by a Lieutenant Iida; I think that's his name.*

"So, between the first and second waves, we rushed over to the armament shack and picked up rifles and ammunition. At that time, we were anticipating that the Japanese would be landing on the island. During the second attack, I know a Jap plane went over me. I jumped behind a rock, and I jammed my rifle down into the ground, and I got dirt in the muzzle. It scared me. I said: 'I think the rifle is all right, but I do not want to fire it!' Before that happened, I did do some firing at the planes, but

---

*Lieutenant Fusata Iida was shot down over Kaneohe shortly after 9:00 A.M. For more details on his death see Gordon W. Prange et al., *December 7, 1941: The Day the Japanese Attacked Pearl Harbor* (New York: McGraw-Hill, 1988): 283–86.

I don't know if I hit any. After I got dirt in the muzzle, I did not shoot anymore. I set the rifle down and walked away, but somehow I got hold of another one. In all I probably shot around fifteen rounds at Japanese planes.

"I think we all were just throwing a lot of lead in the air out of frustration and fear and wanting to do something. We really shot a lot of ammunition. We were even shooting .45s in the air. It was every man for himself; nothing was organized at all. I think the gunner's mate on the .50-caliber knew what he was doing, and some of the PBYs had guns on them, and their gunners were possibly qualified. But, since the rest of us got no guidance, no direction, we felt helpless. We were strictly untrained, unprepared, unready . . . it's an embarrassing spot to be in because we were supposed to be a fighting force. I don't think we had any fear. I think fear came later.

"After the attack we just wandered around and talked to our buddies. We said: 'Did anybody get hurt? Is he still around?' We didn't lose all that many people at Kaneohe. But there was a lot of talking: 'Who's this? What's this all about? What does this mean? What's the future going to be? What do we do now?'

"I don't think we ever did get any direction. After a week we settled into duty. As far as my job as a painter, I had to black out lights. They set up a system with the metal shop building shields that fitted on car headlights. They had to be according to specifications and put on at a certain angle out from the lamp. They would bring them to me, and I would spray red lacquer on the top part and then put masking tape in the crack between the shield and light so that white light would not come through. Then I would paint the light all black, except about an inch below the shield; it had a two-inch long, one-eighth of an inch wide, clear light. The light would shine down on the pavement maybe about 15 or 20 feet in front of the car. It couldn't be seen from the air. This was part of the stuff I had to do after the attack.

"Of course, immediately after the attack, I had volunteered for a machine-gun squad. I thought: 'Man, this is war! We get a gun, and we go fight!' I volunteered. We got tommy guns, and they instructed us how to deploy. The Japs were supposed to have landed in the northern end of the island, and they could have. There were all sorts of rumors. I believed they were going to land on the island. We stayed up all night long, shooting the breeze. I don't know if I slept that night, maybe an hour or so. I don't even know if I ate that day. This kind of excitement and chaos can put a check on your appetite. I don't know if the mess hall was available for food.

"Anyway, at the mess hall we made big vats of coffee, and we were supposed to take one or two suits of whites up there and drop them in this vat and bring them back and let them dry out. This would be our brown khaki uniform. Looking back on it now, it was idiotic. We could have worn blue jeans and have been as camouflaged. I think this was a good indication of how unorganized we were. We wore those coffee-stained uniforms for three or four months. We were wearing them as part of the uniform of the day.

"On the landing strip that night, there were guys on both sides, and, of course, one guy said: 'Hey, there goes a Jap now! Here they come! They're here!' So he started firing, and the guy on the other side of the strip said: 'They're here!' So he fired back. Pretty soon everybody was firing at everybody else. Of course, the Japanese never did land. There was some real shooting going on at the airstrip, and I was glad to be away from it.

"The next day, I went to Pearl Harbor. I heard it was pretty bad over there, and, being in the transportation department, I had to go over and get supplies and equipment and ammunition from Ford Island. So we made a run over to Pearl Harbor, and I still saw flames in the bay and the debris—the ships and the bodies. They had the bodies stacked up behind the dispensary up there. I just got a faraway glimpse; I didn't care to see that. There was a lot of chaos over there in spite of the fact that they were much more militarily organized than we were at Kaneohe.

"All that happened that day made me feel a lot younger than my years. You have a feeling of anger. You realize that somebody has come over here and done this to you and your country and your friends and your possessions—your Navy. You want to strike back. 'Let's do all we can!' This was war, but what does war mean? I didn't know. At that particular time, I don't think anybody knew what war really meant. I would say that, within four or five days, I realized that, even if we were at war, this didn't mean that we were all going to grab our guns and fight in the battlefield like in the movies. We were going to have to maintain the equipment and paint the vehicles and paint the blackout lights and operate the base like we did before. It took me at least three or four days to realize this. So I went back and started to maintain my paint shop, paint trucks, and do the job I had done before.''

Retzloff continued to work as painter, letterer, and designer at Kaneohe until he left the service in April 1946. He returned home to Lansing, where he became an airbrush artist and retoucher of photographs. In 1954 he and his family moved to Little Rock, Arkansas, where he continued to work as a commercial artist, eventually opening his own studio in 1965 and operating it until he retired in 1986.

After the formation of the Pearl Harbor Survivors Association in the early 1970s, Retzloff became active in the Arkansas chapter and served as the group's first president. His primary focus in life, other than his vocation, became the association. He labored unsuccessfully to have a commemorative stamp of the Pearl Harbor attack issued by the U.S. Post Office. Proud of serving at Pearl Harbor and in the Navy, he held fondest memories of the times he spent with his fellow survivors. Hank Retzloff died on June 29, 1987.

40
Lieutenant Phillip Willis
Bellows Field

Phillip Willis entered the Army Air Corps on October 14, 1940, because he realized war was coming, and he ''intended to help defend my country as a pilot.'' Born in Peeltown, Texas, forty miles southeast of Dallas, on August 2, 1918, Willis was twenty-two and had just completed two years of college at North Texas State Teachers College in Denton. His sixty hours of college credit qualified him for the Air Corps.

After induction at Glendale, California, where he trained briefly, Willis spent time learning to fly first at Randolph Field and then at Brooks Field, both of which were located near San Antonio. He received his wings on August 15, 1941, and, requesting duty in the Hawaiian Islands, was sent to Hickam Field near Honolulu, where he joined the Seventh Air Corps. He was quickly assigned temporary duty with the Eighty-sixth Observation Squadron at the makeshift base called Bellows Field, located on the southeast corner of Oahu. From there he flew the O-47, or what he and others called the "pregnant pigeon, a big old fat, single-engine plane."

On December 6, 1941, Willis was preparing to leave Bellows to accompany the body of a comrade killed in a flight accident back to Tulsa, Oklahoma. He was scheduled to depart on December 8 and planned to meet his girlfriend in Tulsa and return with her to Honolulu, where they were to be married on Christmas Day. As he describes below, he spent the evening of December 6 at the officers' club at Hickam, celebrating his approaching departure.

"I really had a hell of a party the night before [the attack] in my honor because I was leaving to bring my buddy's body back to the States on Monday morning. Everybody had to buy you a drink when you were coming back. I had no orders other than to be on that ship on Monday morning. So we had a ball. We got back to Bellows Field about 3:00 or 4:00 in the morning. I had such a big party that I still had my tux on when the machine-gun fire came through the roof the next morning. I had my shoes off, but I had my tux pants on."

Willis next traces his activities from the opening sally at Bellows Field until the second attack, which destroyed his aircraft.

"My condition wasn't worth a damn when I got back from Hickam to Bellows. But when the machine-gun bullets came through the roof, it got pretty good. We were young, and in those days I could drink and get up in the morning and suck on that oxygen and fly just as good as anybody. I did it a lot of times.

"So, when the bullets came through the roof, and we heard the bombs going off, we all ran out. I made a smart remark. I said: 'Us Texans like to die with our boots on.' I ran back and reached in my footlocker and got my cowboy boots and put them on with the tuxedo pants and shirt and grabbed my flight jacket and helmet.

"We ran out and saw these planes just diving and strafing with the red balls on their wings. We knew it was for real. There'd been maneuvers and mock warfare and stuff with the fighters, but, when we saw what was happening, we knew danged well what it was, and we recognized the Zero. We had studied identification of Japanese aircraft.

"It got so hot that I had to find a hiding place. There was a ditchdigger out there, a trenching machine, where they were laying utility lines. The ditch was about 2 feet wide and probably 4 of 5 feet deep. I ran toward it. Then I saw one of my buddies. He was a fighter pilot. We had several P-40 fighters there, along with our planes.

"This fighter pilot was getting ready to try to take off. Well, every time one of our P-40s would buzz down the runway, a Jap would be right on top of him strafing him, and he'd blow up or go in the ocean. If he got off the ground, by the time he got his wheels up, they'd get him because they were swooping down on him.

"I was trying to help the pilot into the cockpit. I was pushing him from behind. So while I was pushing on his rear, one of them came down and shot the plane all to hell and killed him instantly. Blood went all over me. When the machine-gun bullets went through his body, they lodged in the pack parachute. That's what saved me, or I'd have gone with him.

"So I ran and jumped in the ditch behind the trenching machine. I jumped down in this trench, and about this time the strafing caused a clod of dirt to hit me in the eye. I screamed because I just knew I'd been shot right through the head. Actually, I got a clod of dirt in my eye. I guess there's something funny about everything bad.

"Well, pretty soon they went away, and I got my plane off the ground. I got up and looked down on Pearl and saw what the hell was happening. We had no ammunition, so we were told just to fly up and down over the treetops up in the valley and try to save our airplanes. When it was apparent that the Japs had left, we got the all-clear signal. They had left, but there was a second attack. In the meantime, I had a chance to see Hickam Field and Pearl all burning up.

"At Bellows they got our gasoline trucks and our little radio shack and the airplanes. They knocked them out. There was nothing operational. There were some B-17s that did come in, that got shot up a little bit but not destroyed. They were fortunate to get in late. They couldn't all land at Hickam, but the ones that did caught hell. The Japanese concentrated their heavy stuff on Pearl Harbor and Hickam Field. They burned hangars full of airplanes over there. Pearl Harbor was just an inferno.

"Well, we got the all-clear signal. We were getting the word by radio about everything that happened. So I came back and landed. Then they came back the second time and got my plane. We were wiped out over there."

After his plane was destroyed, Willis was issued a pistol and told to patrol the beach. He joined with a Hawaiian National Guard unit, and together they captured the first Japanese prisoner to be taken by Americans in World War II. The hastily created unit of Hawaiians, Hawaiian-Americans, and airmen seized Ensign Kazuo Sakamaki, who commanded one of the five midget submarines that the Japanese launched as part of their Pearl Harbor attack. Ensign Sakamaki had made full preparations for dying before leaving his mother ship, but either engine trouble, problems with the gyroscope, or bad navigation caused him to be stranded on a reef, where he was captured. In addition to commenting on Sakamaki's capture, Willis offers his opinion about the loyalty of Japanese residents in Hawaii to the United States.

"The authorities issued us rifles and pistols and told us to take our little bedroll and put it in the trunks of our cars because they didn't know where they'd send us, but we'd be on beach patrol. They assigned us to some quickly mobilized national guardsmen on this side of the island. There was a Japanese colony right near there. That's why we spent the night patrolling the beach and looking for anything.

"There were so many Japanese on the island that there were all kinds of rumors of sabotage. They later captured this Japanese tavern owner over by Wheeler Field. He had all this radio equipment and everything, and he turned out to be a colonel in Japanese army espionage. He'd sell all these GIs drinks on credit and everything and get them to talking about their equipment.

"I was surprised there wasn't more sabotage than there was.* Of course, they had no occupation forces with them. All they wanted to do was knock out our Navy the best they could. I don't think they had any idea in this world that they would be able to get in there and do as good a job as they did. The knockout punch that they delivered, I think, was as much a surprise to them as it was to us.

"Anyhow, as I said, they told us to take our ammunition, bedroll, rifle, and pistol and put our bedrolls in our car trunk because we did not know what was going to happen. But one damned thing was certain—we had to patrol the beaches. So we wandered around and went up and down the beach in different spots.

"We were prepared for parachute troops to land during the night and then for them to come right on in with an invasion force. We knew that, if they had enough men, they could have done it. We didn't have any Air Force or Navy. There was no way we could hold them off. I can remember during that night patrolling the beach with those guardsmen, and I thought: 'Boy, this thing could last four or five years before we get to go home, or they might capture us before tomorrow's over.'

"I was with this group, and, just at the crack of dawn, someone—not me, but one of the others—spotted this black thing sticking out of the water, and then it disappeared. As the tide would come in and recede, that thing would stick out of the water and disappear. It turned out to be the conning tower of this seventy-foot, two-man suicide submarine. We all immediately zeroed in on it to see what the hell was going on.

"As the sun started to come up, and it got lighter, it turned out that one of the two men manning it had drowned. Why they didn't get out sooner, I don't know. We didn't know how long they had been there. Had they been able to get to this little

---

*None of the stories of sabotage has been proven.

Japanese village right nearby, they probably would have been covered up by some sympathizers. We'll never know.

"This two-man submarine had a ring around its propellor, and it got hung up on a coral reef, and it was damaged. They couldn't get loose from this reef. Of course, the submarines had been to Pearl Harbor. I don't know whether this one was on the way to Kaneohe or if they were trying to escape; maybe that was their intention. They had five hundred pounds of TNT in it. After they expended their two torpedoes, they were supposed to ram something, and the five hundred pounds of TNT would blow up the submarine and them and whatever they rammed. Well, they didn't set it off. They didn't want to die, I guess.

"So, while we were watching this thing, one of the guardsmen started firing into the water. I said: 'Don't do that! What do you see?' He said: 'I saw a Jap, sure as hell, sticking his head out of the water!' I said: 'Well, my God, we need a prisoner! If that is one, don't fire anymore!' Finally, [Sakamaki] couldn't take it any longer, and he just came up.

"His toes and fingers were shriveled up. He said later that he'd been in the water for hours, but he couldn't find a place where there weren't some troops. All he had on was a little belt that was fine stitched—the ceremonial deal, a G-string with all of their good wishes from everybody on it. He was clean shaven, hair clipped, ready for the final gesture for the emperor. Evidently, he decided he didn't want to die. So he came out, and we captured him. We took him up to this little old hut that was kind of dug into the side of a hill. It was just a lean-to we had there, and we interrogated him.

"Everybody had pistols on him. He wasn't going anywhere. He was so weak by then. So we took him up there, and he bowed and just clammed up. So we got the word to get an interpreter, a local Japanese. But, before this, we cocked a hammer on a .45 and stuck the barrel right in his eye and jammed his head against the wall when he wouldn't say anything. At first we tried to soften him up. We gave him a couple of boiled eggs, and he bowed. We gave him a cup of coffee, and he bowed. We gave him a cigarette, and he bowed. Then we gave him a paper and pencil and motioned him to start writing. He didn't. So then we started jamming a gun in his eye and pulled the hammer on the .45 back and threatening him.

"Finally, he took the piece of paper and pencil, and he sat down and wrote in these Japanese characters. When the interpreter got there, it turned out to be: 'I am Japanese naval officer. I expect to be treated as same. I failed in yesterday's battle. So please kill or let kill self by intimate method—hara-kiri. But I no say about ships.' He slammed his pencil down and clamped his arms together and flexed his muscles and just looked us straight in the eye and dared us to kill him.

"So with that we put him in one of those big old military, Navy-type laundry bags and pulled the drawstring on him, tied him up, and pitched him in the back of our truck, and, with him jabbering and kicking like a danged wild animal, they took him over to the stockade at Schofield Barracks. Eventually, they sent him back to the States. He remained in California the whole war. Then, as far as I know, he's still in Tokyo or somewhere over there."*

Soon after the Pearl Harbor attack, Willis volunteered for duty in B-17 bombers. At first he trained on the B-18 but later became a copilot in a B-17 and participated in the Battles of Midway and Guadalcanal and many others across the South Pacific. He and his crew were credited with sinking four ships and shooting down eight planes. Since he had been wounded several times, after the war he took a full medical retirement from the military. He later served two terms in the Texas legislature and is currently a realtor in Dallas.

---

*Willis later reported that Ensign Sakamaki became a successful Toyota dealer in Japan.

Epilogue

Anger, frustration, hatred, and fear were some of the emotions that racked Americans as the Pearl Harbor raid came to an end. In the smoking ruins of Oahu the destruction seemed almost complete. Of 96 ships at Pearl Harbor, 18 were sunk or damaged, including 8 battleships, 3 cruisers, 3 destroyers, 1 repair ship, 1 minelayer, 1 seaplane tender, and 1 target vessel. The Navy also lost 92 aircraft (including 5 from the *Enterprise* shot down by Americans) and had another 31 badly damaged, while the Army saw 96 planes destroyed and 128 severely damaged. Considerable destruction was inflicted also on Army and Navy installations and at the Marine base at Ewa.

The Japanese, on the other hand, suffered very little: 9 fighters, 15 dive-bombers, and 5 torpedo planes destroyed either during the battle or on the return to the strike force. All 5 of the midget submarines used in the attack were sunk, and 1 large, I Class submarine was lost. Although the number of Japanese who died in the attack is an estimate, the figure normally assumed is less than 100.

According to data gathered by the Pearl Harbor History Associates, the American Navy and Marine Corps bore 2,896 casualties, of which 2,117 were officers and enlisted personnel killed or fatally wounded; 779 of the wounded survived. Army losses were 218 killed or fatally wounded and 364 wounded who recovered. Sixty-eight civilians died in the attack, and another

35 were wounded. In all the United States suffered 3,581 casualties.

Americans were perhaps less callous toward war in 1941 than they are today, nearly fifty years after World War II. Having experienced by radio and television the carnage in Korea, Vietnam, and a variety of other places, they have mostly steeled themselves to the inevitable bloodshed. But in 1941 the thought of 2,403 deaths at Pearl Harbor from a "sneak attack" seared itself deeply into the national psyche. Immediately after the air raid the battle cry for Americans became: "Remember Pearl Harbor!" or sometimes, as the song made popular by Sammy Kaye and his orchestra put it: "Let's remember Pearl Harbor as we did the Alamo!" At any rate, those who have remembered Pearl Harbor best are the survivors.

A half century has modified the intensity of feeling for many of those who were there, but, for some, little has changed. Curtis Schulze, for example, continues to feel a distrust of Asians as a result of his experience on December 7. Yet, for Revella Guest, the passage of time has mellowed her emotions; she feels that, after all, "you shouldn't hold a grudge forever." Leonard Webb has said that

> observing hundreds of dead and wounded initiated and has maintained deep and abiding faith in the providence of Almighty God. Upon learning of the atomic bombing of Hiroshima and Nagasaki and seeing pictures of the utter destruction, I experienced a profound sorrow for the Japanese people, notwithstanding their dastardly attack on Pearl Harbor and their endangering my wife and year-old son, who were present there.

Still, Webb concluded these remarks by noting that, "as a nation, Japan is devoid of human gratitude and almost completely insensitive to accepted standards of morality."

One point the interviewees, some of whom helped form the Pearl Harbor Survivors Association, agreed upon is that they have felt closer to one another as a result of the shared experience. William Ellis said that he "makes every effort possible to associate in reverent patriotism, not as a social event, with those who were there." Charles Horner, a life member of the association, has a slide show of the attack that he presents when asked by church groups, senior citizens organizations, military and veteran associations, or service clubs. It is his way of paying homage to and remembering his "buddies."

Like Horner, most are proud to have been at Pearl Harbor on December 7, 1941. "Proud, also," said Emil Beran, "of my sailor response during the attack." Beran, although "shocked and surprised," "did his duty" like the rest. James McClelland, severely wounded during the attack, from that day onward "knew I wasn't immortal," and James Kanaman "finished growing up on that day and realized that life was more than just having a good time."

Jack Kelley remembers on every December 7 "how quickly most everyone else forgets a war and the danger of war." But Dan Wentrcek, Jim Gross, and several others agreed that the United States "must always maintain a strong national defense and never let her guard down again." They would no doubt concur with A. J. Dunn's observation that "the memory of those who gave their lives must be kept alive, and the nation kept ever alert."

When asked what impact being at Pearl Harbor had on them at the time and has had on them ever since, a few of the survivors did not respond with profound or philosophical statements concerning what befell them. Martin Matthews had "lots of memories, some good, some bad," and, like Joseph George and others, "felt lucky to be alive on December 8." Leon Bennett said that he did not think that Pearl Harbor had any impact on him. Archie Wilkerson "found out that day that the Navy wasn't a free ride," while Clifton Bellew "felt trapped by war for five more years."

Not all of the men and women interviewed identified with the feelings Jack White expresses below, but in most cases what he says about being at Pearl Harbor reflects the survivors' sentiments. Electrician's Mate Third Class White, USS *New Orleans*, who now lives in Denton, Texas, answered the question by saying:

Right after Pearl Harbor I felt ashamed—for myself and for the entire fleet—because we hadn't been able to put up a better fight. I felt betrayed by the military brass for letting us be caught by surprise after months of preparations and training. It wasn't until after the Battle of Midway that I felt fully vindicated for the Pearl Harbor disaster. I still have ambivalent feelings about being at Pearl Harbor. It wasn't a battle we won—but neither was the Alamo.

Sources

Despite the historical importance of the attack on Pearl Harbor, only a few books of note have been written about it. Most of these deal with questions related to the success Japan had in opening hostilities and the dispute concerning the culpability of American leaders in allowing such a surprise to happen. Of the purely military studies, two stand out: Gordon Prange et al., *December 7, 1941: The Day the Japanese Attacked Pearl Harbor* (New York: McGraw-Hill, 1988); and Samuel Eliot Morison, *The Rising Sun in the Pacific, 1931–April 1942* (Boston: Little, Brown, 1948).

Morison's book is the third volume in his *History of United States Naval Operations in World War II*, 15 vols. (1947–1960). Only Chapter 5 deals with the raid, but in many respects his work established the parameter of coverage that has been followed by other writers. This is true in part because he, like subsequent researchers, followed the information provided in various Navy reports, hearings before committees of Congress, and the report given by the committee of the 79th Congress that investigated the attack in 1946. Admiral Morison's stature as a naval historian also conditioned students to accord his work careful attention. In Chapter 5 of *The Rising Sun*, he covers events before, during, and after the attack yet provides very little embellishment of the data presented, including none of the individual testimony and stories common to many of the other works.

Prange's book is by far the most scholarly and detailed of all the studies written on the attack to date. It outlines what happened that fateful Sunday in much greater detail than either Morison's volume or an earlier, better-known book by Prange and his associates, *At Dawn We Slept* (New York: McGraw-Hill, 1981). The colleagues who wrote *December 7, 1941* after Prange's untimely death used notes he had made during a lifetime of researching the topic and included many colorful vignettes and tales to heighten interest. Despite their obvious desire to appeal to a large audience, they still accurately reported events as they transpired. Their presentation was fully within the accepted canons of academic history. In addition to employing materials that Morison consulted, the Prange group made greater use of ships' logs and statements by ships' officers. Prange also had interviewed a large number of people involved in the battle, and portions of these conversations were used in *December 7, 1941*.

Both the *Hearings before the Joint Committee on the Investigation of the Pearl Harbor Attack, Congress of the United States*, 79th Cong., 1st sess., 39 parts (Washington, DC: Government Printing Office, 1946), and the *Report of the Joint Committee on the Investigation of the Pearl Harbor Attack*, 79th Cong., 2d sess., 1946, S. Doc. 244, Serial 11033 (Washington, DC: Government Printing Office, 1946) provide a wealth of charts, maps, documents, photographs, data, and observations germane to the military phase of the attack. Of course, the purpose of the inquiry, like many of the earlier investigations, was to pinpoint responsibility and determine blame for the disastrously successful assault.

Less official, but a fine source of information about the attack, is John H. Bradley and Jack W. Dice, *The Second World War: Asia and the Pacific*, West Point Military History Series (Wayne, NJ: Avery Publishing Group, 1989). Chapter 3 deals with Pearl Harbor.

Paul Stillwell's *Air Raid: Pearl Harbor! Recollections of a Day of Infamy* (Annapolis: United States Naval Institute, 1981) is an excellent collection of first-person presentations. Stillwell includes about fifty articles, varying in size from two to seven-teen pages, that primarily recount what happened at specific places during and after the attack as witnessed by naval officers. The essays are clear and make excellent reading.

Another book somewhat in this genre is Rear Admiral Edwin T. Layton's volume, which he wrote cooperatively with Captain Roger Pineau and John Costello, *"And I Was There!" Pearl Harbor and Midway—Breaking the Secrets* (New York: William Morrow, 1985). Layton was Admiral Chester Nimitz's intelli-gence officer. The book has some value as a study of the battle but is better as a defense of the Navy at Pearl Harbor on Decem-ber 7.

An early, interestingly written volume that contains a variety of errors but is nonetheless worthy of mention is Walter Lord's well-known work, *Day of Infamy* (New York: Holt, Rinehart, 1957). One of the nation's better popular historians, Lord con-ducted a large number of interviews for his book, which, prior to the 1970 movie *Tora! Tora! Tora!* was probably the major source of Americans' knowledge of the Pearl Harbor raid.

Five other presentations that make worthwhile reading are Blake Clark, *Remember Pearl Harbor!* (New York: Modern Age Books, 1942); Commander Walter Karig and Lieutenant Wel-bourn Kelley, *Battle Report: Pearl Harbor to Coral Sea* (New York: Farrar and Rinehart, 1944), which uses official sources and was authorized by Secretary of the Navy Frank Knox; A. A. Hoehling, *The Week before Pearl Harbor* (New York: W. W. Norton, 1963); editors of the Army Times Publishing Company, *Pearl Harbor and Hawaii: A Military History* (New York: Walker, 1971); and A. J. Barker, *Pearl Harbor*, Ballantine's Illustrated History of World War II, no. 10 (New York: Ballan-tine Books, 1969). The last volume's pictures are of poor quality and low resolution, but the discussion of events surrounding the action at Pearl Harbor is interesting and appears to be amazingly accurate. As the titles of the other volumes indicate, they have a variety of uses for students of the attack.

Two pictorial histories are of value. The best is Stan Cohen, *East, Wind, Rain: A Pictorial History of the Pearl Harbor Attack* (Missoula, MT: Pictorial Histories Publishing, 1981), which is the volume sold at the monuments at Pearl Harbor. Its photographic quality is good, its picture selection is outstanding, and the continuity of essays and photographs provides a compelling account.

Not nearly as professionally written is the Pearl Harbor Survivors Association's *Silver Anniversary Commemorative Book* 1 (Santa Ana, CA: Taylor Publishing, 1984). This volume, which commemorates the twenty-fifth anniversary of the founding of the association rather than the attack, has some outstanding photographs not published elsewhere of events and some of the young men involved. The work includes a brief history of the association, short statements by participants in specific events, and biographies of a number of the survivors.

As noted above, the military history of Pearl Harbor has not been overwritten. Certainly, the attack is a topic that could be further developed by scholars and popularizers. We hope that our effort has shed a bit more light on that fascinating episode that assuredly was, as President Franklin D. Roosevelt described it, ''a date which will live in infamy.''

Index

Duels with unseen snipers in ruined villages and skirmishes against Hitler's panzers are just some of the battles you can read about in this true account of one US soldier's war

---

Roll Me Over:
An Infantryman's World War II

---

by Raymond Gantter

Published by Ballantine Books.
Available at a bookstore near you.

The classic account of tank warfare in World War II by a German general who was there

---

Panzer Battles

---

by Major General F. W. Von Mellenthin

Published by Ballantine Books.
Available at a bookstore near you.